Decisions for War, 1914–1917

This work poses an easy but perplexing question about World War I – Why did it happen? Several of the oft-cited causes are reviewed and discussed. The argument of the alliance systems is inadequate, most agreements lacking compelling force. The argument of an accident (or "slide") is also inadequate, given the clear and unambiguous evidence of intentions. The arguments of mass demands – those focusing on nationalism, militarism, and social Darwinism – it is argued, are insufficient, lacking indications of frequency, intensity, and process (how they influenced the various decisions).

Decisions for War focuses on the choices made by small coteries, in Austria-Hungary, Germany, Russia, France, Britain, and elsewhere. In each case, the decision to enter the war was made by a handful of individuals – monarchs, ministers, military people, party leaders, ambassadors, and a few others. In each case also, we see separate and distinct agendas, the considerations differing from one nation to the next. The leaderships of not only the major countries, but also Japan, the Ottoman Empire, Italy, the Balkans, and the United States are explored.

Richard F. Hamilton is Professor Emeritus of Sociology and Political Science and Research Associate of The Mershon Center at Ohio State University. He is coeditor, with Holger Herwig, of *The Origins of World War I* (Cambridge, 2003). His previous books include *Who Voted for Hitler?* (1982) and *The Bourgeois Epoch* (1991).

Holger H. Herwig is Professor of History and Canada Research Chair in Military and Strategic Studies at the University of Calgary. Among the many books he has written are *Biographical Dictionary of World War I* (1982), co-authored with Neil M. Heyman, *The First World War* (1997), and *The Destruction of the Bismarck* (2001).

Advance praise for *Decisions for War, 1914–1917*

"The debate on the origins of the First World War remains one of history's most important and hotly contested topics, and this excellent book does it justice by presenting up-to-the-minute research in a refreshingly accessible way. The breadth of its coverage is especially impressive, with Hamilton and Herwig treating the outbreak of the war as a global rather than merely a European event. Quite simply, this is the best introduction to the origins of the 1914–18 war yet published."

 – Dr. Gary Sheffield, Senior Lecturer in History, King's College London

"The First World War – was it an accident or was it design? Historians have debated this question for 90 years, and this latest contribution, aimed at a general audience, offers comparative conclusions about the major and minor powers' motivations for fighting in World War I. Hamilton and Herwig make a convincing case for the importance of human agency in the decisions for war, ranging from a forced hand, blunder or miscalculation, to decisions calculated to provoke a conflict. This book is a welcome contribution to the continuing debate on the origins of the First World War and will provide readers with a useful guide through the maze of conflicting interpretations on this controversial subject."

 – Annika Mombauer, The Open University, UK

"This book is an abridged version of the collection of essays edited by the same two authors, The Origins of World War I (Cambridge University Press, 2003). The footnotes have been removed and its text and bibliography skillfully abridged in order to produce a shorter and cheaper edition that can be made more readily accessible to students and the general reader. This wider accessibility is greatly to be welcomed. The book is the most comprehensive and up-to-date account available of the decisions that led first to the outbreak of the First World War and then to intervention by most of the global powers. A strong feature is the authors' comparative approach, which focuses attention on who made the crucial decisions in each country, how they did so (in what institutional context), and why they acted as they did. The presentation is clear and cogent, and corrects the widespread but misleading view that the war happened by accident or through inadvertence. On the contrary, the book rightly insists that the governments of the day made deliberate choices to fight rather than give way."

 – Prof. David Stevenson, Department of International History,
London School of Economics and Political Science

Decisions for War, 1914–1917

Richard F. Hamilton
The Ohio State University

Holger H. Herwig
University of Calgary

CAMBRIDGE
UNIVERSITY PRESS

CAMBRIDGE UNIVERSITY PRESS
Cambridge, New York, Melbourne, Madrid, Cape Town, Singapore,
São Paulo, Delhi, Dubai, Tokyo, Mexico City

Cambridge University Press
32 Avenue of the Americas, New York, NY 10013-2473, USA

www.cambridge.org
Information on this title: www.cambridge.org/9780521545303

© Richard F. Hamilton & Holger H. Herwig 2004

First published 2004

A catalog record for this publication is available from the British Library

Library of Congress Cataloging in Publication data
Decisions for War, 1914–1917 / Richard F. Hamilton, Holger H. Herwig.
    p. cm.
    Abridgment of: The origins of World War I / edited by Richard F. Hamilton,
Holger H. Herwig.
    Includes bibliographical references and index.
    ISBN 0-521-83679-4 – ISBN 0-521-54530-7 (pbk.)
    1. World War, 1914–1918 – Causes. 2. World War, 1914–1918 –
Diplomatic history. I. Hamilton, Richard F. II. Herwig, Holger H.
III. Origins of World War I.
  D511.D245 2004
  940.3′11 – dc22   2004048596

ISBN 978-0-521-83679-1 Hardback
ISBN 978-0-521-54530-3 Paperback

For Irene and Lorraine

Contents

List of Maps

Sources: Maps 1 and 5 are from Annika Mombauer, *Helmuth von Moltke and the Origins of the First World War* (Cambridge, 2001); maps 2 and 3 are from Hamilton and Herwig, eds., *The Origins of World War I* (Cambridge, 2003); map 4 also appears in Hamilton and Herwig, and is reprinted with permission of the publisher from William McCagg, *History of Habsburg Jews, 1670–1918* (Bloomington, 1989), p. 168. Map 6 is adapted from Bruce W. Menning, *Bayonets Before Bullets: The Imperial Russian Army, 1861–1914* (Indiana University Press, 2000).

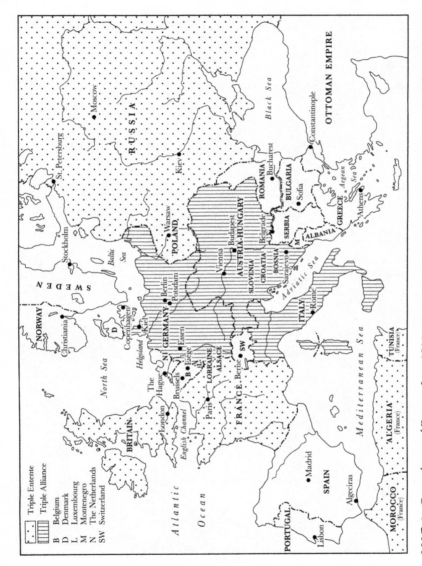

MAP 1. General map of Europe: June 1914

Acknowledgments

In 2003, Cambridge University Press published our lengthy, detailed, and heavily annotated volume entitled *The Origins of World War I*. Therein, ten scholars contributed chapters addressing a key question that we sensed had been missed in many "origins" books: Which individuals or groups wielded the "war powers" in 1914? The authors addressed this question on the basis of the extant documentary record.

In all twelve nations studied, the decisions for war were made by small coteries, most of them having fewer than ten persons. In three cases, the decisions had to receive some kind of legislative approval. In half of these nations the "war powers" were held by a single person, the monarch, who was aided by a small coterie of decision-makers, usually the prime minister, the foreign minister, the minister of war, the chief of the General Staff, and in one case even the minister of agriculture. In the nations with some kind of republican regime, the key decision-maker was a prime minister (or a president), one aided by a different kind of coterie, its members, typically, being leaders of parties (or of party factions). The second question addressed was the obvious one: What were the grounds for their decisions?

As editors of that larger work, we agreed with Cambridge editor Frank Smith's suggestion to pare down that tome and to make it available to instructors and students in an abridged (and revised) version designed for classroom use and discussion. We made deep cuts, a process we found troubling and painful. Our coauthors gave us permission to proceed with this work. The text that follows, most of it, retains the words of the original authors. We have made a few changes, mostly bridge passages and, here and there, some needed explanation. We wish once again to acknowledge their contributions to the individual chapters: John Milton Cooper, Jr. (United States), Frederick R. Dickinson (Japan), Richard C. Hall (the Balkan states), J. Paul Harris (Great Britain), Eugenia C. Kiesling (France), David Alan Rich (Russia), Ulrich Trumpener (Ottoman Empire), and Graydon A. Tunstall, Jr. (Austria-Hungary).

This work was supported by the Mershon Center at The Ohio State University. We are indebted to Richard Ned Lebow and Richard Herrmann, the Center's directors, and to Mershon's superb staff.

We hope that with this volume, we can contribute to a broader and deeper understanding of what George Kennan called "*the* great seminal catastrophe of this century." Decision-makers are still using war as a tool of statecraft. Coteries are still debating the pros and cons of armed state intervention. Scholars still debate the wisdom of those actions. Our intent is to keep that thought process alive.

Richard F. Hamilton
Holger H. Herwig
15 March 2004

CHAPTER 1

The Great War: A Review of the Explanations

World War I, once called the Great War, seems to defy explanation. Why did it happen? Numerous books on the subject carry the words "causes" or "origins" in their titles. The literature on the subject is extensive, probably the largest for any war in human history.

To address that basic question, a review of wars over the previous three centuries proves useful. And for this purpose a key term, world war, needs definition. We define a world war as one involving five or more major powers and with military operations on two or more continents. Since central Europe tore itself apart during the Thirty Years' War (1618–48), eight wars fit this definition. They are the War of the Grand Alliance, 1689–97; the War of the Spanish Succession, 1701–14; the War of the Austrian Succession, 1740–48; the Seven Years' War, 1756–63; the French Revolutionary Wars, 1792–1802; the Napoleonic Wars, 1803–15; then, after a ninety-nine-year interlude, World War I, 1914–18; and, two decades later, World War II, 1939–45. Following our definition and within this time span, the "Great War" was actually World War VII.

Those wars were massive and destructive. We have one crude measure of their "intensity," defined as "total battle fatalities suffered by the involved great powers per million of European population." Of the first six struggles, the Napoleonic Wars (1803–15) were by far the largest, with a fatality rate of 16,112. By this measure, the Great War was much more destructive at 57,616. That "intensity" was far exceeded in World War II at 93,665. Twenty-three smaller wars were fought within Europe between 1815 and 1914, these typically involving two or three powers. The largest had a fatality rate of 1,743.

These intensity figures are the best available estimates. They involve fair-sized margins for error, in most instances errors of underestimation. Civilian deaths, principally those from hunger and disease, are not included, nor are the deaths suffered by smaller countries. The absolute number of deaths due to World War I was clearly enormous, one source giving a total of 14,663,000. The European losses in the war have been estimated at "about 4.1 percent" of the total population.

Seen in relative terms (losses per 1,000 of population), some other wars were much more destructive. The victorious Athenians put to death "all the grown men" of Melos in 416 B.C. The destruction of Carthage in 146 B.C., it is said, "was essentially total." The German states lost one-fifth of their population in the Thirty Years' War, Prussia one-seventh of its population in the Seven Years' War. The most destructive war of all, one that receives very little attention, was a civil war, the Taiping rebellion in China (1851–64) with a loss of more than 30 million lives. We routinely focus on wars as big killing events but often neglect another even more lethal killing event. In March 1918 an influenza epidemic broke out among army recruits in Kansas. Subsequently called the Spanish flu, it spread within a year to all continents. Estimates of total deaths range from 25 million to 39 million, more than twice the World War I total.

World wars are costly ventures. The principal "actors" have to be rich nations with substantial intercontinental "outreach." Rich, of course, is a relative term. The masses in a given nation might have been poor but that nation, relative to others, may be rich, sufficiently so as to allow it to sustain large armies and navies in distant struggles for extended periods. The Netherlands could do that in the seventeenth century when it was a rich nation. In the eighteenth century, when relative to other nations it was not so rich, the Netherlands was no longer a "great power." China presents the opposite experience. It was once a rich nation with a demonstrated ability to "reach out," but in 1433 by imperial decree the voyages ceased, overseas trade was severely restricted, and the construction of ocean-going ships stopped. Confucian-trained officials, it seems, "opposed trade and foreign contact on principle." China's foreign involvement ended.

The eight world wars were initiated by well-off, indeed rich, European nations. Most history textbooks emphasize the battles fought on the European continent, but in each case those wars were fought also in Asia, Africa, and the Americas. In three of those wars, the English and French fought in India, with France ultimately losing out. And in four of them, the same contenders fought in North America. In 1763 the British gained the vast territories of New France. In the course of the same war, the British "took" Martinique, Grenada, Havana, and Manila (all later returned).

World wars, as defined here, require extensive economic, technological, and political development. Five or more nations had to generate considerable wealth, create capable naval forces, and acquire overseas empires. Basically, they had to establish and maintain relatively large military forces and send them enormous distances. That initially meant transport with large seagoing vessels that were effectively armed. Later, in the nineteenth and twentieth centuries, railroads, motor vehicles, and air transport came to be the decisive factors.

A military revolution occurred in the early modern period. The most important of the many changes was a considerable growth in the size of the armies. Those large forces could no longer "live off the land" – steal supplies from the populace. That change forced the creation of "the train," a large number of horse-drawn wagons to carry foodstuffs, munitions, medical supplies, and so forth. The size of military operations increased accordingly with armies marching over several roads and converging later at the site of battle. For several reasons, the military was forced to give much greater emphasis to drill and discipline. Much more elaborate arrangements for command and control became necessary. War offices and admiralties were created to provide both the training and the command structures.

The military revolution increased the costs considerably. There were more soldiers to be fed, clothed, housed, armed, and trained. The number of infantry and artillery pieces required grew and, with the technological advances, the unit costs of those weapons also increased. The sources of wealth allowing this revolution were diverse – New World gold and silver as well as trade and commerce in commodities. Machine manufacture had a considerable impact, increasing national wealth and making new weapons possible.

A nation's military capacity is limited by its economic strength, by its ability to pay. Our histories generally focus on monarchs and generals when discussing wars. But that overlooks another important figure: the finance minister. When the tax monies reach their limit and no further loans are possible, the war ends. Austria's participation in the Seven Years' War is a classic case in point. Campaigns were budgeted for 10 million to 12 million florins per annum, but a single campaign in 1760 cost 44 million florins. Overall, the costs for the Seven Years' War came to 260 million florins. The war ended in large part when the finance minister told Maria Theresa that Vienna had reached its financial limit. The focus on political and military outcomes of wars sometimes leads to neglect of the economic consequences. The debts incurred by France in the Seven Years' War had serious impacts, especially with the added costs of its involvement in the American Revolution. The debt and resultant tax problems were important sources of the 1789 revolution.

Another economic linkage should be noted. Britain was likely the richest of the European nations on the eve of the French Revolution. Famous for its small army, its wealth allowed the nation to hire mercenaries and to provide subsidies to its allies. Above all, Britain's wealth, combined with its insular position and command of the seas, allowed it as much or as little of a European war as it desired. In raw figures, Britain spent £1,657 million on wartime expenditures between 1793 and 1815, up more than £1,400 million from the period 1776 to 1783. Much of that was to finance the various coalitions it formed against Napoleon Bonaparte.

The French Revolutionary Wars brought a second revolution in military affairs, the engagement of the citizenry. For the first time, rulers dared arm their subjects in vast numbers. Nationalism and patriotism rather than impressment and bad fortune would, presumably, prompt young men to take up arms. Military practice was dramatically altered, the number of men directly involved escalating considerably. Again, some words of caution should be added. The *de facto* achievements fell far short of the aspirations. Legislative decrees do not transform mass sentiments. Monarchists did not become Jacobins; faithful Catholics did not become ardent secularists.

Napoleon Bonaparte put the new principle into practice in his imperial wars from 1803 to 1815, the sixth of the world wars. For twelve years, the emperor and his subjugated allies fought wars against the Revolution's major-power opponents. Once again, the conflict extended well beyond the European continent: to the West Indies, Turkey, Egypt, and it had indirect effects in North America (the Louisiana purchase, the War of 1812) and Latin America (the wars of independence).

The first six of these world wars depended on "executive decisions" – rulers initiated and others responded. The decision-makers typically consulted within an immediate circle of advisors. Imperialism, intercontinental outreach, was clearly involved although different in character from later efforts. The causal factors that gained prominence in the nineteenth century – nationalism, militarism, newspaper agitation, and "aroused masses" – scarcely appear in discussions of the first six of the world wars.

After the Napoleonic Wars there was a ninety-nine-year interlude without a world war. That did not mean years of peace but rather twenty-three smaller, more contained wars. The largest of these were two Russo-Turkish Wars (1828–29, 1877–78), the Crimean War (1853–56), and the Franco-Prussian War (1870–71). Recognizing the enormous costs of the Napoleonic Wars, the leaders of the major powers agreed to form a Concert of Europe to prevent such outbreaks. But in July and August 1914 it failed completely. That ninety-nine-year interlude and the events leading to the breakdown will be reviewed in the following chapter.

Of the eight world wars, the Great War, called World War I, poses the most serious challenges with regard to explanation. The heir presumptive to the Austro-Hungarian throne was assassinated on 28 June 1914. The Austrian government alleged official Serb involvement, issued an ultimatum, and, rejecting negotiation, began hostilities on 29 July with a bombardment of Belgrade. In a linked series of decisions, four other major European powers – Russia, Germany, France, and Britain – joined the struggle. In all instances, the decision-makers recognized the hazards involved. They knew their choices could enlarge the conflict and significantly escalate the dimensions of the struggle. One German participant, Kurt Riezler, had argued, "Wars would no longer be fought but calculated." The assumption underlying this "calculated risk" was that one power could enter the conflict without motivating the next power to make the same choice. Bluff, or offensive diplomacy, could be played, forcing other possible participants to desist. Ultimately, however, twenty-nine nations would be involved.

Most university-level history and social science courses that consider "the causes" of the Great War focus on "big" events, processes, or structures. Many accounts of the war's origins begin with the alliance system and continue with discussions of nationalism, militarism, and imperialism. All of these factors are "big" and all are routinely said to have had "powerful" impacts. They are, accordingly, treated as acceptable causes. Accounts that focused on individuals, on Emperor Franz

Joseph, Kaiser Wilhelm II, or Tsar Nicholas II, and on their outlooks, whims, and fancies, and on those of their closest advisors are viewed as "small." The peculiar traits of an individual or the chance presence of a given person are treated as somehow unacceptable.

Alexis de Tocqueville anticipated the big-cause preference. "Historians who write in aristocratic ages," he observed in his most famous work, "are inclined to refer all occurrences to the particular will and character of certain individuals: and they are apt to attribute the most important revolutions to slight accidents. They trace out the smallest causes with sagacity, and frequently leave the greatest unperceived." Historians writing "in democratic ages exhibit precisely opposite characteristics. Most of them attribute hardly any influence to the individual over the destiny of the race, or to citizens over the fate of the people: but, on the other hand, they assign great general causes to all petty incidents."

Tocqueville did not analyze modern societies in either–or terms, either general or particular causes, or, to use current terms, either structure or contingency. "For myself," he wrote, "I am of the opinion that, at all times, one great portion of the events of this world are attributable to very general facts and another to special influences. These two kinds of cause are always in operation: only their proportion varies." As may be seen in any of Tocqueville's writings, his main concern was to sort things out, to generalize where it was appropriate and, where it was not, to particularize. The obvious imperative is that one should be guided by evidence, by the "facts of the case." This is also our position.

The preceding discussion may be summarized with four generalizations:

First, World War I resulted from the decisions taken by the leaders of the great powers, Austria-Hungary, Germany, Russia, France, and Britain.

Second, in those nations the decision to go to war was made by coteries of five, eight, or perhaps ten persons. Three of those nations were authoritarian regimes and there the decision-making was the work of a monarch and his chosen civilian and military leaders. France and Britain, with parliamentary regimes, had somewhat more complicated procedures, but there too the decisions were taken by small coteries.

Third, explanations for the war's origins must center on the considerations that moved the members of those five groups of decision-makers. One must delineate the information, perceptions, and motives involved in each case. The key question is what were the concerns that moved them? If the review of motivations reveals a common tendency – that the five coteries were moved by nationalism, militarism, and imperialism – a general conclusion, a focus on those big causes might be warranted. If, however, the agendas differed, some other explanatory "strategy" is appropriate.

The fourth generalization is concerned with constitutional arrangements. All countries have procedures, formal and informal, that specify who will participate in the decision to go to war. A curious gap appears in many narrative histories, also in comparative government and international relations texts, in that the question of "war powers" is rarely addressed. How did it happen that a given set of, say, six individuals made "the decision"? A few others may have played ancillary roles, but everyone else (persons, groups, or elites) in the nation was "out of it." The procedures specifying "the war powers" provide "the cast" of decision-makers. They stipulate which individuals (or office holders) will be present. And those arrangements, in turn, would have impacts on the agendas brought to bear on the decisions. A narrowly based coterie consisting of the monarch, his chosen political leaders, and the heads of the military, might readily agree on a given agenda. Other elites – bankers, industrialists, press lords, clergy, or intellectuals – might have had different concerns and, if present, might have argued for other options.

Four of the five major powers had written constitutions, Great Britain being the exception. But the importance of those documents should be neither assumed nor exaggerated. Russia had a constitution after the 1905 revolution, but the tsar announced he would pay it little attention. The actual arrangements in those nations were loose, informal, and easily altered depending on *ad hoc* needs or personal fancy. A determined ruler could bring others into the decision-making. A lazy monarch could, either by plan or indifference, delegate power. An aggressive and/or astute minister could enhance his power or, at minimum, could cajole an easily influenced ruler. The authoritarian regimes showed unexpected capacities to resist the "advance of democracy" and, in some instances, to reverse the movement.

We are trained to think of constitutions as indications of progress, as steps setting limits to arbitrary rule. But these constitutions were not as "progressive" as one might think. One of the powers that remained, unambiguously, in the hands of the old-regime elites in Austria-Hungary, Germany, and Russia was the power to declare war. The German constitution specified that the powers "to declare war and to conclude peace" rested solely with the kaiser. His decision for war required the approval of the Federal Council, or Bundesrat, the Upper House of the legislature. In republican France, the decision-makers, officially, were the premier, the Cabinet, and the Chamber of Deputies. In fact, however, the decision was largely the work of the president and the premier. Britain was a constitutional monarchy with cabinet government. Formally, the prime minister and his Cabinet (fifteen or twenty of his appointees) had "the power." The decision for war required a majority vote in Cabinet and a tiny minority led by Edward Grey, the foreign secretary, generated that majority and brought about the final decision. The American constitution is strikingly different: it stipulates that "Congress shall have the Power . . . to declare War." But the decision in 1917, as will be seen, was largely the work of one man, Woodrow Wilson.

Another constitutional factor needs consideration. In all of these countries the "power of the purse" was vested with a broadly based legislature. In Germany, for example, the Reichstag had the authority to say "no" to the war budget. It is one of the great "what ifs" of history: What if a majority had voted "no" on 4 August? But that did not happen, a problem that deserves attention. The issue comes up regularly in leftist historiography, the Socialist parties, presumably, being the most likely nay-sayers. In a moment of crisis, when the nation appears to be under attack, a "no" vote is a difficult choice.

One important implication follows from these guiding assumptions. A decision for war made by a small coterie means that contingency is highly likely. Misinformation, weak nerves, ego-strength, misjudgment of intentions and of consequences, and difficulties in timing are inherent in the process. Put differently, diverse choices are easy to imagine. In the midst of the crisis, two monarchs, Tsar Nicholas and Kaiser Wilhelm, did say "no" to the war. But both men were then convinced by others in their coteries to reverse those decisions.

As of 1919, the dominant explanation, one written into the Versailles Treaty, was intentionalist: basically, that Germany was to blame for the catastrophe. But revisionist views came quickly, some expressed by leaders of the victorious powers. The new readings were summarized in a compendious history by Sidney Bradshaw Fay, *The Origins of the World War* (1928). In an opening chapter on the "Immediate and Underlying Causes," Fay discussed the early readings on the subject, reviewed and commented on recently published documents,

and finally considered five "underlying" causes – the system of secret alliances, militarism, nationalism, economic imperialism, and the
press. Four of those causes appear routinely in present-day histories but
the argument of newspaper agitation has largely disappeared. Many accounts add another cause, social Darwinism, to the basic list. Some
authors argue "domestic sources," that some or all of the powers chose
war to head off internal dissent. Another option, one that appeared immediately after the war's end, is the argument of a "slide." This declares
the Great War to have been an accident, an event neither intended nor
foreseen by any of the decision-makers. Some authors argue multiple
causation, combinations of the above. Social Darwinism, for example,
stimulated imperialism which in turn required the expansion of armies
and navies.

We will discuss first the alliance-systems argument and then consider the others in the following sequence: nationalism, social Darwinism, imperialism, militarism, the press, domestic sources, and the
argument of a "slide."

The "alliance system" refers to treaties that, allegedly, determined
the August 1914 choices. As of 1907 Europe was divided between two
power blocs: the Triple Alliance of Germany, Austria-Hungary, and
Italy and the *entente cordiale* of France, Russia, and Great Britain. The
1920s' revisionists argue the binding character of those treaties. If a
member of the Alliance were attacked (an unprovoked aggression), the
others were obliged to come to that member's defense. The members
of the *entente* also, it was said, had similar obligations.

A review of the initial steps taken by the major powers in July
and August of 1914 shows the inadequacy of this position. Austria-
Hungary's leaders decided to punish Serbia for the killing of Archduke
Ferdinand. Their first action was to consult with Germany's leaders,
who readily assured the Austrians of their support. A month later, after much discussion and vacillation, Russia's leaders decided to help
Serbia and announced a partial mobilization directed against Austria-
Hungary. The next day, pressed by his generals, Tsar Nicholas ordered
a full mobilization, one directed also against Germany. That nation's
leaders defined Russia's mobilization as an act of war and, arguing
the need for defense, announced a general mobilization. On 28 July
Austria-Hungary declared war on Serbia. The first military action
came the next day with the bombardment of Belgrade. On 1 August
Germany declared war on Russia and its troops entered Luxembourg.
On that day also, France ordered general mobilization for the following

day. On 3 August Germany declared war on France; on 4 August their forces entered Belgium, whereupon Britain declared war on Germany.

None of those decisions for war was mandated by treaty obligations. Those choices were all "situational," decisions made in response to immediate events. Germany was obliged by treaty to aid Austria-Hungary only if one or more of the *entente* powers engaged in unprovoked aggression. The Dual Monarchy's move against Serbia, accordingly, did not in any way obligate Germany. Italy's leaders recognized that move against Serbia as a provocation and, citing the terms of the Alliance, declared their country's neutrality.

The logic of the alliance-system argument is improbable. The "men of 1914" are routinely depicted as tough, aggressive, and ruthless in pursuit of their aims. Yet here they are portrayed as honorable men faithfully defending the "sanctity" of treaty agreements no matter the costs. But political leaders repeatedly have rejected that course. In 1870, for example, William Gladstone, Britain's prime minister and a very honorable man, said he could not accept "the doctrine [that] a guarantee is binding on every party to it" irrespective "of the particular position in which it may find itself . . . when the occasion for acting on the guarantee arises." The great authorities on foreign policy, he declared, "never, to my knowledge, took that rigid and, if I may say so, that impracticable view of a guarantee." In 1908 Italy's King Vittorio Emanuele III, unhappy with the action of one of his Alliance partners, made this comment: "I am more than ever convinced of the utter worthlessness of treaties or any agreements written on paper. They are worth the value of the paper." In short, the leaders of major powers recognized the tenuous nature of treaty terms.

Only the Franco-Russian alliance was unambiguous: both powers agreed to mobilize their forces in case one or more of the Triple Alliance powers mobilized. Quite apart from "the letter" of the agreement, French and Russian leaders were generally disposed to accept those terms. But even here there were sources of concern and anxiety. Would the partner honor the commitment? Or would fear and anxiety obviate formal contractual agreements? Again, when Britain and France signed their *entente* in 1904, St. Petersburg feared this accommodation might prompt Paris to renege on its treaty obligation in case of a Russian clash with Britain. In the wake of the Russo-Japanese War, there was deep-seated fear in Russia whether France might reassess the value of the alliance in the wake of Russia's humiliating defeat. Thus, during joint staff talks held at Paris in April 1906, the tsar's General Staff "consistently" but "fraudulently" reassured their French counterparts that the war and the resulting revolution had not reduced Russia's defense capabilities.

The Belgian "case" is relevant here. In 1839 Austria, Britain, France, Prussia, and Russia signed a treaty in which they agreed to respect and defend this "Independent and perpetually Neutral State." But, for a decade prior to 1914, Germany's strategic plan involved the violation of that neutrality. France's strategic planning also, at various points, involved an incursion into Belgium. Just before Germany's 1914 invasion, leaders in Berlin made two attempts to finesse the problem, offering to reward Belgium and Britain if those nations would permit the passage of German troops. But both offers were refused. Germany's leaders were surprised at the lack of "realism" in those responses.

The next four causes – nationalism, social Darwinism, imperialism, and militarism – all supposedly have cultural roots. All four involve attitudes or preferences said to be widely held among "the masses." For that reason then, they may be subjected to some common lines of criticism. Each of these causes ought to be considered at three "levels" – one must inquire about those mass beliefs, the efforts of advocacy groups, and the responses of decision-makers.

The key problem with respect to the mass outlooks is their indeterminacy. Many assertions put forth with respect to these factors are merely unsupported statements of frequency followed by judgments of weight or importance. The problem: with no serious public opinion surveys prior to the mid-twentieth century, we have no satisfactory evidence of prevalence, intensity, or import with respect to any "mass" attitude. It is easy to declare that "fervent nationalist" views were held by some tens of millions. But, given the lack of serious evidence, the appropriate response to such judgments is another declaration, an unambiguous "don't know."

We have better evidence with respect to the advocacy groups although even here, the quantity is limited and the quality often questionable. We can often find data on the membership of such organizations. But rarely do we find indications of intensity – how many of the members were active, how many inactive, how many lapsed? We rarely find a time series showing membership trends over the course of key decades. Associations, with rare exceptions, inflate membership figures and exaggerate their influence. Another frequent problem is partial or one-sided presentations. Information on nationalist sentiments and organizations is reported at length but no equivalent account of internationalist tendencies is provided. The same holds with respect to the militarism–pacifism pair. Social Darwinism was "widespread," to be sure, but opposition to it was probably much more frequent, especially in the major religious bodies.

In contrast to our knowledge of "mass sentiment" and of the organizations, our knowledge of the decision-making coteries is extensive. But here too one finds a serious gap. Were the decision-making coteries responding to the demands of the masses or to the pressures of organizations representing them? Or were they fending off mass demands? Or, another possibility, were they simply indifferent to such importunities? Kaiser Wilhelm II, upset by the July Crisis, referred to the coming struggle as one between "Teutons and Slavs." Was he moved by social Darwinist beliefs when he made the key decision for war? Or was that decision based on some strategic concerns, on Germany's place within Europe? The basic problem here is the failure to specify the connections: how did the alleged cause, those "mass" sentiments, impact on the decision-makers in July 1914?

Nationalism, the second cause reviewed here, gained in importance in the nineteenth century. But we have no serious evidence on the extent or intensity of those views in the general population. Many accounts of this growth have a "broad brush" character, meaning they are best seen as plausible but untested hypotheses. The extension of public schooling would have eroded local and regional loyalties providing instead some sense of a larger national heritage. Teachers and textbooks created a common language and probably instilled patriotic sentiments. Reviewing evidence on these matters for France, Eugen Weber thought the schools very effective in creating "cultural homogeneity" but conceded the evidence was "rather thin" since no broad survey of "national consciousness and patriotism" was ever undertaken in the nineteenth century. In a later period, 1905–14, he declared the nationalism to be "a product of Paris. It never went much beyond, and, even in Paris, it remained a minority movement, trying to compensate in violence and vociferation for the paucity of its numbers." In July 1913 France passed a law increasing the period of military service from two to three years. Weber argues that majority opinion in France was opposed to the change, and that paying the costs brought strenuous opposition. The principal theme, in elections fought in the spring of 1914, was "no new taxes."

If we know very little about the frequencies, we know even less about the intensities of these feelings. How many adult French citizens were ardent supporters of "the national interest" in the spring of 1914? How many would have put that interest ahead of the lives, health, and the well being of their immediate families? How many would have been indifferent – or opposed – to involvement in Bosnia, Serbia, or East Prussia? How many citizens of the *Midi* would have been indifferent to the fate of Alsace and Lorraine?

Some accounts focus on pressure groups, the Pan-Germans and Pan-Slavs receiving much attention. Few accounts, however, give information on the size of those organizations and few tell of their impacts. Roger Chickering provides relevant information on the Pan-German League. Although the founders expected it to be "a massive organization," after the turn of the century numbers declined steadily from "a peak of a little over 23,000." Most of the members were upper or upper middle class, a category estimated to have contained 2.75 million families. The Navy League, by far Germany's largest patriotic society, is said to have had "well over 300,000 members" in 1913. One obvious question: is that a credible number? The League's paper, *Die Flotte*, gives an even larger number, 331,493, for 1914. Although presumably a powerful organization, naval appropriations had recently been cut and funds were shifted to the army.

Military service may have helped generate nationalist outlooks. But an opposite hypothesis should also be considered, that service in the military generated hostility, resentment, or disdain. Civilian careers were interrupted, apprenticeship and on-job training was postponed, and marriage delayed. For a couple of years, one had to suffer the daily importunities of officers and noncommissioned officers. Unfortunately, we have little serious evidence dealing with "mass" reactions to military experience.

A third cause, one not on Sidney Fay's list, is social Darwinism. Put simply, the "men of 1914" were smitten with the notion that Charles Darwin's theories of "natural selection" could be transferred to the development of human society. The social Darwinists argued that life was a constant struggle to survive. Those most fit survived, the others perished. The history of nations and empires was a constant pattern of "rise and fall." To stand still meant to decline – and to die.

Again one must put the critical questions: how many people subscribed to such views? What influence did they have? And, did this "background factor" lead to the decisions of August 1914? What were the mechanisms linking the ideology and the decisions? Were the decision-makers driven by that belief or were they moved by more immediate political concerns?

The fourth argument, imperialism, also requires further discussion beginning with a need for differentiation. Britain had the world's largest empire. Russia had the second largest. France had a much smaller empire, one-tenth the size of Britain's. Germany had some modest holdings, most of them economic losers. Austria-Hungary had no off-continent empire and showed no interest in gaining one. An obvious lesson: the five major powers would have had markedly different imperial agendas. An analysis of this subject must specify the "interests" or "needs" sensed by the various decision-makers.

One can again point to the role of advocacy groups, to Britain's Empire League or Germany's Colonial Society. But, as with the other factors discussed here, one must ask about frequencies, intensities, and impacts. To counter the insistent magnification bias, one should again consider an alternative hypothesis: for every member one might find 99 nonmembers, persons either indifferent or opposed to imperial ventures, or not enthused by the nation's "presence" in Fashoda, Ethiopia, South Africa, Southwest Africa, the Philippines, or China.

Obviously, the decision-makers of most of the powers (and those of some minor powers or aspirants) were driven by some imperialist concerns. That "interest" often proved an astonishing mistake because the colonies, on the whole, were not profitable. The returns, typically, were limited and the costs of policing, administration, and defense often enormous, a conclusion insistently argued by British liberals.

Imperial Germany provides a convenient test. The aggregate value of German's commerce with its colonies between 1894 and 1913 remained less than what was spent on them: Kiaochow alone received more than 200 million Goldmark in subsidies. Of the Reich's total trade, a mere 0.5 percent was with its colonies. Only one in every thousand Germans leaving the homeland chose to go to the colonies (5,495 people by 1904). Russia provides another test. At enormous cost, it pushed to the East, building the world's longest railway line, developed Pacific ports, and, ultimately, took over an important Chinese province – Manchuria. But the Russian colonization efforts were unsuccessful and the expectation of monetary gain proved illusory. Despite all efforts to "secure a captive market," Russia continued to run a huge trade deficit with China. As for investment opportunities, only two factories were started in Manchuria – "distilleries that produced liquor mainly for the Russian army of occupation."

Elites are regularly depicted as well informed, rational, and calculating. But opposite hypotheses are always useful, in this case the possibility that the decision-making coteries were uninformed or ignorant. One might also consider a social–psychological possibly, that some kind of conformity was operating. The logic of imperialism seemed plausible because "everyone" was doing it. Otto von Bismarck, strikingly, was an exception, one not moved by such "peer pressures." Recognizing the costs, he ended Germany's limited imperialist effort while recommending it to others, to France, for example.

An important lesson about the causal dynamics appears in the Austro-Hungarian experience. In 1912–14 Foreign Minister Count Leopold Berchtold saw an opportunity for "empire" in Anatolia. But his plans faced a serious difficulty – "the almost complete lack of interest on the part of commercial circles in the Monarchy." He found "absolutely no pressure to found colonies – this had to be stirred up artificially by the government." The Anatolian venture, F. R. Bridge states, "was based on the old quest for prestige, or, rather, on that concern to avoid losing prestige which was to become a neurotic obsession in Vienna in the last years of peace."

The imperialism argument surfaced again in 1961 when the Hamburg historian Fritz Fischer published his provocative book *Griff nach der Weltmacht*, wherein he posited that Germany in July 1914 had embarked on an explicit "grab for world power." Fischer's opus outraged his colleagues and ushered in two decades of debate concerning both the origins of the war and the place of German imperialism therein. The argument was as brutal as it was simple. From 1890 on, Fischer argued, Germany had pursued world power. In its drive for colonies and imperial trade, it had offended established powers such as Britain and France as well as upstarts such as Japan and the United States. This course of *Weltpolitik* was deeply rooted within German economic, political, military, and social structures, he argued, with both civilian and military leaders steering a course of aggressive imperialism under Wilhelm II. In the wake of the Fischer debate, no historian could ignore his emphasis on the centrality of imperialism among the causative factors behind the decision for war in July–August 1914. We will return to Fischer's "imperialism" argument in Chapter 4.

Militarism is the next factor on the "standard list" of causes. Discussions ordinarily begin with a review of the arms race, of the competition between the powers before 1914. Many of these come without figures on appropriations, size of the military, capacity of weapons, and the like. Again, there is the need for differentiation. The five powers were doing different things. Germany was the most zealous in its effort, first with naval expansion, then, between 1911 and 1913, with a shift to the army. In 1913 it spent £118 million on defense, while Britain spent £76 million. One of the powers, Austria-Hungary, made no serious increase in the decades before 1914. Russian army effectives actually declined slightly from 1911 to 1913. Between 1910 and 1913, France increased army expenditures by 7.6 percent, Russia by 20.8 percent, and Germany by 104.6 percent. The "broad brush" depiction suggests a common response – "they were all doing it" – but the diversity of these efforts is far more striking.

Per-capita expenditures on the defense budget of 1906 (in Austrian Kronen) were: Britain 36, France 23.8, Germany 22, Italy 11.6, Russia 9.8, and Austria-Hungary 9.6. As late as 1903, Habsburg subjects spent as much on tobacco and more on beer and wine than on defense. The ethnic conflicts in Austria-Hungary blocked provision of requisite funds for modernization of the armed forces. As a result, the Dual Monarchy each year trained only between 22 and 29 percent of draft-eligible males (compared to 40 percent in Germany and 86 percent in France).

The undifferentiated portraits of "the arms race" also overlook the markedly different financial and political restraints faced by the major powers. They pay little attention to the opposition, to the anti-imperialists, Socialists, pacifists, and liberal internationalists, who argued that war was no longer an option by 1914. And they pay virtually no attention to business leaders, many of whom were also opposed to militarism. In 1911 in a private conversation, Heinrich Class, leader of the Pan-Germans, pleaded for a preventive war. His partner in the conversation was Hugo Stinnes, Germany's most aggressive industrialist and a leading figure in the steel industry. Stinnes counseled restraint: after "3–4 years peaceful development" Germany would be "the undisputed economic master of Europe." Max Warburg, an influential Hamburg banker, was shocked by Wilhelm II's question at a dinner, one week before the Sarajevo murders, whether it was better "to attack now" rather than to wait for Russia to complete her rearmament. Warburg counseled the kaiser not to draw the sword. "Germany becomes stronger with every year of peace," he declared. "We can only gather rewards by biding our time." Also opposed to arms programs were farmers, shopkeepers, small businesses, civil servants, and workers who would pay more taxes.

Many accounts point to the "war euphoria" seen in European capitals in August 1914, this presumably attesting to the militarization of the masses. But the signs of euphoria came after the key decisions had been made. While the enthusiasm was no doubt genuine, one must again consider the questions of frequency and typicality. Jeffrey Verhey's review of 85 German newspapers and periodicals found evidence of that euphoria, most of it among intellectuals, students, and the upper middle classes. He also noted other responses (mixed feelings, dismay, fear, anxiety) being much more frequent than suspected. And he found frequent reports of tears. Theodor Wolff, editor of the *Berliner Tageblatt*, writing in 1916 on the anniversary of the outbreak, denied the mass euphoria claim, declaring as "false" the notion that "the German people greeted the outbreak of war with joy." The censors forbade "indefinitely" any further publication of such claims.

The euphoric crowd in Berlin, the "centerpiece" of the myth, appeared there on 25 July, at first awaiting news of Serbia's reaction to the Austrian ultimatum. Verhey describes the event and attempts some quantification: "That evening 'Germany' had not paraded. Only a small minority of the Berlin population had participated – no more than 30,000, or less than 1 percent of the population of greater-Berlin."

Those four sentiments – nationalism, social Darwinism, imperialism, and militarism – were probably more frequent in the spring of 1914 than at any earlier time. That said, however, some cautions should be noted. We know little about the prevalence of those views – was it 5, 30, or 65 percent of the adult population? What percent of the adherents expressed their views, urging support for their demands? How many joined and were active in the pressure groups? The members of voluntary associations are drawn disproportionately from the upper and upper-middle classes, which means the sentiments of other classes, those forming the vast majority, remain largely, or for the most part, unheard. Advocacy groups, at all times, exaggerate the size of their membership, the urgency of their message, and the extent of their influence. At one time or another, Chickering reports, the Pan-Germans had almost 400 chapters. But "the majority or these groups – more than two-thirds – existed only on paper or were dormant on all but select occasions." One further question: did the nation's leaders view these advocacy groups as valued supporters or as a troublesome nuisance?

What about that vast majority, the voiceless masses? What, for example, were the views of those other Berliners, those not demonstrating? Had they been asked, what demands would they have made? One hypothesis might be expressed as follows: "my family and my family's welfare, first and foremost." But that possibility is regularly bypassed, the noisy demonstration by the tiny minority being judged as more important, and more representative, than the lives of ordinary people struggling with the tasks of everyday life.

The sixth argument focuses on the newspaper agitation that was said to have "created" the mass sentiments. And those sentiments, in turn, supposedly forced political leaders to choose war. There is no denying the bellicosity of much of the press, but here too there are many complications. The press in most countries was differentiated, most newspapers linked to political parties (some also with links to governments). To assess influence, one would have to review the contents, have circulation figures, know the audience characteristics, their reactions to those contents, and their subsequent actions. One can research the contents, the easiest of those tasks, and occasionally one can find circulation figures. But beyond that, for all practical purposes, we have nothing. Another relevant factor, basic literacy, also needs consideration. Illiteracy was still widespread in Europe in 1914, the rates everywhere being higher in the countryside and among older citizens. They were also higher in Eastern Europe. For many people, clearly, a direct press influence was impossible.

Another problem is that of sequence. The argument holds that the press agitation led to the subsequent decision. There was much agitation in Vienna in July 1914, much of it focused on provocative comment in the Belgrade press. But that agitation came after Austria-Hungary's leaders had made the key decision. In Germany, Verhey reports, newspapers brought out many "extras" in the first days of August. The practice was a profitable one and played some role in sustaining the enthusiasm. But that too came after political and military leaders had made the basic decision. Research to date has not demonstrated a direct influence of "the press" on decision-making in 1914. This position, accordingly, has fallen into abeyance.

The seventh argument, domestic causes, is a late entry in the field. The argument, basically, is that conservative elites, faced with serious internal threats, chose war to save their positions. Arno J. Mayer, a leading advocate of this position, writes that in Britain, France, and Italy, the "vital center" of parliamentary liberalism "was heavily besieged" while in Germany it was "almost completely emasculated." For conservative elites then, the choice was "armed repression at home" or "preventive war abroad – with the resolve of thereby arresting or reversing the course of history." The argument is that the choice of war was counter-revolutionary, an attempt to counter serious domestic threats.

Subsequent research on the topic has found little support for this position. Most political leaders knew the hazards involved. The Franco-Prussian War (1870–71) ended with a revolution, the Paris Commune. More recently, the Russo-Japanese War (1905–06) also brought on a revolution that took months to subdue. Mobilization alone caused severe dislocations. Banking and trade were immediately disrupted; large numbers of workers were thrown out of work; young men ordered into the military were taken from jobs and families; incomes declined just as food prices were increasing significantly. One British leader, Ramsey MacDonald, "predicted that by November there would be bread riots and a socialist government." For conservative leaders, war was a very dangerous weapon, one far more likely to destabilize than to maintain any regime.

The eighth argument, the accident thesis, sees the Great War as the unintended consequence of decisions aiming for some other outcomes. The most famous statement of this argument of "inadvertence" came from David Lloyd George when in December 1920 he claimed that "no one at the head of affairs quite meant war" in July 1914. "It was something into which [the statesmen] glided, or rather staggered and stumbled." Later, in his postwar memoirs, Britain's wartime prime minister reiterated this argument of inadvertence: "How was it that the world was so unexpectedly plunged into this terrible conflict? Who was responsible?" His reply became the classic statement of innocence for July 1914: "The nations slithered over the brink into the boiling cauldron of war without any trace of apprehension or dismay." The theme is developed, a few pages later, under the heading: "Nobody Wanted War."

This shift from arguments of intention to those of inadvertence occurred within a few months. Lloyd George suggested the change was based on his wide reading of diplomatic records but, in the late months of 1920, that is unlikely. It reflected, rather, a new political concern, reconciliation, that would be aided by the new "no-fault" reading. Political leaders on both sides of the previous conflict, and many political commentators, adopted the new view. The "slide" image also found favor with many scholars.

Lloyd George's notion of an unintended "slide" stands sharply opposed to the evidence now available (reviewed in later chapters). The argument relativizes, making King George V as culpable as Wilhelm II, Sir Edward Grey as culpable as Count Leopold Berchtold. And it is a digression. The commentator thereby avoids the essence of decision-making: that human beings made the choices. Hew Strachan provides a useful summary: "what remains striking about those hot July weeks is the role, not of collective forces nor of long-range factors, but of the individual."

Two more options should be added to the eight hypotheses reviewed to this point. The ninth is the possibility of joint effects, that two or more factors, nationalism, militarism, and imperialism for example, somehow worked in combination to generate a decision for war. The problems reviewed above – poor measures of incidence (extent and strength of views) and equivalence (they were "all doing it") – apply also in this case. And there is a problem of weighting: how much importance should be assigned to factor A, B, C, and so forth?

Discussions of some of these causes present the possibility of *post hoc ergo propter hoc* errors. The alliances, nationalism, imperialism, social Darwinism, and so forth, all preceded the outbreak of war, but without further specification it is not clear they had causal impact. A listing of factors that occurred prior in time is easy; establishing their causal significance is much more difficult. The appropriate test: if a given factor were causal, it should figure in the thought and discussions of the July 1914 decision-makers.

A tenth possibility, a routine scientific requirement, is the open-ended option usually referred to as "other hypotheses." We argue one such claim: that the decision-makers of the five major powers sought to save, maintain, or enhance the power and prestige of the nation. We refer to this as the strategic argument. On this we agree with Hew Strachan – "By July 1914 each power, conscious in a self-absorbed way of its own potential weaknesses, felt it was on its mettle, that its status as a great power would be forfeit if it failed to act."

The analysis of the decisions made in the capitals of the five major powers that opted for war in 1914 must consider three components: the institutional arrangements, the persons involved, and the grounds or motives for their choices. Among the latter, their readings and assessments of the events of the previous two or three decades and their readings of events from 28 June onward must be central.

Our sense is that a differentiated analysis is required. Nationalist sentiments had been aroused in each of the five major powers. They certainly had greater salience in 1914 than in the previous five, six, or seven decades. One might point to imperialist concerns in each of the great powers. But the problems facing those "empires" were so diverse as to make any general analysis of this causal factor impossible. One might point to the needs of "capitalism" as somehow causing the catastrophe, but the "specific form" of those arrangements, the needs and interests of five sets of capitalists, also differed significantly from one nation to the next. Our hypothesis is that the leaders in each of those nations were moved by separate and distinct sets of concerns.

In each of these settings, a small coterie made the decision for war, findings that will come as no surprise. It has been known for years that in Austria-Hungary Kaiser Franz Joseph acted on the advice of his foreign minister, chief of the General Staff, war minister, finance minister, and the premiers of the two halves of his empire. Similarly, in Germany Kaiser Wilhelm II and a small group of his close advisors – chancellor, foreign secretary, chief of the General Staff, chief of the Military Cabinet, and war minister – made the decision for war. Likewise, in Russia, Tsar Nicholas II reached his fateful decision for war on the advice of a similarly small cadre of advisors: foreign minister, chief of the General Staff, war minister, and (somewhat of a surprise) agricultural minister. Austria-Hungary, Germany, and Russia were ruled by dynastic coteries, ones headed by the monarchs (who might not have dominated the discussions). The decisions made in France and Britain were also taken by coteries. But these were of different composition and are best described as party coteries.

After dealing with the July Crisis and the reactions of the five major powers, we turn to consideration of several important later participants in the struggle, to Japan, the Ottoman Empire, the Balkan States, Italy, and the United States. One might think the United States would be an exception to this pattern of rule by coterie, but in the world's oldest and most open democracy, President Woodrow Wilson, in the words of Arthur Link, his official biographer, exercised "almost absolute personal control" over foreign affairs. Wilson routinely bypassed the State Department via private agents, conducted negotiations behind the backs of his secretaries of state, and generally "acted like a divine-right monarch in the conduct of foreign relations."

In making the case for coterie and contingency, for what Tocqueville called "the particular will and character of certain individuals," we are *not* overlooking the importance of social history, of the "big" factors. We are sensitive to the mindset, the *mentalité* of the coteries. Did common, long-term patterns of education, training, and public rhetoric contribute to the "mood of 1914"? Put differently, what assumptions, both spoken and unspoken, did they bring to the table in 1914? We are sensitive also to the contributions of economics, psychology, and sociology (beyond those provided by diplomatic, military, and political history) toward explanation of what George F. Kennan called "*the great seminal catastrophe*" of the twentieth century. We will be considering the role of public opinion, financial institutions, academic leaders, church fathers, and press lords. And, especially in the case of the Balkan states, we consider also the role of secret societies, some with ties to governments though not in all cases controlled by the governments that supported them.

Among the many items of information brought to the July 1914 decision-makers, among the various grounds for their choices, were representations of mass attitudes, of public opinion. One conclusion about those outlooks may be stated as an absolute: no precise measures of public opinion were available at that time. More, we believe that decision-makers by and large proceeded independently of perceived mass opinion, that they probably were moved by "larger" strategic considerations – their conceptions of the nation's power and prestige. The implication: one should avoid gratuitous "democratizing" assumptions.

CHAPTER 2

European Wars: 1815–1914

Throughout most of this 99-year period, Europe was dominated by five great powers: Britain, Austria (after 1867, Austria-Hungary), Prussia (after 1871, Germany), Russia, and France. The first four were the victorious powers of 1815. At the Congress of Vienna they rearranged the map of Europe, reducing France to its 1792 boundaries, putting Prussia in the Rhineland as a buffer and Austria in northern Italy for the same purpose. France was present at the Congress, still viewed as a major power, but at that point and throughout most of the following century, that nation was viewed with suspicion, as one harboring dangerous revolutionary tendencies.

Two lesser contenders were present on the European scene. The Ottoman Empire, once a formidable power, located in the southeastern "corner" of the Continent (and in the Near East, the Middle East, and across North Africa), was manifestly in decline, a condition that was key to much of subsequent history. A new state was created in 1861, a unified Italy, which toward the turn of the century also sought "great power" status.

The guiding concern for the victorious powers was the maintenance of peace on the European continent. Having the disasters of the French Revolution and the Napoleonic era clearly in mind, the leaders of the victorious powers sought to prevent war through collegial discussion and agreement about any major actions to be taken. This arrangement was called the Concert of Europe. The leaders substantially agreed on "the basics," favoring the established (or restored) monarchical regimes and opposing international conflict. The assumption of consensus, however, proved tenuous since, as quickly became evident, the powers saw their interests somewhat differently.

Britain chose to remain free of continental ties; it would help to maintain the balance from outside, from its island "base." British leaders, with evident pride, later referred to this stance as one of "splendid isolation." Continental leaders judged the practice differently, referring to the United Kingdom as "perfidious Albion." Austria's leaders did not care for Russian involvement in central European affairs. And four of the powers viewed even restored France with some suspicion.

At the Congress of Vienna the victorious powers – the original Concert of Europe – rearranged the map of the Continent and restored a few displaced monarchies. Among other things, they reunited the Netherlands after more than two centuries of division and installed a new monarch. Napoleon's creation, the Duchy of Warsaw, was abolished and Poland was again divided among three of the powers. The understanding, especially on the part of the three victorious continental powers, was that they would oversee and protect the new arrangements. On several occasions, when faced with insurgency, the powers undertook armed intervention to make appropriate corrections. These police efforts were directed largely by the Austrian chancellor, Prince Clemens von Metternich. The Metternich system was generally successful until the initial collapse with the revolutions of 1848. The basic aims of the Concert were carried over in the years that followed but the problems faced were more serious and wars within Europe, accordingly, were more frequent.

Three major problems surfaced in the years after 1848. First, changes in the status of the major powers brought serious problems. Second, changes in southeastern Europe, the "retreat" of the Ottomans, brought another set or problems. And third, European imperialism had "spillover effects," consequences affecting other members of the Concert.

A first major change in status came with the 1848–49 revolutions – Austria suffered a serious loss of position. The restored regime, rescued by Russian troops, was no longer the "policeman of Europe." Austria would suffer serious losses in three subsequent episodes, the Crimean War, the unification of Italy, and the unification of Germany. With nationalist movements rising throughout the Balkans, this multi-ethnic empire was easily the most vulnerable, the most threatened of the major powers. Russia was recognized as the major continental power, second only to the British Empire in population and territory. But that changed with a major defeat in the Crimean War, a later defeat in the Russo-Japanese War, and the 1905 revolution. France was a major power but its defeat by Prussia in 1870–71 showed its strength to be limited. The newly united Germany was clearly strong, a nation perhaps best described as "a comer," one looking for its "place in the sun." Italy was also "a comer," but its efforts were repeatedly thwarted. Britain was unquestionably a great power with the largest empire in the history of the world. But, as indicated, it generally avoided involvement in continental affairs.

The Ottoman Empire was clearly in decline. The Ottomans crossed into Europe in 1345 and conquered Hungary and much of Austria until their "forward movement" was stopped with defeat at Vienna in 1683. The Empire had been in retreat ever since, a process that accelerated in the decades just before 1914. That retreat created the second major problem for the European powers: what states, or what arrangements, would replace the Ottomans? Called "the Eastern question," the problems posed were prime concerns for Austria-Hungary and Russia and of considerable interest to Great Britain.

The European powers showed varying degrees of interest in imperialism, in gaining and maintaining control over other peoples and territories. Although beginning earlier, much of this effort, a "second wave," occurred in the last decades of the nineteenth century. The European Concert operated with a clear double standard: the major powers sought peace and civility "at home" in Europe, but war and rapacity was the accepted practice elsewhere, most of that occurring in Asia and Africa. Great Britain undertook four military interventions on the European continent in this period, three minor "police actions" in Greece, Portugal, and Belgium, plus the Crimean War. In that same period, according to one account, Britain engaged in twenty-two conflicts elsewhere, that is, on other continents. Byron Farwell reports that there "was not a single year in Queen Victoria's long reign [from 1837 to 1901] in which somewhere in the world her soldiers were not fighting for her and her empire." Those off-continent ventures occasionally had effects that "spilled over" and threatened the European peace. The Fashoda affair, for example, was "the worst crisis in Franco-British relations since Waterloo." The Boer War and the two Moroccan crises also had very serious consequences for the European powers. Still more serious was an incursion into North Africa by Italy in 1912.

The European "social contract," the so-called Concert, was always in need of repair and adjustment. The strains became greater with the growing importance of the "Eastern question" and of the imperialist scramble elsewhere in the last decades of the century. Some accounts of the origin of the Great War begin with the assassination of Archduke Franz Ferdinand, the mobilizations that followed, and the first acts of war. The reading of the war's origins offered here takes a longer view, emphasizing first the remarkable fact – 99 years without a world war. We turn then to the breakdown of the restraints or, put differently, the failure (or refusal) to either maintain or reestablish "the Concert."

By our count, twenty-three European wars were fought in that 99-year span. These wars fall into three general categories depending on the causal dynamics. Some are best described as restorationist, where one or more of the powers sought to put down political or national insurgency. Some were fought to either gain or enhance great power status (or alternatively, to maintain it). And others involved "the Eastern question," these stemming from problems posed by the decline of the Ottoman Empire. For some populations, these wars were simultaneously national liberation struggles, efforts to create new states.

Most of the restoration efforts came in 1815–47, in the Metternich period. In July 1820 in Naples, the capital of the Kingdom of the Two Sicilies (an Austrian satellite), members of a secret sect, the Carbonari, together with army officers forced their king to accept a liberal constitution. In March 1821 in Turin, the capital of Piedmont in northwest Italy, a part of the army revolted and demanded a constitution. The royalists responded with an appeal for Austrian aid. Metternich sent Austrian troops into both kingdoms and put down the insurgencies. Two years later, France, under Louis XVIII, the restored Bourbon king, sent troops into Spain for the same purpose.

The uprising of Greeks against their Turkish overlords in 1821 posed a different set of problems and, ultimately, yielded a different outcome. Metternich was opposed to intervention. This insurgency was in the Ottoman Empire, outside the Concert's chosen jurisdiction. And he feared the implications of Russian involvement. Eventually, an "unnatural" coalition was formed and, over Metternich's objections, Russia, France, and Britain sent naval forces to encourage a compromise. But the planned nonviolent intervention went astray and in the Battle of Navarino Bay the Ottomans suffered a major defeat. Britain, France, and Russia then arranged a settlement, without either Greek or Turkish participation, in which Greece was declared an independent state, guaranteed by the three powers. The new nation was to be a monarchy. The allies found someone willing to serve, the seventeen-year-old son of the Bavarian king. The Greek civil war gave Russia an opportunity for expansion. The resulting Russo-Turkish War (1828–29) brought another defeat for the Ottomans and further loss of territory.

In 1830 three revolutions disturbed the domestic peace. But all three were contained and yielded outcomes that, while not entirely pleasing, were nevertheless acceptable to the leaders of the major powers. The July revolution in Paris ousted the Bourbons and replaced them with the Orleanist branch of the same family. The new monarch, Louis Philippe, agreed to some modest constitutional restraints. Later that year, Belgium broke away from the United Netherlands, this insurgency stemming from resentment over the monarch's anti-Catholic and pro-Dutch policies. The Dutch king sent troops to regain the lost provinces but the major powers intervened, forced an armistice, and arranged the division of the unitary kingdom they had established fifteen years earlier. Like Greece, the new state would be a monarchy and a kinsman by marriage of the British royal family was chosen as king. In 1839 the great powers signed an agreement declaring that Belgium would be a "perpetually neutral" state. The third revolution occurred in the Russian satellite state, Congress Poland, in November 1830. Some 100,000 Russian troops were required to defeat it, the struggle ending only in September the following year.

The Metternich system collapsed with the 1848 revolutions. Although frequently portrayed as class struggles, several of these were national in character. The uprisings began in January at Palermo in the Kingdom of the Two Sicilies. The Neapolitan army had to abandon Sicily and three weeks later the king granted a constitution. Revolutions occurred in Paris, Brussels, Karlsruhe, Munich, Dresden, Vienna, and Berlin, most of these involving demands for basic rights and constitutional reforms. Insurgents in Piedmont again battled the Austrians. National revolts occurred also in Bohemia and in Hungary. Insurgents in the largely German-speaking provinces of Schleswig and Holstein rejected Danish rule and briefly gained independence. In June 1849 Russia came to Austria's assistance and sent troops into Hungary to suppress the revolt there.

The 1848–49 revolutionary efforts were all ultimately defeated. "Reform" involved, at best, some modest moves in the direction of constitutional monarchy. The French overthrew the monarchy and created the Second Republic. But a few years later, Louis Napoleon, a nephew of the great Napoleon, overthrew the republic and established a dictatorship, the Second Empire. Overall, the immediate achievements, political, social, and national, are best described as meager.

A significant reordering of priorities was manifest in the second period, 1849 to 1871. Several nations now chose war in preference to the peacekeeping efforts of the European Concert. Three major international conflicts were fought in this period, the Crimean War, the wars of Italian unification, and those of German unification. In all three conflicts, for the first time since 1815, major European powers fought each other. Britain and France fought Russia in the Crimean War. France joined Piedmont in the struggle against Austria that led to Italian unification. Prussia, seeking to enhance its status, moved first against Denmark, then against Austria, and finally against France, inflicting serious defeats in the two latter conflicts. As of 1871, the relative positions of the European powers had been decisively altered.

The Crimean War (1853–56) was a curious, unexpected, and unusual conflict. Britain and France reached across the Continent and together with the Ottomans (and later with token support from Piedmont) fought a war against Russia. Judged in terms of the losses incurred, the Crimean War was the largest European war of the ninety-nine-year period. The central concern for the three major participants was the Straits. For Russia, it was the key to any naval effort in the Mediterranean or in more distant locations. Without the assurance of unhindered passage, Russia could have no serious impact. Britain was concerned with its connections to India and other points in the East. France claimed some rights in the eastern Mediterranean, protection of Roman Catholics in the Holy Lands, rights that were more boldly asserted by Napoleon III than by his predecessors. Given their aims, both Britain and France saw the Ottoman Empire as a useful buffer state. Some elements of "realism," in short, underlay their involvement in this struggle. The tottering buffer state would be supported and the Russian naval threat would either be limited or removed entirely.

Piedmont joined with the allies, sending 15,000 men to the Crimea. That small state had no immediate interest in the distant struggle, but Premier Camillo di Cavour anticipated that his nation would gain prestige and be represented at the future peace conference. There was also a *quid pro quo* – his allies would be under some obligation to Piedmont in future conflicts. Unexpectedly, Austria did not come to the aid of Russia but instead undertook actions that favored the Ottomans, Britain, and France. For the Russians this was a betrayal, no fit compensation for the aid provided in 1849 to pacify Hungary. Subsequently, in the wars leading to Italian and German unification, Austria found itself without allies. Russia, its "natural" ally, did not intervene in 1859 or in 1866 when Austria was in serious difficulty.

"Public opinion" had some impact in the origins of this conflict. Monarchs in previous ages did not have to "consult with" the general populace; they were not pushed or constrained in any serious way by mass sentiment. But the extension of education and the consequent growth of literacy provided the basis for mass circulation newspapers, which could inform and mobilize opinion as in no previous era. The long dispute prior to the outbreak of hostilities stretched over nine months during which it was "continuously ventilated" in British and French newspapers. The Russian actions, it is said, aroused a patriotic fervor. Press reports and public sentiments would be factors in all subsequent crises. Political and military leaders, accordingly, had to "stylize" the beginnings of conflicts in such a way as to make engagement seem plausible and justified.

The Crimean War ended with the Treaty of Paris (1856). For Russia it was a major defeat. The most important of the losses was the neutralization of the Black Sea: its waters were "to be open to merchantmen of all nations and closed to all warships." M. S. Anderson describes the settlement as "extremely harsh and indeed unprecedented. . . . Its greatest single achievement was to make Russia a revisionist power, to end the stress on conservative solidarity and maintenance of the *status quo* . . . [it led to] a concentration on purely Russian interests." In a separate treaty, Britain, France, and Austria "guaranteed the independence and integrity of the Ottoman Empire." In 1858, with some French assistance, Romania was created out of two Ottoman principalities previously under Russian control. Russia's leaders opposed this move but could do nothing to stop it.

Much of Russia's influence in international affairs prior to the Crimean War, Barbara Jelavich writes, was "due to a gross overestimation" of its military strength. From the Napoleonic Wars through to the early 1850s, Russia had faced no real test of that strength and the empire's opponents accordingly "remained hypnotized by the mass of the Russian territory and the size of the Russian army." But the loss in this war demonstrated Russia's weakness, making clear it could no longer be the "gendarme of Europe." With Russia's "restraining hand" removed, Napoleon III's France "was able to assist in the unification of Italy and play a generally disruptive role in regard to other national movements."

The Austro-French-Sardinian War was fought in 1859, three years after the Crimean War. In a prior secret agreement, Napoleon III arranged with Cavour to support Piedmont in its efforts to gain Lombardy and Venetia, two Italian-speaking territories then under Austrian rule. Austria suffered serious defeats at Magenta and Solferino. In the settlement, Vienna gave up Lombardy and Austrian leaders were removed from three satellite states, Tuscany, Modena, and Parma. Napoleon III backed out of a promise to liberate Venetia and for a few more years that state remained with Austria. After further struggles, Italian unification was achieved in 1861. More was to be gained later, Venetia in 1866, the Papal States in 1870, and Trentino-Alto Adige in 1918. The "rise" of Italy, it will be noted, meant losses for Austria.

Three other wars occurred in this second period, these initiated by Prussia. Usually referred to as the wars of German unification, these were the Danish-Prussian War (1864), the Austro-Prussian War (1866), and the Franco-Prussian War (1870–71). In the first, Prussia and Austria took Schleswig and Holstein from Denmark with Austria occupying Holstein. In the aftermath, Otto von Bismarck engineered a falling out with his Austrian partner and brought about the second war. Although generally called the Austro-Prussian War, most of the smaller German states were involved, siding primarily with the Habsburgs. Austria was quickly and definitively defeated. The settlement, directed largely by Bismarck, gave Prussia clear dominance among the German-speaking states. Italy was also a participant and, in the settlement, was given Venetia.

The war had a further consequence: it brought about the reorganization of the Austrian Empire. Prussia had, among other things, used subversion as a weapon in that conflict. Facing an ethnically diverse opponent, Berlin gave support to nationalist movements, specifically to the Hungarians, the aim being to fragment and immobilize its opponent. After the war, to address that problem, Austria produced the Compromise (*Ausgleich*) of 1867, giving a wide range of powers to a newly created Hungarian government and parliament. The empire at this point became Austria-Hungary, or the Dual Monarchy. The arrangement still left out the nation's majority, consisting of nine other national groups. Austria-Hungary was easily the most fragile of the five major powers. In a period of growing nationalist sentiments, this multinational empire was a vulnerable entity.

The Franco-Prussian War (1870–71), the third of Bismarck's wars, was also brief. The result was a stunning and humiliating defeat for France, which, by the Treaty of Frankfurt, was obliged to pay large reparations. The sum fixed was "exactly proportionate with the one imposed by Napoleon I on Prussia in 1807." One province, Alsace, and part of another, Lorraine, were taken from France and added to the new German Empire.

The creation of a unified Germany on 18 January 1871 was easily the most important result of the war. The centuries-long history of small-state fragmentation was now ended. The new Germany, a large unified nation with a rapidly growing economic base, would be a major power, one of much greater strength and importance than tottering Austria-Hungary and seriously weakened Russia and France. Informed observers recognized the importance of this development. Benjamin Disraeli, the British Conservative Party leader, told Parliament that the struggle between France and Germany "is no common war" like the two preceding European conflicts. This war, he said, "represents the German revolution, a greater political event than the French revolution of last century. . . . Not a single principle in the management of our foreign affairs, accepted by all statesmen for guidance up to six months ago, any longer exists."

The Concert of Europe, clearly, was not operating in this second period. Beginning with the Crimean War and ending with the Treaty of Frankfurt, the collective concern had been all but abandoned. As of 1871 the new "balance sheet" read as follows: Prussia, now Germany, had achieved significant gains; it was soon to be the major economic power of Europe and also a major military power. Piedmont, now Italy, also made major gains; it was now "a power" although clearly not of the same rank as the original Concert members. France had experienced major losses; it would never again have the stature it held from the time of Louis XIV to the end of Napoleon's rule. Russia's weakness had been amply demonstrated; from 1856 on, it was no longer the ultimate arbiter of central European affairs. And last but not least, Austria had lost its long-standing dominance in central European affairs and was now replaced by the Prussian "upstart."

After German unification in 1871, central and west Europe experienced more than forty years of peace. All of the wars fought between 1875 and 1913 were based in East Europe; all involved "the Eastern question." The main contenders were the Ottomans, Austria-Hungary, Russia, and the emerging Balkan states. As the Ottomans retreated, or were beaten back, the key question was that of succession: which state (or states) would take its place?

Austria had experienced a series of losses. Unable to defeat the 1848 revolution on its own, it needed Russian assistance to recover Hungary. One important result of the Crimean War was that Russia was no longer an ally. In 1859 Austria lost a war to France and was deprived of some Italian territories. Then in 1866 it was defeated in the contest for dominance in central Europe, losing power, prestige, and more Italian territory. A few years later, Austria-Hungary sat out the Franco-Prussian War hoping, vainly, for gains if Prussia foundered. To maintain the nation's historic position as a great power, Austria-Hungary's leaders had to demonstrate its continuing political capacity.

One might think that Austria-Hungary would seek to demonstrate that "capacity" through "expansion" into the Balkans, still largely under Ottoman hegemony, but that inference would be mistaken. In 1875 Count Julius Andrassy, the Habsburg foreign minister, declared that Turkey's presence in the Balkans was "essential to our well-understood interests. She keeps the *status quo* of the small states and hinders their aspirations to our advantage. Were there no Turkey, then all these heavy duties would fall on us." Several decades later, with continued Ottoman decline, Austria-Hungary was forced, as best it could, to undertake those "heavy duties."

A. J. P. Taylor made a similar claim about Russia's Balkan aims. Russia, he wrote, "had no ambitions in European Turkey nor interest in the Balkan states, except as neutral buffers versus Austria-Hungary and Germany." There were "no Russian banks in the Balkans, no Russian-owned railways, virtually no Russian trade." The principal concern of Russian policy was the waterway, the "fear of being strangled at the Straits." Anderson offers a similar reading: "The Russian government did not wish to destroy the Ottoman Empire; but for a good many years Russian policy had envisaged the creation in its Balkan provinces of a series of autonomous states under Christian rulers somewhat on the lines of Rumania and Serbia." Both Austria and Russia wished to see small and divided states in the region, ones that were allies or satellites, or, at minimum, nonthreatening neutrals.

But the leaders of the existing and now emerging Balkan states had other plans. Their prime aim was independence and that required, first, the removal of the Ottomans, and second, the achievement of national unification. All Serbs, for example, should be brought together in the new nation. The same would hold for Croats, Slovenians, Romanians, and so forth. The new states, in short, aimed to repeat the Piedmont experience. The Serb nationalists advertised that fact in the title of their newspaper, *Pijemont*. Some Italian-speaking populations were still under Austrian rule; for Italy's nationalists unification was not yet complete. All of those aspirations, as the Austrian and Hungarian leaders well knew, threatened losses of population and territory.

Recognizing the many sources of instability in Europe after unification, Bismarck sought to alleviate the most obvious problems. First, he arranged an easy peace for Austria after the 1866 war, taking no Austrian territory and imposing only a token indemnity. This left the door open for a reconciliation that came quickly. Second, to the other European powers he declared that Germany was "satiated," that it had achieved its goals and would now concentrate on internal development. Third, fearing a war of revenge, he sought to counter a possible French threat. The worst combination would be France joined with Russia leaving Germany caught in middle and facing a two-front war. Thus, he cultivated a Russian alliance and, simultaneously, encouraged the French to seek "glory" elsewhere, that is, overseas. The French leaders did just that. The nation's foreign affairs crises in this period – Indochina, Fashoda, Morocco 1905, and Morocco 1911 – were all linked to the colonial aspirations, not to the recovery of "the lost provinces," Alsace and Lorraine.

In October 1879 Bismarck opened negotiations with Austria-Hungary that produced the Dual Alliance. This linkage, which lasted to 1918, was to be of pivotal importance in European affairs over the next four decades. In 1882 the alliance was extended to include Italy, thus the Triple Alliance.

Recognizing the unique problem stemming from Germany's central position in Europe, the nightmare of a two-front war, Bismarck in June 1887 arranged a highly secret treaty with Russia. Called the Reinsurance Treaty, the parties agreed for a three-year term to remain neutral in a war waged by the other. Two exceptions were specified: if Russia attacked Austria or if Germany attacked France. Since those options were unlikely, from one perspective the treaty would appear pointless. But by separating Russia from France, it was an important achievement.

Gordon Craig judges Bismarck's foreign policy, on the whole, as a success with the "warmongers in France and the Pan-Slavs in

Russia . . . in eclipse." But his achievement was undone by events beginning in 1888. Kaiser Wilhelm I died that year and was succeeded by his son, Friedrich III. He was dying of cancer and within months his son, Wilhelm II, became kaiser. Unlike his grandfather, who rarely interfered with Bismarck, Wilhelm "was determined to rule his empire himself." He dismissed Bismarck and set out on a "New Course," one focused on *Weltpolitik*, to make Germany a great imperial power.

In the week following Bismarck's resignation, an important decision was made. It has been described as "the most crucial of all those made between 1890 and the outbreak of the First World War [one which] set in train the whole chain of calamity that led toward that catastrophe." On the unanimous advice of his advisors, Wilhelm II decided to let the Reinsurance Treaty lapse. The news was devastating for the Russians, who offered concessions to maintain the treaty, but these were to no avail. Those advisors, both in the Foreign Office and the General Staff, thought it was "incompatible in spirit . . . with the Austro-German treaty and would compromise Germany's relationship with Vienna." But for their intervention and advice, Wilhelm II would probably have renewed it.

Recognizing the opportunity, France's leaders proceeded to consider the otherwise "unnatural" link – republican France allied with authoritarian Russia. Discussions moved slowly and erratically until in December 1893, after a year and a half of negotiation, the tsar signed the agreement. The principal clause read: "If France is attacked by Germany, or by Italy supported by Germany, Russia shall employ all her available forces to attack Germany. If Russia is attacked by Germany, or by Austria supported by Germany, France shall employ all her available forces to fight Germany." As Donald Kagan put it, "Bismarck's worst nightmare had become reality."

The Franco-Russian alliance forced a reconsideration of Germany's military strategy. Count Alfred von Schlieffen, chief of the General Staff, devised a plan to counter the possibility of a two-front war. With some important changes, it remained Germany's basic operational concept until its implementation in August 1914. The plan was based on the assumption that Russia, the stronger enemy, would be slow to mobilize. The first aim, accordingly, was a powerful move with overwhelming force against France, this to bring a quick victory in the west. Then, with those forces transferred to the east, Germany could begin a full-force attack on Russia. To defeat France, the plan called for an invasion of two neutral countries, Luxembourg and Belgium. Massive German armies would sweep through Belgium, cross into

France, and encircle the French forces then moving into Lorraine and Alsace. That sweep would allow the Germans to attack the French flank and rear. The conflict would be over in six weeks.

One aim of the kaiser's "New Course" was to bring about an alliance with Britain, a goal that was never achieved. His bullying tactics certainly did not help. In 1894 Germany "challenged or quarreled with Great Britain about Samoa, the Congo, the Sudan, Morocco, Turkey, and Portugal's African colonies." The tactics were unpleasant and the apparent lack of motive "confused and annoyed" the British without producing any serious gain for Germany. In 1896 the kaiser made a pointless and annoying intervention in the Transvaal, sending a telegram of support to President Paul Kruger after the Jameson raid. In the course of the South-African War, much of the German press was openly pro-Boer. To many, this anti-British content reflected the sentiments of the German government.

Ideas of empire, of *Weltpolitik*, were propagated within Germany by political, military, and intellectual leaders and by various pressure groups. In 1897 Bernhard von Bülow, the state secretary of the Foreign Office (and later chancellor), provided a key slogan – Germany was demanding its "place in the sun." These aims required a strong navy and, accordingly, the kaiser and his people, led by Admiral Alfred von Tirpitz, undertook a major program of naval expansion. This too caused Britain's leaders much concern. That program was one of several factors that led Britain to move away from its long-term policy of "splendid isolation." In 1902 Britain reached an accommodation with Japan. And in 1904 it concluded a loose agreement with France called the *entente cordiale*, which settled some continuing colonial disputes.

In 1905 the French government, in violation of a previous international agreement, moved to extend its control over Morocco but the German government challenged the move. Wilhelm II made "a theatrical landing at Tangier . . . asserted [Germany's] demand for free trade and equal rights . . . and confirmed the Sultan's status as ruler of an independent country." The resulting crisis, one involving an obvious threat of war, ended with the Algeciras Conference of 1906 and a humiliating defeat for Germany. The result was that "the French got exactly what they wanted, and the Germans found themselves isolated except for the support of Austria-Hungary." Italy, from the outset, sided against its Triple Alliance partner.

After this crisis, Germany's leaders were even more concerned with the problem of *Einkreisung*, of encirclement. Their reading, Germany-as-victim, was accentuated by the inherent weakness of the Triple

Alliance. Italy had not provided expected support. And Austria-Hungary, because of its internal weakness, was thought to be not entirely reliable. The German move, intended to break up the emerging alliance, had just the opposite effect. France solidified its relations with Russia and now provided financial support to upgrade its military. The Anglo-French *entente cordiale* was also strengthened, this episode encouraging talks between their military staffs.

The imperialist ambitions of the major powers brought frequent conflicts that had lasting consequences. Early in 1904 Russia was attacked and defeated by "upstart" Japan. For Russia, the outcome was both humiliating and costly. Apart from the prestige loss, the army and navy were seriously damaged and in need of repair. A revolution broke out in 1905 and, although ultimately put down, it too brought heavy costs for a weak economy. Some German leaders considered the possibility of a preventive war at that point. Russia was incapacitated and Britain was recovering from the Boer War. A move against France could, at little cost, remove that power and break up the developing alliances. No action, however, was taken.

Russia's leaders, recognizing the empire's weakness and its "over-extension," in "rare unanimity" agreed to a rapprochement with Great Britain. The result was the Anglo-Russian *entente* of 1907 that sought to deal with the many points of contention along their central Asia frontiers (Tibet, Afghanistan, and Persia). This move, encouraged by France, was an important change from the long-standing hostility between the two powers. A new alignment was being formed – France, Russia, and Britain – soon to be called the Triple Entente, or simply the *entente*.

A range of problems in the Balkans, those centering on the "eastern question," were also concerns for the major powers. As of 1815 some areas there were ruled by Austria, but most of the region was still under Ottoman control. Ottoman rule was weak, erratic, and decentralized, occasionally operating with shared sovereignty arrangements. The years 1815 to 1914 saw much contention; it was, basically, a history of independence movements forcing the Ottoman retreat. The European powers intervened on occasion, seeking peace and/or some advantage. And, with increasing frequency, the new Balkan states fought each other, struggling for people and territory.

Bosnia and Herzegovina engaged in an extended struggle from 1875 to 1877 against their Turkish overlords. In 1876 Montenegro and Serbia, under considerable domestic pressure, came to the aid of their kinfolk and declared war on the Ottomans. Six months later, after the Turks had defeated the Serbs and repressed a rising in Bulgaria, Russia joined the struggle. The conflict appears in most textbooks as "the Russo-Turkish War." After some initial reverses, Russian forces overwhelmed the Ottomans, swept through the Balkans, and approached the outskirts of Constantinople. Alarmed by the Russian advance, Disraeli, the British prime minister, sent a squadron to Istanbul and mobilized troops elsewhere. The Russians, close to the end of their resources, quickly ended the war and, in the Treaty of San Stefano, dictated terms that would have driven the Ottomans from all but a tiny scrap of European territory. A large Bulgarian satellite state was planned, one reaching from the Black Sea to the Aegean, thus separating Turkey from the rest of Europe.

Alarmed by this Russian success, the other European powers convened the Congress of Berlin in June 1878. Presided over by Bismarck, it was the most important international gathering between the Congress of Vienna in 1815 and Versailles in 1919. The Congress substituted "a smaller, weaker, and divided Bulgaria" with part of it remaining under nominal Turkish rule. Russia recovered the part of Bessarabia lost in 1856 and was allowed to keep some territories gained east of the Black Sea. Britain received revisions of the Straits agreements. Turkey transferred Cyprus to Britain "for use as a base in the eastern Mediterranean."

Earlier, in January 1877, Russia and Austria-Hungary had signed a secret agreement according to which the latter would remain neutral in the imminent Russo-Turkish War. In exchange, Russia promised that it would create no large state in the Balkans and that Austria-Hungary would be allowed to occupy Bosnia and Herzegovina, two Turkish provinces, when it chose. Those provinces, with their Croatian, Serbian, and Moslem populations, would then be administered by Austria-Hungary although officially remaining Ottoman possessions. This transfer of administration was the subject of intense discussion at the Berlin Congress. The Ottomans, understandably, opposed it but they were overruled. Germany, Austria-Hungary, and Britain, for diverse reasons, approved the change. The Russians were divided but ultimately agreed to it. The Berlin Congress produced a disaffected Russia: the "gang-up" by the other powers denied it the fruits of victory and ended further cooperation.

Late in July 1878, a month after the Berlin agreement was signed, Austro-Hungarian troops entered Bosnia and Herzegovina.

A "ferocious and sanguinary struggle" followed. Four years later, following an order for conscription into the Habsburg army, a second revolt occurred. This took six months to subdue. Three decades later, in 1908, Austria-Hungary annexed Bosnia-Herzegovina, formally ending Ottoman rule. That move upset the Ottomans, Serbs, Russians, and others in the region. Austria-Hungary had not informed its Alliance partners of their intention. Germany's leaders, with growing economic ties to the Ottomans and the prospect of the Berlin-to-Baghdad railway connection, were "disagreeably surprised." But for the sake of the Alliance, they continued to support their partner.

Austria-Hungary's takeover was motivated by a concern with Serbia's aspirations, one aim being to block access to the sea. In the years immediately following the Berlin Congress, Serbia had been a compliant Austrian satellite. But in June 1903, the Austrophile monarchy was overthrown. Serbia's new leaders were now pushing their "larger" aspirations hoping to unify all their compatriots still under Habsburg and Ottoman rule. For support of those aims, the new Serb regime looked to Russia.

Austria-Hungary's annexation of Bosnia and Herzegovina in 1908 brought widespread opposition by the Serb population in those provinces. Russia's leaders were angered by the move but, still recovering from war and revolution, could do nothing about it. For them, it was a serious loss of prestige. The Serbian government, because of internal problems, was forced to accept the outcome, even to the extent of being compelled to repress anti-Austrian movements. The annexation left a heritage of unresolved tensions.

A second Moroccan crisis came in 1911 when France inserted troops in a clear attempt at a takeover. Germany sent a gunboat, the *Panther*, and put forward its demand for "some kind of territorial compensation," later specified as "almost the entire French Congo." France resisted and Britain reacted with strong support. Germany's leaders decided to back off and agreed to settle for "a large, but worthless, tract in Central Africa." This demonstration of Germany's ambitions further strengthened the British-French *entente*.

This crisis provided an opportunity for Rome to pursue its ambitions in Africa. Italy had first moved into Africa in 1890 with the proclamation of a new colony, Eritrea, on the Red Sea. An attempt to establish a protectorate over Ethiopia followed, but that ended with a major military disaster. Eritrea was retained and a protectorate was established over much of Somaliland, a desert acquired at great expense.

Undaunted by the limited returns, Italy saw Libya as a next opportunity. But the resulting war of conquest, in 1911–12, proved very costly in men and money. Italy did ultimately conquer Libya but economically this imperialist venture was also a major disaster.

The Libyan venture again demonstrated Ottoman weakness, and this stimulated a war in the Balkans. In the summer of 1912 the newly formed Balkan League (Serbia, Bulgaria, Greece, and Montenegro) moved toward war with the Ottoman Empire. The goal, one of formidable importance, was "the destruction of Turkey-in-Europe." The major powers showed concern but, occupied with other matters, undertook no decisive action. A last-minute flurry of diplomatic activity produced a note, transmitted by Vienna, announcing the resolve of "the powers" that "no change of the status quo would be permitted." It was transmitted on 8 October, the day Montenegro declared war on the Ottomans. A few days later, Serbia and Bulgaria joined. Unexpectedly, by the end of that month the League had defeated every Turkish army in Europe.

This conflict, the First Balkan War, was significant for several reasons. It was the first time in modern experience that small states had proceeded independently, or perhaps more appropriately, in defiance of the major powers. The European powers did intervene and in mid-December peace talks began in London. These dragged on for several months; the final agreement was not signed until 30 May 1913.

In the course of this struggle, a serious confrontation occurred in central Europe. Russia, concerned about possible Austro-Hungarian intervention in the Balkans, announced a "trial mobilization" in the Warsaw military district. Vienna countered with troop increases in Galicia. Count Leopold Berchtold, Austria's foreign minister, sent a representative to Berlin to check on German intentions should a conflict result. He was told that Germany, not sensing sufficient cause, would not come to Vienna's support. In early March the two contenders agreed to troop withdrawals and for the moment tensions eased.

The settlement of the First Balkan War effectively pushed the Ottomans out of Europe, leaving that empire with only a tiny enclave on the north shore of the Straits. Some Aegean islands were transferred to new owners; the disposition of some others was to be undertaken by the great powers. Austria-Hungary achieved two explicit demands. Serbia was denied an Adriatic port; and an independent Albania was established to counter possible Serb dominance in the area. But for

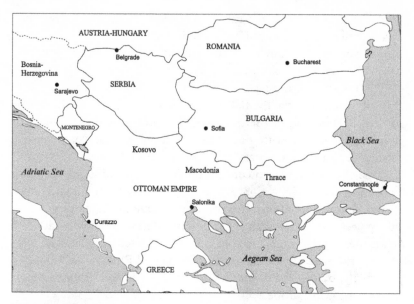

MAP 2. The Balkans, 1912

Austria, one result, an enlarged Serbia, was a source of alarm. Taylor describes the victory of Balkan nationalism as "a disaster beyond remedy for the Habsburg monarchy."

In June 1913, a month after the signing of the peace, the Second Balkan War began. The members of the League were now struggling over the division of Macedonia. Bulgaria attacked Serbia and Greece. Romania joined with the latter two and together quickly routed Bulgarian forces. Turkey joined in at that moment and regained Adrianople. Bulgaria agreed to a settlement, the Peace of Bucharest, which was signed on 10 August. Serbia emerged as the biggest winner, nearly doubling its territory and increasing its population from 2.9 to 4.4 million. Montenegro was joined to Serbia as a satellite. Still, the Serbian victories remained incomplete. Large numbers of Serbs remained under Austro-Hungarian rule in Bosnia, Croatia, Dalmatia, and Slavonia. For Austria-Hungary this new, large, aggressive, and antagonistic Serbia on its Balkan frontier was seen, understandably, as a serious threat. The settlement, it should be noted, was achieved without any great power involvement.

Initially, Austria's leaders had welcomed the breakup of the League, anticipating a long drawn-out struggle in which all participants, most especially Serbia, would lose. As events developed, Vienna wished

MAP 3. The Balkans after the Peace Settlement, 1913

to help Bulgaria but found no support from Germany or Italy. The German position is worth noting – according to Samuel R. Williamson, Berlin did not see that "Serbia posed a fundamental threat to Austria-Hungary." Later, when Austria was considering a possible intervention, it again found that the "threat posed... by Serbia remained unappreciated and minimized." The result was a "badly strained" relationship. The problem, as Williamson puts it, was one of discrepant agendas. "What was fundamental to Vienna was but part of a larger mosaic of German *Weltpolitik*."

The August settlement did not end the contention. Serbia, it was discovered, had not evacuated Albanian territory as per the agreement but had occupied still more. Austrian leaders reviewed many possible responses. One thread common to all of the options was agreement on a "military solution if diplomacy failed." Their outlook is summarized in a message from Count István Tisza, the Hungarian minister-president, to Berchtold, the Austrian foreign minister – the "border issue would show whether Austria-Hungary was a 'viable power' or had fallen into a 'laughable decadence'." Without informing Germany or Italy, its alliance partners, Austria sent an ultimatum to Belgrade. Serbia complied and withdrew the troops from Albania. This victory carried a lesson for Austrian leaders – the threat to use force would win.

It was against this background that, on 28 June 1914, the assassinations of the Austrian heir-presumptive, the Archduke Franz Ferdinand and his wife, occurred.

Following the coup d'état of 1903, Serbia was ruled by King Peter Karadjordjević, Prime Minister Nikola Pashich (Pašić), and a small coterie of civilian and military appointees. All Serbian politicians after 1903 sought national unification. All were in agreement on the anti-Austrian direction of Serb affairs, differing mainly on means and timing. Another influential person was the Russian minister in Belgrade, Nikola Hartwig. He acted more as advocate of Serbian interests than as a representative of the Russian government, which caused leaders in Belgrade to overestimate Russian support.

Secret societies were also involved in "the national struggle." They had support from active and reserve military officers and close links with the military establishment. Operating outside the official hierarchies, their actions were not subject to the constraints that might be imposed on public agencies. These societies typically had murky origins and went through various incarnations. Some of the officers who overthrew and murdered King Alexander Obrenovich in 1903 formed the secret society Union or Death (*Ujedinjenie ili Smrt*) in 1911. Popularly known as the Black Hand (*Tsrna Ruka*), its constitution declared "the aim of realizing national ideas – the unification of Serbdom." It stated further, "the organization prefers revolutionary struggle to a cultural one." The Black Hand had close ties with Serbian military leaders. In 1913 its leader, Colonel Dragutin Dimitrijevich (called Apis because his bull-like physique recalled the ancient Egyptian god) became head of Serbian military intelligence. That organization had a central role in the assassination at Sarajevo. The key question arising after that event was the involvement of the Serbian government: were the assassins acting on their own? Or were they acting as agents of the government?

Early in 1914 Pashich and Crown Prince Alexander visited St. Petersburg. There, on 2 February, in a private audience, Tsar Nicholas II gave Pashich some welcome news – "We will do everything for Serbia." But no assistance followed this bold assurance and in the spring Pashich again appealed to St. Petersburg for aid against a possible Austro-Hungarian attack. By June, "nothing had arrived" and on 18 June the Serbian legislature, somewhat reluctantly, "voted an extraordinary credit of 123 million dinars to re-equip the army."

Ten days later, on 28 June, a group of young Bosnian Serb nationalists with connections to the Black Hand assassinated Franz Ferdinand and his wife Sophie in Sarajevo. The archduke provided an appropriate target both because of his known hostility to Serbia and, supposedly, because of his support for trialism, a federalist plan with a South Slav state to be contained within the Austrian Empire. Such a reform would undermine Serbian aspirations to unite with the Serbs of Austria-Hungary. It would also hamper attempts to create a Greater Serbia including Croats and Slovenes.

The precise role of the Black Hand in the plot remains unclear. The organization did facilitate the acquisition of weapons for the plotters. Nevertheless, just as the Serbian government and the Serbian military were unable to control the Black Hand completely, so was the Black Hand unable to manage all of its agents. The assassin, 19-year-old Gavrilo Princep, who was not a member of the Black Hand, subsequently claimed the plot had been his own idea. Even if the Black Hand had wanted to prevent the killings, it would probably have faced the obstacles of youthful enthusiasm and obstinacy.

Since the beginning of June 1914, Pashich and several others in his government had been aware that a plot involving the Black Hand was underway. The government tried to investigate but, because the military was implicated in the effort, failed to clarify the situation. Pashich took limited steps to frustrate the plot, but his vague words of warning to Vienna were ineffective. Knowledge of the plot placed the Serbian government in a difficult position. If the plot were thwarted, it would uncover much of the Serbian intelligence network and run the risk of a coup d'état. If the plot succeeded, a punitive military response by the Dual Monarchy was likely.

Several other factors complicated decision-making. On 24 June King Peter temporarily retired due to ill health and Crown Prince Alexander, then 26 years of age, became head of state as regent. New elections were scheduled for 14 August. Thus, in the midst of the crisis, Pashich was conducting an election campaign. When the Austro-Hungarian ultimatum was delivered in Belgrade on 23 July, the prime minister was campaigning in the provinces. With national questions passionately debated at home, Pashich had limited room for diplomatic maneuvering. He had to be conciliatory to Austria-Hungary but, at the same time, had to undertake a strong defense of Serbian national interests.

The Serbian government showed "correct respect" in response to the killings, curtailing festivities (28 June was Vidovdan, the most important Serb national anniversary) and ordering mourning. Official condolences were dispatched to Vienna, and personal condolences to Kaiser Franz Joseph. Pashich also sent a circular to Serbian embassies, stating that the Sarajevo assassinations found the sharpest criticism in Serbian society. Official and unofficial circles were aware of the bad impression that the murders would have on relations between Vienna and Belgrade – as well as on the "position of our compatriots in Austria-Hungary." Last but not least, Pashich allowed that "anarchistic elements" (doubtless, the Black Hand) might have been responsible for the crime, but he was reluctant to identify them as the perpetrators.

Austro-Hungarian authorities at once assigned responsibility to the Serbian government. Belgrade quietly solicited support among the powers, great and small, to moderate the anticipated Austro-Hungarian demands. More importantly, it sought a promise of military support from Russia, its most likely ally. Whatever Vienna decided, the Serbs, still recovering from the losses of the Balkan Wars, had to rely on foreign and especially on Russian support. Despite the tsar's promises earlier in the year, no support was forthcoming.

Almost three weeks passed with no decisive move from Austria-Hungary. As Mark Cornwall explained, "Vienna had been partially successful in lulling Belgrade into a false sense of security." Only on 18 July did Pashich have information, from several credible sources, indicating the seriousness of the forthcoming demands. At midnight that day urgent telegrams were sent to all Serb legations (except Vienna) asking them to request foreign governments to act for reconciliation.

Baron Wladimir Giesl, the Austro-Hungarian minister in Belgrade, delivered the ultimatum at 6:00 p.m. on 23 July. It began with a direct charge: "It is clear from the statements and confessions of the criminal authors of the assassination of the twenty eighth of June, that the murder in Sarajevo was conceived in Belgrade." It then made ten demands on the Serbian government. The most contentious of these was for judicial inquiries against all those involved in the events of 28 June found on Serbian territory, this with the participation of Austro-Hungarian authorities. Belgrade was given forty-eight hours to accept. These were by any measure imposing demands. Upon learning of them, British Foreign Secretary Sir Edward Grey pronounced them "the most formidable document" he had ever seen "addressed by one state to another that was independent."

Pashich returned to Belgrade early the next morning. The attitude of the powers, especially of Russia, toward Serbia was critical in the formulation of the Serbian reply. Pashich realized that little sentiment in favor of Serbia existed in London and Paris. But clear and forceful Russian support would allow Serbia to reject much of what was demanded. Crown Prince Alexander telegraphed Tsar Nicholas II to indicate the Serb position: "We are prepared to accept those Austro-Hungarian demands which are in keeping with the position of an independent country as well as those which Your Majesty might recommend. We shall severely punish all persons who can be proven to have participated in the assassination." The message continued with an urgent statement: "[T]he Austro-Hungarian army is massing on our border. It is impossible for us to defend ourselves, and therefore we beg Your Majesty to hasten to our aid as quickly as possible."

Serbia's last-minute efforts were to no avail. None of the powers, in the words of Cornwall, "appeared to be doing anything definite to influence Vienna; all of them wanted Serbia's reply to be as conciliatory as possible, with a view to keeping the peace and then arranging some compromise." For Serbia's leaders, the most serious concern was the lack of a clear statement of support from Russia. Romania, its ally in the war with Bulgaria, recommended acceptance of the Austrian ultimatum "without reservation." That advice, along with some bland words from Greece, arrived after the ultimatum had expired.

By any measure, the Serbian government's response was remarkably conciliatory. Pashich agreed to most of the demands, albeit with the proviso, pending production of appropriate evidence. But Pashich refused the demand for Austro-Hungarian investigators empowered to act within Serbia, a point that, if accepted, would amount to a humiliating sacrifice of national sovereignty, one that would risk a backlash from the Serbian military and unpredictable actions from the Black Hand.

Pashich personally delivered the Serbian reply to the Austrian legation, just before the expiration of the time limit. Baron Giesl, following his instructions, rejected the Serbian response and immediately left for Vienna. Three days later, on 28 July, Austria-Hungary declared war on Serbia. At 5:00 a.m. the next morning gunboats of the Dual Monarchy bombarded Belgrade. This was the first "act of war" in the long struggle.

Many commentators have focused on the murders of the archduke and his wife, declaring them, in a familiar image, to have been "the spark" that set off "the conflagration." But unlike a spark in the tinderbox, the killings, by themselves, caused nothing. It was the use made of this event, initially by Austria-Hungary, that brought the nations to war. The key event, one recognized by the decision-makers of all the major powers, was the delivery of the Austro-Hungarian note to Serbia on 23 July. It was this note with its formidable demands that brought the involvement of the other powers.

CHAPTER 3

Austria-Hungary

Austria-Hungary declared war on Serbia on 28 July 1914. The first act of hostilities came the next day with the bombardment of Belgrade. Using the 28 June assassination of Archduke Franz Ferdinand as the pretext, the leaders' aim was to end the Serbian agitation that, in their view, posed a serious threat to the Dual Monarchy. In the thirty days that intervened between those dates, they took a series of steps whose purpose was to eliminate Serbia. The most important step, taken early in July, was to secure the assurance of support by Germany, their powerful ally. A second central concern was to prevent Russian participation, to limit the conflict to a "localized" Austro-Serbian war.

Two conclusions deserve special emphasis, ones that might easily be lost in the complexities of this and the following chapters: in July 1914 Austria-Hungary's leaders were the first to opt for war, and they did so with plan and foresight. The latter point may be expressed negatively – their action was not inadvertent, it was no accident, or, to use the most frequent cliché, this was no "slide into war." In short, the timing and the pace of the July Crisis were set in Vienna.

The Cast of 1914

A small coterie, not more than eight or ten persons, made the key decisions of July 1914. This coterie consisted of the emperor, Franz Joseph, the political leaders, the senior diplomats, and the top military leaders – collectively, the Council of Ministers (to be discussed later).

Franz Joseph became emperor in the midst of the tumultuous events of 1848. In July 1914 he was 84 years old; he had presided over the Habsburg heritage for 65 years. In that time he had witnessed a series of Austrian losses, and now faced still another threat. Throughout his reign he had maintained close supervision and control of Habsburg foreign and military affairs. The historian F. R. Bridge writes that the emperor was "ultimately responsible" for the most momentous decisions taken during the seven decades of his reign, "either directly or through his choice of advisers [who] almost without exception were men after his own heart." By 1900, however, that "ultimately responsible" phrase, while accurate, is misleading. During the 1908 Bosnia crisis, Foreign Minister Count Alois Lexa von Aehrenthal and Chief of the General Staff Baron Franz Conrad von Hötzendorf continued to provide the monarch with memoranda but they "increasingly behaved as if he were in virtual retirement." In the three and a half years prior to World War I he attended none of the Council's thirty-nine meetings. The governance of the empire, in short, was being delegated.

The emperor appointed the leaders of the political, diplomatic, and military branches of government after consultation with, and influence by, other officials. The foreign minister and most of the high-ranking officials at the Ballhausplatz (home of the Foreign Ministry) were members of the aristocracy; they were also graduates of either the Theresianum or the Consular Academy, and had long experience in the Foreign Service. Most importantly, they were chosen for their reliability and loyalty to the Habsburg dynastic state.

The emperor often delegated the leadership of foreign policy to the Imperial and Royal Minister of the Household and of Foreign Affairs. From 1906 to 1912, this was Aehrenthal, a forceful personality, a man of considerable charisma, and one with a sense of mission. His aim, basically, was to see the revival of the empire. The takeover of Bosnia-Herzegovina in 1908 was his work, for better or for worse, his most important achievement. As he put it: "We have reconquered again the place that belongs to us among the Powers."

Aehrenthal took on and trained the next generation of diplomats, imbuing them with his sense of purpose. They were staunch admirers of their mentor, his loyal and devoted disciples. They had entered the diplomatic corps at the turn of the century and had served in varying capacities in the Balkans. They held social Darwinist viewpoints with respect to the "lesser Balkan peoples." Sometimes called the Young Turks or the Young Rebels (rebelling against Austria's easy-going ways), they would have considerable influence on Aehrenthal's successor.

Aehrenthal died in February 1912 and was succeeded by Count Leopold Berchtold. At age 49 years he was the youngest foreign minister in Europe. For five years Berchtold had been Vienna's ambassador to Russia where he served with distinction. But he lacked experience in the management of foreign affairs, never having been a section chief in the Ministry. He also lacked experience in domestic affairs and in military matters, a persistent problem for the monarchy. A reluctant office holder, Berchtold served in what he once called the "simmering cauldron at the Ballplatz" against his own will and better judgment. One authority describes him as "intelligent and hard-working and possessed of a great personal charm," but "entirely lacking in that self-confidence that carried Aehrenthal through." Berchtold showed "indecisiveness and diffidence," and quick reversals of policy became serious problems.

Berchtold's feelings of inadequacy made him heavily dependent on the advice and opinions of his personal staff at the Foreign Ministry and to compensate, he quickly adopted a "consultative" style. During the July Crisis the leading officials met regularly with Berchtold late in the evening to discuss the day's events and prepare for the next. Some scholars have portrayed Berchtold as a pawn in the hands of Aehrenthal's aggressive disciples, but in July 1914 that does not appear to have been the case. Samuel R. Williamson, Jr., writes that on this occasion Berchtold "commanded and managed the process."

The leading members of the Young Turk faction at the Ballhausplatz constituted the most vocal pro-war diplomatic cadre during the July Crisis. At their head stood the assertive Count Alexander Hoyos, a personal friend of Berchtold with diplomatic experience in Europe and Asia. In 1912 he became *chef de cabinet* in Berchtold's ministry. At age 36, "Alek" Hoyos headed the foreign minister's small immediate staff and thus was at the center of decision-making. Early in July Berchtold dispatched Hoyos to Berlin with Vienna's pleas for German support in its planned campaign against Serbia.

Just below Hoyos were the Foreign Ministry's five section chiefs. Count János Forgách had served as minister to Belgrade from 1907 to 1911. Thus, he played a significant role during the Bosnian crisis of 1908, but the following year discredited himself by providing forged documents for a highly publicized treason trial at Agram (Zagreb).

Sent into professional exile at Dresden, in the fall of 1913 Forgách returned to the Foreign Ministry as chief of its Political Section. The major participants in the July Crisis assign Forgách (along with Hoyos) a prominent role in those events. As head of the Political Section, he was responsible for preparing Berchtold's personal correspondence and material for Common Ministerial Council meetings. During the July Crisis, Forgách maintained daily telephone contact with both Minister-President Count István Tisza at Budapest and Baron István Burián, the Hungarian emissary to Vienna.

Next in importance came Baron Franz von Matscheko, a senior section chief and Berchtold's Balkan expert. On 24 June, just four days before the killings at Sarajevo, Matscheko had counseled a more aggressive diplomatic policy, one requiring the support of both Tisza and the Germans. He had spoken of Russia's "encirclement" of the Dual Monarchy and demanded "energetic" steps to break that alleged iron ring. As well, Matscheko identified Bulgaria as a potential ally and Romania (an ally) as a potential foe. After Sarajevo, Matscheko replaced his strident call for a more militant diplomatic policy with one for an aggressive military policy. And finally, there was Baron Alexander von Musulin, a diplomat and bureaucrat in the Foreign Ministry who was entrusted by Forgách with drafting the ultimatum to Serbia in July 1914.

Among senior Habsburg ambassadors, the two most important were at Berlin and St. Petersburg. Count Frigyes Szápáry von Szápár had been Forgách's predecessor as head of the Political Section; late in 1913 he was named ambassador to St. Petersburg, the first Russophobe to hold the position for some time. Personal problems forced Szápáry to leave St. Petersburg almost as soon as he had arrived, leaving much of the work to Legation Secretary Count Ottokar Czernin. During the first weeks of the July Crisis, Szápáry was again absent due to the illness of his wife, which of course hindered both intelligence and diplomatic efforts. But in Vienna during those weeks he participated in several important sessions dealing with the crisis. He returned to his post in the Russian capital in mid-July.

Count Ladislaus Szögyény-Marich had held the critical ambassadorship to Berlin since 1892. The most senior Habsburg ambassador, Szögyény loyally acted as a conduit for diplomatic messages rather than as a shaper of relations with Berlin. The arrival of Hoyos in Berlin as a special envoy of both Franz Joseph and Berchtold effectively reduced the ambassador's role during the most sensitive phase of the July Crisis.

The two minister-presidents, Counts Karl Stürgkh of Austria and Tisza of Hungary, like Berchtold were also members of the Common Ministerial Council. Their primary concerns, ordinarily, were with internal affairs. Each ruled his half of the monarchy on the basis of separate Austrian and Hungarian constitutions. Each appointed a Cabinet directly responsible to the two respective legislatures at Vienna and Budapest. And while the conduct of foreign policy was assigned to a "common" foreign minister (Berchtold) for the entire monarchy, in reality war could be declared (and conducted) only with the consent of the two minister-presidents, who thus had what *de facto* if not *de jure* amounted to veto powers.

Stürgkh was a professional bureaucrat, a man of limited vision whose career should have ended with his appointment as minister of education in 1908. Instead, he was appointed minister-president in November 1911. A bureaucrat of German centralist tendencies, Stürgkh proved to be disaster. In July 1913 he overthrew the Bohemian constitution, and in March 1914 he prorogued the Austrian parliament, the Reichsrat. As a result, Austrian politicians played no role in the events following the Sarajevo assassination.

Tisza was cut from a different cloth. Minister-president since June 1913, the Magyar aristocrat firmly believed in the Compromise of 1867 as the supreme guarantor of Hungarian rights against Germans, Romanians, and Slavs. Tisza ruled his half of the Dual Monarchy with an iron first. No decision could be reached at Vienna without his support. Early on in the July Crisis, Tisza indicated some concerns, some grounds for dissent with respect to war with Serbia, but he eventually yielded.

Tisza's activities, understandably, were based largely in Budapest. For this reason, his emissary in Vienna, Count Burián, during the July Crisis was an influential participant in Council discussions. Serious, unimaginative, and prone to strict legalistic approaches to issues, Burián in July 1914 was little more than Tisza's mouthpiece in Vienna.

The common finance minister, Ritter Leon von Biliński, was an avowed "hawk." Already during the Balkan Wars, he had demanded that Habsburg forces intervene not only in Montenegro, but also that they march against the Serbs – even if this brought about war with Russia. A victorious war against Montenegro-Serbia, Biliński counseled in May 1913, alone could bring new territories to the Dual Monarchy and arrest the forces of nationalism. During the July Crisis, Biliński, not surprisingly, reiterated his strident calls for military action against Serbia, with or without German support. After the Great War, he admitted to a friend that Austria had decided on a war course at the latest by 3 July.

And finally, there was the common minister of war, Ritter Alexander von Krobatin. The son of an army officer, he had been schooled exclusively in military institutions. He taught at the Technical Military Academy and later headed the Artillery Cadet School. From 1896, he served in the War Ministry and, in 1912, was named as its head. Krobatin worked tirelessly to modernize the Austro-Hungarian artillery. In July 1914 he vigorously supported the "hawks" in calling for an immediate military strike against Serbia.

The two minister-presidents and the several ministers listed above operated through the Dual Monarchy's Common Ministerial Council, the highest agency in the empire's complicated governmental system. Officially, the emperor presided over its meetings but more often his appointed foreign minister chaired it. This select group had the authority to summon others, such as the chief of the General Staff, to participate in their discussions. At its disposal were all of the resources of the government, which for July 1914 meant effectively all the personnel of the Foreign and War Ministries.

The Common Ministerial Council, in the words of John Leslie, was "more a discussion group than an executive cabinet." In fact, between October 1913 and July 1914 it met only three times. It was not regulated by any constitution or laws. Apart from an ineffectual oversight agency, called the Delegations, it was not subject to any serious restraints. The Dual Monarchy was constructed so as to preserve, as best it could, the empire's absolutist character. But, as stated earlier, it should not be overlooked that its decisions could be enacted only if the governments of both halves of the monarchy were united behind the Council's decisions. The Common Ministerial Council would make the decision for war in July 1914.

The Council's consideration of war required the services of still other military specialists, the most important of whom was the chief of the General Staff, Conrad von Hötzendorf. He had participated in various campaigns most notably in the Balkans, had taught at the War Academy, and had held regimental, divisional, and corps commands. Conrad met and became a friend of the heir apparent, Franz Ferdinand, who helped him acquire the chief of staff position late in 1906. Over the next five years Conrad sought to update the antiquated Habsburg forces, especially the artillery. His advocacy of a preemptive

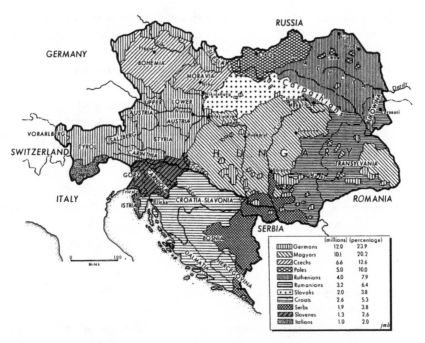

	(millions)	(percentage)
Germans	12.0	23.9
Magyars	10.1	20.2
Czechs	6.6	12.6
Poles	5.0	10.0
Ruthenians	4.0	7.9
Rumanians	3.2	6.4
Slovaks	2.0	3.8
Croats	2.6	5.3
Serbs	1.9	3.8
Slovenes	1.3	2.6
Italians	1.0	2.0

MAP 4. Ethnic Groups of the Habsburg Empire, 1910. *Source:* William McCagg, *History of Habsburg Jews, 1670–1918* (Bloomington: Indiana University Press, 1989), p. 168. Reprinted with permission of the publisher.

strike against Serbia brought him into conflict with the emperor and with Aehrenthal in 1911. Later that year, following his call for a pre-emptive strike against Italy (an ally then engaged in the Tripolitanian War), Conrad was dismissed. Renewed difficulties in the Balkans in 1912 led to his return as chief of staff.

Conrad was an insistent advocate of war against the empire's "congenital enemies." He counseled action against Italy, Serbia, Montenegro, and, on occasion, Romania, and Russia – or combinations of the above. His prime targets, the objects of several plans, were Serbia and Montenegro. He "argued repeatedly that the use of armed force alone could retard the centrifugal forces of nationalism in the 'multinational empire'." In July 1914 he was the most vigorous advocate of war with Serbia; in this matter, he received strong support from his close friend Krobatin, the minister of war.

Most of these key decision-makers were long-term veterans of either the Foreign Ministry or the War Ministry. Those two elites in Austria-Hungary and elsewhere were driven by somewhat different concerns, the diplomatic and military "necessities" not always converging. Another lesson should be noted, a negative one, namely the groups that were not present. Other elites, the leaders of industry, finance, church, universities, and the press, were absent from the deliberations that led to war in 1914.

Last but not least, it should be remembered that whatever decisions the members of the Common Council took, these required final blessing by the emperor. The "Fundamental Law Concerning the Exercise of Administrative and Executive Power" of December 1867 left no room for doubt on this matter. Article 1 stated clearly: "The Emperor is sacred, inviolable, and cannot be held accountable." Article 5 gave the emperor "supreme command of the armed forces" and the right to "declare war, and conclude peace." In short, the July Crisis could end with a declaration of war only with the consent of Franz Joseph.

The Run-up to 1914

The Austro-Hungarian annexation of Bosnia-Herzegovina in 1908 was viewed in most European capitals as a colossal error of judgment. The immediate consequence, a leading scholar writes, was "the disgrace and isolation of Austria-Hungary." In the years following, Foreign Minister von Aehrenthal sought to repair the damage. Vienna tried to conciliate Serbia and to convince the powers that the annexation was "the final rounding off of the Monarchy's southern frontiers; and that Vienna was now genuinely desirous of maintaining the status quo."

Russia's leaders were not convinced. Instead, they continued to believe that Vienna would seek to extend Habsburg influence or frontiers, a view that in St. Petersburg acquired "the force of an immutable political law." Indeed, the belief that Austria-Hungary's leaders had imperialist ambitions in the Balkans was widely shared. While the logic might be compelling, readily available evidence points to a different conclusion. Conrad was the most persistent advocate of the imperialist position, but he generally stood alone on this issue. In January 1909 Conrad argued "that Serbia should be attacked in March and annexed." Aehrenthal, however, declared that the Dual Monarchy "could never absorb Serbia." Any action "must be restricted to consolidating the position in Bosnia and Hercegovinia." If Serbia could not be "contained," the preferred solution was division; some parts would go to Romania, some to Bulgaria, some to newly formed Albania.

One prominent member of the leadership group was the heir apparent, Franz Ferdinand. His hope was that "the Monarchy could stay clear of Balkan entanglements." Whenever Conrad pressed for a "settling of accounts" with Serbia, the emperor and the archduke would sharply reject those demands. In a discussion in early February 1913 Franz Ferdinand declared that war and a conquest of Serbia would be "nonsense." "Let us even assume," he added, "that no one else will contest us, [that we] can in peace and quiet settle accounts with Serbia." But, he asked rhetorically and most undiplomatically, what could Vienna gain thereby? "Only a pack of thieves and a few more murderers and rascals and a few plum trees. In other words, more rabble at the cost of so many soldiers lost and several billions spent. That most favorable case, that no one contests us, is more than unlikely." At a later point, commenting on another of Conrad's plans for war on Serbia, the archduke prophetically declared:

> War with Russia means the end of us. If we take the field against Serbia, Russia will stand behind her, and we will have the war with Russia. Should the Austrian emperor and the Russian tsar topple one another from the throne and clear the way for revolution? Tell Conrad that I categorically reject further suggestions in this vein.

Because of its importance, an extended quotation on the subject is useful. These are the words Archduke Franz Ferdinand wrote in a letter of 1 February 1913 directed this time to Berchtold:

> It would be a misfortune if we were to get involved in a big war with Russia. Who knows whether we can count on protection for our left and right flank; Germany has its hands full with France, and Romania will use the Bulgarian threat as an alibi. So this is a very unfavorable time. Suppose we wage a separate war against Serbia. In no time at all, we will overpower it, but what then, and what good will it do us? First of all, we will have all of Europe after us and viewing us as a disturber of the peace. And God save us from annexing Serbia: a country over its head in debts, brimming with regicides and scoundrels, etc. As it is, we cannot even cope with Bosnia, and that nonsense alone is costing us huge sums of money and creating a host of constitutional problems. And Serbia will be far worse! We can throw away billions there and still be faced with a terrible irredenta.

Over and over, the archduke advised the Ballhausplatz along similar lines. "The best policy is to remain an onlooker while others bash in each other's skulls, *egg them on in their quarrels, and keep the monarchy at peace.*"

For most of Austria-Hungary's decision-makers, the preferred arrangement for the Balkans was fragmentation, not takeover. They wished to see a cluster of small, nonthreatening states, either harmless neutrals or docile satellites. Any additions of new Balkan populations to the Dual Monarchy would only add to the problems of what already was a nearly unmanageable multinational empire.

The transition from Aehrenthal to Berchtold brought no immediate change in the Dual Monarchy's Balkan policies. The new minister, one authority writes, "was no expansionist, but, like Aehrenthal, a firm believer in the Monarchy's role as a conservative, status quo power." But the Young Turks continued their mentor's basic directions: Forgách, Hoyos, Matscheko, and Musulin were "all advocates of a tough, confrontational approach towards the Monarchy's opponents." Berchtold responded to the difficulties posed by the Balkan wars by resorting to "concert" principles, calling on intervention by the European powers. But, as circumstances worsened, Vienna's decision-makers shifted to the use of that "tough, confrontational approach."

The Dual Monarchy was poorly prepared for such an approach. Throughout the prewar period, its military expenditures lagged far behind those of the other European powers. In 1911 Austria-Hungary's expenditures were less than a third those of Germany, barely more than a third those of Russia and Britain, less than half that of France, and only marginally greater than that of Italy. This circumstance had profound implications for any Austro-Hungarian military initiative. The obvious preferred option would be limited war, the monarchy versus one or two minor contenders. A more problematic next-best option would be a war fought with German support.

There were other difficulties. The Habsburg military was not a single unified body but instead consisted of three distinct organizations: the Imperial and Royal Army, which drew its recruits from throughout the monarchy; the Landwehr, comprised of the Austrian National Guard; and the Honvéd, the royal Hungarian National Guard. The Habsburg Army was critical to maintaining a unified empire and keeping its multinational populace loyal. Although dominated by Germans, that army faced serious nationality problems. In the event of an armed conflict, it would have to mobilize its reservists, which, depending on the character of the conflict, would add further elements of uncertainty. Another difficulty: the most likely opponents,

Serbia and Russia, had armies with recent combat experience. Austria and Hungary had not fought a major war since 1866.

The creation of the Balkan League in 1912 was followed immediately by two wars in the Balkans. Vienna was very much concerned about this development, sensing that enlarged and more aggressive Slavic states would threaten the Monarchy's integrity. Worse still, during both Balkan wars Berlin proved indifferent to what Vienna viewed as its vital interests. As a result, all Berchtold could do was to adopt a "wait and see" attitude and to keep Habsburg forces in a state of readiness. At a Common Ministerial Council meeting on 3 October 1913, not only the military but also the so-called Young Turks in the Foreign Ministry voiced preferences for a more forceful approach especially to Serbia. The Treaty of Bucharest in August 1913, which ended the Second Balkan War, was a severe diplomatic defeat for Berchtold. Most important for the events of July 1914, Vienna's leaders were now even more convinced that the South Slav "problem" could only be resolved by Serbia's demise.

The Dual Monarchy's leaders found further cause for alarm. While Romania was a fourth member of the Triple Alliance, albeit a secret one, there were signs of a possible defection – and worse, that it might join with Russia and the *entente* powers. Indeed, the possibility of Romania and Serbia as allies with Russian backing gave Austria-Hungary's political and military leaders nightmares. Czernin, then the monarchy's ambassador to Romania, communicated his sense of pending danger in a long letter to Berchtold on 22 June 1914. He summarized with a hypothetical statement, with "the lesson" that the French and Russians would give to the Romanians:

> 'Do not tether yourselves to a death-stricken carcass' – 'leave the sinking ship while there is still time' – 'do not cast in your lot with that of the Monarchy; Vienna can only drag you down into its own destruction, whereas the Entente, at the sharing out of the spoils, will reward you with the gift of Transylvania.'

The ambassador's final words were laced with ultimate pessimism: "Before our eyes in broad daylight, plain for all to see, the encirclement of the Monarchy proceeds glaringly, with shameless effrontery, step by step.... And we stand by with folded arms interestedly observing the carrying out of this onslaught."

Italy presented the Dual Monarchy with still another source of concern. There was uncertainty as to whether it would stay in the

Triple Alliance or, in an attempt to regain Trentino and Trieste and possibly some advantage in the Balkans, would move against the Monarchy. If that happened, Austria-Hungary would face a very difficult two- or even three-front conflict.

Countering these evident or feared losses were two possible gains. Germany was cultivating relations with the Ottoman Empire. And Bulgaria, once a dependable Russian satellite, now showed signs of defection. Still, those two nations were off at some distance to the southeast. Of greater importance, by far the more urgent concern, were the nations close at hand, those on the borders to the north, east and south.

The newly enlarged Serbia was a central problem. The Austrian military attaché in Belgrade sent Berchtold a summary of "Easter Greetings" that appeared in the Serbian press. These promised "the Resurrection," that is, "the liberation of the Slavs in the Monarchy." The problem was made worse by manifest – or apparent – Russian backing. The Russian minister in Belgrade, N. V. Hartwig, was a "ubiquitous presence" in Serbian politics and an active supporter of Pan-Slav groups there. Especially galling to Austro-Hungarian leaders were his "frequent references" to the Dual Monarchy as "the next sick man of Europe."

A further complication was that the two allies, Austria-Hungary and Germany, had markedly different readings of Balkan affairs. German leaders thought that Romania, if properly cultivated, would remain loyal to the alliance. They also thought that Serbia could be enticed to affiliate if the right incentives were provided and if the Dual Monarchy made appropriate friendly overtures. If successful, the expanded alliance, with Italy remaining loyal to it, would form a solid bloc within central Europe. The Russian threat would be removed from the Balkans. The leaders of the Dual Monarchy viewed this reading of things as hopelessly unrealistic. It was, not too surprisingly, a source of great concern for them.

In reaction to these developments, Berchtold and his staff prepared a memorandum calling for and justifying a new and more aggressive policy in the Balkans. Called the Matscheko Memorandum, as earlier noted, it was completed on 24 June 1914 and intended for Franz Joseph, Franz Ferdinand, Tisza, and the Germans. The hope was to bring all four around to recognizing the new and urgent necessities. Its most striking feature, Williamson reports, was the "fixation on Russia's more active, assertive foreign policy." Matscheko's new threat assessment held that "St. Petersburg would press every advantage." Vienna wanted Berlin to realize just how dangerous the Russian threat had become "and that some action now, rather than later, might be preferable." Surprisingly, Serbia was not the focus of Matscheko's position paper. Rather, he trained his diplomatic guns on Russia – and on Italy. Chaos reigned in Albania, Matscheko argued, largely because the former Turkish commander, Essad Pasha, now in the pay of the Italian consul at Durazzo, incited the populace against their new ruler, Prince Wilhelm zu Wied, an Austrian. Put differently, Albania, Berchtold's major triumph in the Balkan Wars, seemed threatened by alleged Italian disloyalty.

The assassination of the archduke and his wife on 28 June 1914 shifted the Ballhausplatz focus back to Serbia. Austria-Hungary's tough, aggressive responses had proven successful between 1908 and 1913. To halt the sensed loss of position, to fend off the threat, the need now was for a more decisive action, this time for the definitive punishment of Serbia.

In the wake of the Sarajevo assassinations, a series of decisions were taken, all conscious and calculated, all designed to bring about war with Serbia. The few objections, the few signs of demurral, were largely over tactics and timing, the concern being for alternatives that would put "a better face" on things. One serious difficulty was posed by the scheduling of the Monarchy's reaction. The delay stemmed from two insurmountable problems – the needs of the economy and those of the military. Apart from these questions of implementation, the most striking feature of Austria-Hungary's decision-making was the consensus on the immediate goal, war with Serbia, even in the face of a very serious threat, that of Russian intervention.

The July Crisis

When news of the assassination arrived in Vienna late on 28 June, most of the monarchy's leaders were away for a long weekend or on vacation. There was neither panic nor even a sense of great grief. Franz Ferdinand was not a beloved figure: the emperor and the court had been scandalized by his morganatic marriage to Sophie Chotek; the Magyars detested what they perceived to be his anti-Hungarian stance; the imperial bureaucracy was concerned about his alleged reform plans for the empire; and Conrad von Hötzendorf feared for his job as long as the archduke was alive. There was no hard evidence that the Serbian government had a hand in the assassination – the Vienna press, in fact, presented its readers with a host of possible "conspiracies" to commit murder by the likes of German intelligence, Freemasons, and even Minister-President Tisza of Hungary! Almost unanimously, the sympathy of Europe's royal families (only France was a republic) was squarely with Austria-Hungary; regicide appealed to few crowned heads. Moreover, members of royal houses and aristocratic families had been murdered before without serious consequences. Recent wars in the Balkans and in northern Africa had not led to a wider war. Why should 28 June 1914 be different?

The Austrian case is striking in that a great power, without certain knowledge of the regicides and their putative handlers, decided almost immediately on war. There was much informal debate about "punishing" Serbia for its alleged support of the archduke's murderers, but the real discussions at the Ballhausplatz focused almost at once on using the assassination to advantage. As one senior Habsburg diplomat, Baron Leopold von Andrian-Werburg, indelicately stated, "precious fruits for the Monarchy were to ripen" from Franz Ferdinand's spilled blood. Put differently, leaders in Vienna quickly grasped that an aggressive stance against Belgrade could change the perception of Austrian weakness, decadence, and decline not only in Serbia but also in much of the rest of Europe. Two of the Young Rebels at the Foreign Ministry, Forgách and Matscheko, met right after news of the assassination arrived. They rewrote Matscheko's 24 June memorandum, which called for a more aggressive diplomatic policy at the Ballhausplatz, and instead counseled a military solution to the Serb "problem."

Foreign Minister Berchtold "commanded and managed" the decision-making at Vienna in the aftermath of the killings at Sarajevo. His primary concern was to learn the reactions of Franz Joseph, Tisza, and Wilhelm II. Several members of the Common Ministerial Council, most notably Austrian Minister-President Stürgkh, Common Finance Minister Biliński, and War Minister Krobatin, pressed for immediate action against Serbia. Chief of the General Staff Conrad von Hötzendorf announced that the murder was "Serbia's declaration of war on Austria-Hungary [and that] the only possible response to it [was] war." He wished to mobilize on 1 July without further discussions with Serbia. Berchtold later summarized Conrad's views during the July Crisis with three words: "War, war, war." Despite those pressures, the foreign minister moved cautiously in the first days after the assassination.

On Tuesday, 30 June, Berchtold met with Franz Joseph. Both agreed that they should "await the judicial investigation," that they should learn Tisza's views, and, most importantly, that they should inquire about Berlin's attitude. They learned the same day that Tisza opposed an immediate military confrontation. Fearing new annexation of Slav subjects to Hungary, Tisza wrote letters to Franz Joseph on 1 July and later on 8 July to seek assurance that diplomatic actions preceded any military effort.

By Thursday, 2 July, some information based on the interrogation of the conspirators revealed links to Serbia. Three of them, including Gavrilo Princep, had just returned from Belgrade where they had been given pistols and bombs. Complicity by several members of Serbian military intelligence – most notably by Colonel Dragutin Dimitrijević ("Apis") – was suspected. This incomplete report (which said nothing of the "Serbian" leaders' involvement) helped reinforce the already existing consensus. Oskar Potiorek, the governor-general of Bosnia (and the man most responsible for the failure of security at Sarajevo), also argued for an attack on Serbia, this to help put down the alarming and pervasive "unrest" he now, with generous distortion, reported in the recently annexed territory. That same day Berchtold drafted a private letter from Franz Joseph for presentation to Wilhelm II. It placed the blame for the assassination on Russia and on Serbian Pan-Slavs. While not specifically calling for war, it stated that "the band of criminal agitators in Belgrade" could not go "unpunished." The intention was unmistakable.

Berchtold made clear his bellicose stance on 3 July in conversation with Heinrich von Tschirschky, Germany's ambassador to Vienna. He spoke of the need for a "final and fundamental reckoning" with Belgrade. While Tschirschky reacted with great caution, Wilhelm II fully endorsed Berchtold's demand with the marginal note, "now or never." The kaiser's terse comment on Tschirschky's warning against "precipitate steps" was "nonsense."

Ordinarily, the monarchs of Europe would have come to Vienna for a state funeral at which time some discussion of appropriate responses could have occurred. But because of Franz Joseph's advanced age and infirm condition, other arrangements were made. That change meant that the Dual Monarchy's leaders had to make a special effort to ascertain Germany's response. A member of the Foreign Ministry was sent, secretly, to Berlin for this purpose. "Alek" Hoyos, Berchtold's personal friend and *chef de cabinet*, volunteered for the mission. One of the most articulate "hawks" in Berchtold's circle, Hoyos would be a most competent advocate of the "pro-war" position. By choosing Hoyos, Berchtold made sure that the Germans would hear of Vienna's resolve to strike at Serbia; that the aged and unimaginative Ambassador Szögyény at Berlin would, as much as possible, be bypassed; and that any further intrusions by Tisza into the diplomatic process would be preempted. The secret mission had only one purpose: war.

On 5 July Szögyény and Hoyos reviewed the two documents from Vienna. Szögyény then had lunch with the kaiser at Potsdam. Hoyos had lunch with Arthur Zimmermann, the under-secretary of the Foreign Office (Gottlieb von Jagow, the foreign secretary, was away on his honeymoon). At 10 p.m. Szögyény cabled Berchtold the kaiser's pledge of "full German backing" in any action that Vienna took, requesting only that it proceed promptly. It would be deplorable, Wilhelm had counseled Szögyény, if Vienna did not exploit "the present situation which is so favorable to us." The kaiser's only reservation was that he would have to consult with Chancellor Theobald von Bethmann Hollweg before taking a final decision. Independently, Zimmermann conveyed much the same sense to Hoyos.

Late that afternoon, the kaiser and the chief of his Military Cabinet, Baron Moriz von Lyncker, met with Bethmann Hollweg and Erich von Falkenhayn, the Prussian minister of war. These four men "considered the question of Russian intervention and accepted the risk of a general war." And on the 6th, Bethmann Hollweg and Zimmermann ratified the commitments made by Wilhelm II. Ambassador Szögyény cabled Berchtold that evening that Bethmann Hollweg regarded Austria-Hungary's "immediate intervention" against Serbia as the "most radical and best solution" of its "difficulties in the Balkans."

These declarations of support for Austria-Hungary's imminent war on Serbia have been referred to as the "blank check." The Dual Monarchy could "fill in" the contents when it chose. Those issuing "the check" urged them to do so quickly. These promises of backing were of immense importance. Without them, Austria-Hungary could not have moved to war.

Upon his return to Vienna on 6 July, Hoyos met secretly with Berchtold and the two minister-presidents, Stürgkh and Tisza. The

German ambassador, Tschirschky, also participated in their discussion and informed the Austrians of what they already knew – namely, that Bethmann Hollweg considered the present moment to be more suitable for action than a later occasion.

The following day, Tuesday, 7 July, the Common Ministerial Council met to determine the next steps to be taken with respect to Serbia. The promise of German backing strengthened the predominant sentiment, that of "settling accounts with Serbia." Over four hours, the ministers (Berchtold, Biliński, Stürgkh, Tisza, Krobatin) as well as a guest, Conrad von Hötzendorf, examined each option. The decisions taken, in the words of Williamson, were "carefully evaluated choices." A consensus developed on the possibility of a "strongly worded ultimatum to Belgrade," one which Serbia would have to reject, thus providing the justification for a "local" war. In the afternoon, Conrad reviewed the military plans including the possibility of Russian intervention. He minimized the risks involved and, to Tisza's objections, repeated his "better now than later" phrase.

Given the decisions taken on 7 July, it follows that Austria-Hungary's leaders would seek to avoid, or block any later peacemaking efforts. Those decisions, it should be noted, were taken before any official "Serbian" role in the murders had been established. And, despite that problem, the decisions enjoyed the full support of the German Foreign Office. On 8 July Zimmermann informed the Austrians that "now was the right moment – a moment, which might not ever reappear under such favorable conditions – energetically to move against Serbia."

Then, curiously, a period of quiet followed. The ordinary citizen would have read of the assassination in Monday morning newspapers on 29 June. The next major event, signaling the alarm, was the delivery of Austria-Hungary's ultimatum to Serbia on 23 July, three and a half weeks later. For Germany's leaders, that period of quiet became a source of concern: why was the move against Serbia being delayed?

Three factors led to the postponement of the Monarchy's response. Tisza, as indicated, wished that an effort be made to establish Belgrade's role in the assassination so as to legitimate the Austro-Hungarian response. His concern led to the dispatch of an investigative body to Sarajevo, headed by a prominent lawyer and member of the Foreign Ministry, Ritter Friedrich von Wiesner. This source of the delay, however, does not appear to have been decisive.

A second and more compelling consideration was that the Monarchy's troops were not immediately available. As a concession to agrarian interests, Conrad had instituted a policy of harvest-leaves allowing men in the military to return home on temporary leave to help harvest the crops. On 6 July Conrad "discovered" that many units were on leave and not scheduled to return until 25 July. To cancel those leaves would disrupt the harvest, upset railroad schedules, and, most importantly, alert Europe to Vienna's "possible military intentions."

A third factor was the scheduled visit of France's President Raymond Poincaré and Premier René Viviani to St. Petersburg. To block a concerted response by the two *entente* partners, Vienna's leaders planned to deliver the ultimatum on 23 July, after the visit ended and when the French leaders would, literally, be at sea. The second and third factors meant that "settling accounts" with Serbia could not begin before the last week of July. Since a general mobilization would take some time, the "settlement" could not possibly begin until at least mid-August.

At a meeting on 14 July, Berchtold, Tisza, Stürgkh, and Burián reviewed matters again and agreed on the overall plan and content of the ultimatum to Serbia. The document was to be delivered to Belgrade with a 48-hour time limit. Tisza accepted the harsh ultimatum with its unacceptable demands and short deadline, but only on two conditions: there was to be no annexation of Serbian territory following a Habsburg victory, and defensive military measures were to be initiated immediately along the Romanian frontier.

One crucial aspect of Austrian decision-making deserves special note. Franz Joseph, as discussed earlier, had "the last word" with respect to these fundamental decisions. But he was not present at any of the discussions of the Common Ministerial Council where these policies were being formulated. On the morning of 7 July, prior to the key Council meeting, he left Vienna for his summer estate in Bad Ischl, five hours by train from Vienna. He remained there for the next three weeks. Since all key decisions had to be ratified by the emperor, Berchtold on 9 July had to travel to Bad Ischl to review the Council's decision. He made the journey again on the 19th for the emperor's review of the text of the ultimatum. Berchtold, Krobatin, and Biliński were there with the emperor on the 25th to await word of the Serbian response. Franz Joseph was in complete agreement with the directions chosen but had, clearly, delegated all further questions to his immediate subordinates.

Vienna's leaders at this point were engaged in a "policy of deception." They were "lulling Europe." The aim was to suggest that no exceptional measures would be taken against Serbia. The local press was asked to curtail its comments about Serbia. Attempts were made to obtain more favorable treatment in the foreign press. To allay possible fears of impending war, Generals Krobatin and Conrad left Vienna "with conspicuous fanfare" ostensibly on leave. "No military moves were undertaken, and Habsburg officers on leave were left undisturbed."

On the weekend of 18–19 July, three weeks after the assassination, information regarding Austro-Hungarian intentions was discovered and passed on to several European governments. The "leak" began on 11 July when the German foreign secretary, Jagow, informed the German ambassador in Rome of "the general thrust of Habsburg intentions." The ambassador then "mentioned" the substance of this message to the Italian foreign minister, Antonio di San Giuliani, who passed this information, on 16 July, to the Italian embassies in St. Petersburg, Vienna, and Belgrade. Austrian cryptographers had broken the Italian codes and thus discovered that this information was available in the four capitals, two of them "unfriendly." It is likely that Russian cryptographers also broke the code. Another possibility, of course, is that the Italian ambassadors passed the information directly to their hosts – in St. Petersburg and in Belgrade.

The reactions of the European nations changed dramatically. On 18 July Serbia began calling up reservists. On the same day Vienna received a memo from the Russian minister of foreign affairs, Sergei Sazonov, warning that Russia would not permit an attempt against Serbia's independence. The Habsburg ambassador in St. Petersburg, Count Szápáry, apparently allayed Sazonov's concerns at that point, convincing him that Vienna "planned nothing unusual." Three days later, however, Poincaré, in St. Petersburg, sought out the same ambassador and "left no doubt of France's support of Russia and Russia's support of Serbia." The conclusion, as Williamson puts it, is that "before the French delegation had ever left St. Petersburg, the two allies were able to shape the broad outlines of their policy for the approaching crisis."

On Sunday, 19 July, the Common Council of Ministers met at Berchtold's home, the members arriving in unmarked vehicles. The tasks were simple – to review again the terms of the ultimatum, to confirm the dates of delivery and reply, and to confirm the steps that would follow Serbia's anticipated rejection of the demands. Conrad reviewed the military situation, focusing on his Plan B, the attack on Serbia, largely neglecting the likely Russian response. The ministers "did not probe further." To assuage Tisza (who wished "no more Slavs" in the monarchy) and to fend off possible criticism by other nations, the group pledged that Austria-Hungary would take no Serbian territory. Conrad was not pleased by that decision but assumed it would be altered after the coming victory.

On 21 July Berchtold traveled to Bad Ischl, where he again briefed the emperor. And again, Franz Joseph assented to the plan of action. The same day, a sealed copy of the ultimatum was delivered to the Habsburg ambassador in Belgrade, Baron Wladimir Giesl von Gieslingen. The final version of the ultimatum was delivered to Berlin on 22 July. And, following the plan, Ambassador Giesl handed the note to the acting head of the Serbian government at 6:00 p.m. the following evening. At about the same time, copies of the ultimatum were delivered to the governments of the major European powers. All of the recipients recognized the seriousness of the move.

Serbia had commenced full mobilization three hours prior to receipt of the Austro-Hungarian note. On the following day, 24 July, Russia ordered a "period preparatory to war," a partial mobilization of four military districts bordering the Dual Monarchy. Franz Joseph ordered a partial mobilization against Serbia on 25 July, shortly after Belgrade rejected the Austrian note. The first official day of mobilization would be 28 July. Before then, however, reports of accelerating Russian military measures, initiated on 25 and 26 July, arrived in Berlin and Vienna. It must be remembered that Russia had openly warned Austria-Hungary that it would mobilize if Habsburg troops crossed the Serbian frontier. Thus, senior leaders in Vienna could have no doubt about the wider (European) implications of their actions. This notwithstanding, Berchtold asked Franz Joseph to sign a declaration of war against Serbia. Again the emperor assented and the Dual Monarchy declared war on 28 July. The first hostile action occurred the next day when Austria-Hungary bombarded the Serbian capital. The Russian general mobilization came shortly thereafter.

The Austrian decision for war, as seen, was the end result of a careful, well thought out, and rational process. Early on, the leaders sought and secured a promise of support from their major ally. Then Vienna's senior ministers, diplomats, and military leaders met twice in planned formal sessions to review the issues and to weigh their options.

On 7 July and again on 19 July they reached the same conclusion, namely, that the empire's "Balkan problems" could be solved only by war against Serbia. They then sought, and received, formal approval for their decision from the ultimate decision-maker, Franz Joseph. But then, curiously, having decided on war, they failed utterly in planning for the implementation and execution of that decision.

The impact of the assassination itself should be noted. A rash, impetuous act of murder committed by a teenager at Sarajevo on 28 June 1914 removed the Dual Monarchy's most influential and outspoken opponent of war with Serbia and, consequently, of war with Russia. The killing allowed Conrad von Hötzendorf to remain chief of staff and it emboldened Count Berchtold to act on the "hawkish" advice of Conrad and of the Young Rebels at the Foreign Ministry.

Conclusion

For the past four decades, Fritz Fischer's powerful indictment of the German decision for war (to be reviewed in the next chapter) dominated commentary on the origins of the Great War. Fischer's arguments, first enunciated in 1961 and then sharpened in a follow-up work in 1969, were so radical, so powerful, and so devastating to German conservative historians, that attention was riveted almost exclusively on Germany. Austria-Hungary's part in starting the "great seminal catastrophe" of the twentieth century was glossed over: Berlin, Fischer brazenly stated, had merely taken Vienna "on the leash." Gradually, however, scholarly judgment has shifted to a more complex, to a more nuanced view. The initial decision for war, after all, was made in Vienna, not Berlin.

Today, serious scholarship into the origins of the war focuses, unambiguously, on Austria-Hungary. That country's government, Williamson writes, "clearly initiated the violence in July 1914." Later, in another forceful statement, he declares, "Vienna plunged Europe into war." With regard to relations between Vienna and Berlin, Williamson argues that Vienna made the original decision for war, approached its ally for support, decided the pace and the timing of events, and eventually foreclosed all options other than war.

We have numerous statements by Habsburg diplomats involved in the July Crisis to justify Williamson's conclusions. "Alek" Hoyos openly admitted to Josef Maria Baernreither, a German-Austrian politician: "We want the war, that is why we composed the note [to Serbia] that way." Another senior Austrian diplomat, Andrian-Werburg, writing in December 1918, declared: "We started this war, not the Germans, and certainly not the Entente." Also attesting to that clear intention are the various rejections by Vienna's decision-makers of the last-minute peacemaking efforts originating in London. When Foreign Minister Berchtold on 27 July asked the emperor to sign a declaration of war, he openly stated that he did so because "he did not consider it impossible that the Triple Entente might yet undertake an attempt to reach a peaceful resolution of the conflict, if a clearing of the air was not attained by way of a declaration of war." Berchtold's German counterpart, Jagow, that same day informed Ambassador Szögyény that Berlin would "decisively reject" rumored last-minute peace overtures from London.

The Austro-Hungarian leaders, moreover, determined to fight a war from an early point, effectively from the 7 July meeting. The minutes of that meeting are revealing:

> All those present, with one exception [Tisza], were of the opinion that a purely diplomatic victory, even if it ended with a striking humiliation of Serbia, was worthless; and that therefore such demands should be made upon Serbia as to secure their rejection so that the way for a radical solution along the lines of a military intervention could be opened up.

As the historian Fritz Fellner writes, "in Vienna one decided on a war against Serbia on 7 July and all deliberations and subsequent diplomatic actions up to the declaration of war on 28 July were only consistent executions of the basic decision made on 7 July 1914."

Austria-Hungary's leaders sought a limited war, one in which they hoped the Dual Monarchy would eliminate definitively a troublesome Serbia. Their intention, effectively, was a Third Balkan War. Those leaders knew that Russia was very likely to intervene, in which case the war would be a much larger enterprise. In the course of those key discussions in Berlin, Under-Secretary Zimmermann gave Hoyos his estimate: "Yes, 90% probability for a European war if you undertake something against Serbia." Although the decision-makers knew this, it is curious, astonishing even, that at the Common Ministerial Council meeting of 19 July they "did not even bother to discuss the chances of Russian intervention." Later, when Franz Joseph saw the key document, he recognized the implication – "Russia cannot possibly swallow this note." Those, to be sure, were the German and

Austrian readings. But France and Russia also read matters the same way. President Poincaré "left no doubt" about the French and Russian positions.

Austria-Hungary's decision-making differed from that of the other major powers. They saw themselves as "having no choice," but sensed their opponents were free to back down or compromise. Yet the Dual Monarchy's leaders, in striking contrast, centered their discussions on what in their view was the ultimate threat to their empire. They began their war with Serbia regardless of the likelihood that Russia would not back down, that it would become a much larger war. Those leaders, working together with Germany's, successfully blocked the belated attempts to maintain the peace through negotiation.

CHAPTER 4

Germany

"Even if we go under as a result of this," General Erich von Falkenhayn stated on 4 August 1914, "still it was beautiful." These almost surrealistic words by the Prussian war minister in many ways encapsulate the mood that prevailed among Germany's political and military elite as July yielded to August 1914. Historians since then have hotly debated the *why* of the decision to go to war. Fritz Fischer suggested that it was part of a "grab for world power." John C. G. Röhl has insisted that it was to establish German hegemony over the Continent. Andreas Hillgruber, on the other hand, argued that it was nothing more than an effort to secure the Reich's tenuous position as a European great power.

We wish to state up front that the available evidence supports Hillgruber. There was no talk of a "grab for world power" during the July Crisis. The Imperial High Sea Fleet was eight battleships and thirteen cruisers behind schedule in 1914. To put it differently, the British Royal Navy enjoyed a numerical advantage of nine battleships or battle cruisers, ten light cruisers, and seventy-three destroyers in the North Sea alone. Moreover, it was clear to senior leaders in Berlin that in any war involving Britain, the German colonies were indefensible and would be seized with impunity. Thus, it is not surprising that the discussions in Berlin in 1914 were dark and defensive, of breaking the *entente*'s iron ring of "encirclement," of striking "now or never," of "securing" the gains of 1870–71, and of assuring the "survival" of the "last reliable ally" in Vienna.

The Cast of 1914

The process of decision-making – and, in the case of July 1914, of crisis management – in Imperial Germany was restricted to the small coterie of high-level political and military advisors that surrounded Wilhelm II. Under the Constitution of 16 April 1871, the "war powers" rested with a single individual: Wilhelm II. Article 11 unequivocally stated that the kaiser enjoyed the power "to declare war and to conclude peace"; neither the Reichstag, nor the Foreign Office, nor the General Staff could exercise that power. The only potential curb on the kaiser's "war powers" was that the Upper House (Bundesrat) had to approve a decision to go to war. Made up of the representatives of the various German states, the Upper House by 1914 had, in the words of the constitutional scholar Ernst Rudolf Huber, become little more than "an aristocracy of princes." It readily gave consent to all imperial legislation, and it was unthinkable that the envoys of the German princes would cross the German kaiser and Prussian king on such an important matter. Prussia, after all, made up two-thirds of the German Reich. Its armies had defeated Denmark, Austria, and France half a century earlier.

Furthermore, Article 68 granted the Supreme War Lord the authority unilaterally to declare a "state of war" to exist in case the "security of the Reich" was threatened. The Lower House (Reichstag) could not interfere in foreign policy or military affairs; its powers were restricted under Article 23 to "suggesting" legislation to the chancellor and the Bundesrat. Its only effective power was that it had to approve any future war credits. The General Staff, it should be noted, was but an advisory bureau for the monarch. The kaiser alone enjoyed the "power to command" (*Kommandogewalt*).

The inner circle of Germany's crisis-management team in July 1914 consisted of Kaiser Wilhelm II, Chancellor Theobald von Bethmann Hollweg, War Minister Erich von Falkenhayn, and Chief of the General Staff Helmuth von Moltke. State Secretary for Foreign Affairs Gottlieb von Jagow as well as State Secretary of the Navy Office Alfred von Tirpitz were absent from the capital early in July.

Wilhelm II was a tragic example of a ruler who could not accept and much less live within the range of his limited talents. As soon as he ascended the throne in 1888, Wilhelm announced that he wanted to be his "own Bismarck," to be the "captain of the ship of state." While intelligent, he was weak and vacillating, unable to do sustained work. He admired Great Britain, the home of his mother, yet yearned to supplant it as the premier naval power. He consistently gave bloodthirsty speeches and loved to rattle the saber, yet was unable to steer a steady course in the decisive weeks of July 1914. The kaiser's influence on German politics and history was mostly negative. King Edward VII accurately assessed his nephew as "the most brilliant failure in history." A recent biographer, Lamar Cecil, has depicted the pattern of the kaiser's career as "descendant," moving from "martial tyranny" to "political obtuseness," and from "diplomatic maladroitness" to "military inconsequence."

Chancellor von Bethmann Hollweg was a highly competent bureaucrat who should have reached the pinnacle of his career as state secretary of the Interior in 1907. The complexity of the July Crisis 1914 (and later of war leadership) was beyond the limited talents of this lawyer. A Hamlet-like figure, Bethmann Hollweg all too often fell victim to indecision and half-measures. He was unable to chart a clear course for his country and unable to restrain either his blustering sovereign or the military. In July 1914 he fell victim to the theoretical speculations of Kurt Riezler, his principal advisor.

General von Moltke was perhaps the most complex figure among the German decision-makers. The nephew of the victor of Königgrätz and Sedan nurtured serious doubts about his military abilities, yet he accepted the post of chief of the General Staff when it was offered in 1906. Within five years, Moltke had gravitated into the camp of the "hawks." During the second Morocco crisis in 1911, for example, he wrote to his wife, "If we slink out of this affair again with our tail between our legs . . . then I despair of the future of the German Reich." He advised use of "the sword" or, failing that, sarcastically suggested placing the Reich under "the protectorate of Japan." While Moltke had serious misgivings about the Schlieffen plan, once in command of the General Staff he was content merely to tinker with some of its features.

In terms of social origin, the ruling elite came from a homogeneous and ancient aristocratic class. Bethmann Hollweg's family could trace its roots to 1416, Falkenhayn's ancestors to 1504, Jagow's descendents to 1268, and the German branch of Moltke's clan to 1254. Moltke's deputy, Georg von Waldersee, even had Hohenzollern ancestors, and they had come to Brandenburg in 1415. With regard to the generals, most had been born the sons of East Elbian army officers and landed squires; almost all had attended first the Prussian Cadet School and then the War Academy; and all but a few had served with the General Staff. Service was frequent and consistent. Most noble officers had intermarried and all were closely related both by birth and by mentality.

The Reich's diplomats came from similarly narrow social strata. Of the 548 Imperial German diplomats between 1871 and 1914 studied by Lamar Cecil, 69 percent bore titles of nobility – as did all ambassadors to European states. Of Cecil's cohort, 21 percent were fraternity men – Jagow was Wilhelm II's fraternity brother in the Bonn Borussen – and 57 percent had military service. Almost all had degrees in jurisprudence. Given the social homogeneity of the officer corps and the diplomatic corps, it is not surprising that their professional ties were as close as their social bond.

Unspoken Assumptions

Economic rivalries, alliance structures, or imperial adventures – those "structural factors," the "big" causes often touted by historians seeking to explain decision-making in 1914 – do not cause wars. Nor do operations plans with their imperative railroad timetables. Wars, as indicated in Chapter 1, stem from decisions taken by national leaders. They weigh the options, calculate the risks, and then decide for war as their best choice.

In reaching the decision for war in July 1914, Germany's leaders were motivated by a complex set of assumptions, both spoken and unspoken – these the product of their schooling, specialized training, and subsequent professional experience. Those assumptions centered on the nation's heritage and present position in Europe and the world, the prime concern being to protect or augment its power and prestige. Political and military leaders, James Joll has percipiently argued, will read events in terms of those assumptions. In times of crisis, their reactions will be guided or framed by those received assumptions. It is not at all contradictory to argue for coterie, on the one hand, and then to suggest the influence of "unspoken assumptions," on the other. The key question is the character of the outlook, or *mentalité*, found within the decision-making coterie.

First and foremost among these assumptions was the conviction that war was part of the natural order, a legitimate extension of politics by other means. Most European nations had been forged in war.

Most had consolidated that gain and then expanded overseas by way of war. And most anticipated that the twentieth century would also see its share of wars. On New Year's Eve 1899 addresses by university rectors and editorials in leading newspapers prophesied that the breakup of the British Empire would be the most important event of the coming century. And Germany had to be prepared to do battle for its share of this "inheritance." Some dreamed that the task for the Reich was not simply to defend Bismarck's gains of 1864–71, but rather to take the next steps: fleet, colonies, overseas expansion – all that came to be encapsulated in the term *Weltpolitik*. Their voices were muted by 1914. Still, they saw wars as part and parcel of great power relations. Thus, the recourse to arms in 1914 was not an aberration, but the norm.

Second, some politicians and writers viewed war as a cure-all for what they perceived to be the evils of an age of bourgeois materialism – lethargy, emasculation, and moral rot. General Colmar von der Goltz put it most crassly in 1900, "But I could do with a war, with a truly hard, invigorating, joyful war." A "jolly, little war" could turn back the clock in domestic politics and end the dangerous process of modernization.

Third, German leaders viewed a future war as a contest among "rising" and "falling" races. In December 1912 Wilhelm II spoke of a "struggle to the bitter end between Slavs and Germans." To make certain that the message was not lost on Berlin diplomats, that same day he telegraphed State Secretary for Foreign Affairs Alfred von Kiderlen-Wächter his belief that "the struggle for survival that the Germans in Europe (Austria, Germany) would have to conduct against the Romans (Gauls) supported by the Slavs (Russia), would find the Anglo-Saxons on the side of the Slavs." One week later Wilhelm informed Albert Ballin, a confidante and head of the Hamburg-America Line, that a *racial war* was in the offing between the "Germans" and the "presumptuous Slavs." This *racial war* was for nothing less than "the survival of the Habsburg Monarchy and the *existence* of our fatherland." The popular press gave wide circulation to the kaiser's racialist views. That same December 1912 a lead article in the *Hamburger Nachrichten* warned the nation of the "unavoidable clash between the Germanic and Slavic peoples."

General von Moltke thought along similar lines. In a letter to his wife of November 1914 entitled "Observations and Remembrances," Moltke argued that the "Romance peoples," such as the French and the Italians, had passed their peak of historical creativeness and were in the process of decline and decay. "England pursues only material goals." The "Slavic peoples, first and foremost the Russians," were on the "rise," but not yet ready to lead the Continent. A Slavic victory would subject Europe to "intellectual barbarism" under the "Russian whip." That left the Germans as "the only people who at this time can lead humanity towards higher goals."

The chancellor joined in this chorus of doomsday prognostications. In a speech to the Reichstag in 1913 Bethmann Hollweg couched the prospect of war in racial terms, as an "inevitable struggle" between Slavs and Teutons. Indeed, the diplomatic and political records in Berlin as well as in Vienna by 1914 were filled with references to "Germanic loyalty," *Nibelungentreue*, and standing "shoulder-to-shoulder" with Austria-Hungary against the Anglo-French-Russian *entente*.

Fourth, many members of Germany's ruling elite were taken with the ideas of social Darwinism, of the need to either rise to world power status or to decline. As Bethmann Hollweg reminded Jules Cambon, the French ambassador to Berlin, early in 1914, France had pursued a "grandiose policy" of "immense empire" for the past forty years; now Germany needed its "place in the sun." Germany's growing population, burgeoning commerce, and industry as well as navy cried out for overseas expansion. The Reich, the chancellor averred, "is in a sense condemned to spread outwards." General von Falkenhayn used the English-language term "struggle for life" in his private correspondence. The economist Johann Plenge later depicted the war of 1914 as a clash of civilizations: between the German "ideas of 1914" – duty, order, justice – and the French "ideas of 1789" – liberty, fraternity, equality.

Fifth, European leaders were gripped by what historian Wolfgang J. Mommsen has called "the topos of inevitable war" – a "topos" heavily tainted by a "home-made" fatalism that eventually turned into a self-fulfilling prophecy. Beginning with the first Moroccan crisis of 1905–06, Europe experienced a series of crises: Bosnian annexation in 1908, the second Moroccan crisis in 1911, the Tripolitanian War that same year, and the Balkan Wars of 1912–13. The Foreign Office at Berlin was unable to mount a consistent foreign policy and instead hastily extemporized responses. Some pundits saw the beginnings of a *finis Germaniae*. The Russian "Great Program" of rearmament begun after the Russo-Japanese War of 1904–05 and the French decision of

1913 to raise obligatory male military service from two to three years spawned in Berlin a paranoia bordering on panic that St. Petersburg and Paris were "encircling" Germany and preparing to crush her once their rearmament programs were completed.

The general pessimism shared by Germany's leaders may be seen in one of Schlieffen's last published articles. He painted a frightening future for an "encircled" and endangered Germany. "At the given moment, the gates will be opened, the drawbridges let down, and armies of millions of men will pour into Central Europe across the Vosges, the Meuse, the Königsau, the Niemen, the Bug, and even across the Isonzo and the Tyrolean Alps in a wave of devastation and destruction." In 1912 General Friedrich von Bernhardi published a very successful opus, *Germany and the Next War*, which went through six editions by 1913. There he called for nothing less than "the total destruction of France" by war. For Germany, it posited a clear choice: either "world power or decline."

Indeed, there existed in German ruling circles a desperate belief that time was running against Germany and that war alone could rejuvenate the Reich. Foreign Secretary von Jagow perhaps best captured the fear of Russia that dominated decision-makers in Berlin at the height of the July Crisis. He pessimistically informed Ambassador von Lichnowsky at London that while the Berlin-Vienna partnership was "growing steadily weaker," Russia would soon be "ready to strike" and to "crush us." Bethmann Hollweg had already concluded, in 1911, that the German people were "in need of a war." In July 1912, while showing Ambassador Hans von Flotow the park of his estate Hohenfinow on the Oder River, he had wistfully mused, "whether it made sense to plant new trees; the Russians would be here in a few years in any case." In July 1914, at the very moment at which Vienna asked Berlin to back its play in the Balkans, Bethmann Hollweg instructed the Austrians that because Russia "grows and grows and weighs on us like a nightmare," he felt the "present moment" to launch a war "more advantageous than a later one."

The Younger Moltke likewise felt war to be inevitable. As early as December 1911 he had lectured the General Staff: "All are preparing themselves for the great war, which all sooner or later expect." One year later, at the so-called "war council" of 8 December 1912, at which the issue of solving Germany's strategic problems by way of a "preventive" strike against France and Russia had been raised, the general had forthrightly counseled war, "and the sooner the better." During his last meeting in May 1914 with his Austro-Hungarian counterpart, General Franz Conrad von Hötzendorf, Moltke again demanded war: "to wait any longer meant a diminishing of our chances." Returning to Berlin from Karlsbad, the general informed Jagow that time was running against Germany, that "there was no alternative but to fight a preventive war so as to beat the enemy while we could still emerge fairly well from the struggle." Moltke's deputy, General von Waldersee, in May 1914 argued that Germany had "*no* reason whatever *to avoid*" a European war, "but *quite the opposite*, [good] prospects *today* to conduct a great European war quickly and victoriously."

Sixth, Bethmann Hollweg had developed a "model" for war based on the writings of his principal advisor, Kurt Riezler. According to the latter's so-called "calculated-risk" theory, future wars would be fought not on the battlefield, but around the negotiating table. War had become too expensive and too dangerous for states to risk. "The more one arms," Riezler wrote, "the more the relationship between the advantages and disadvantages of going to war shift in favor of the latter, and thus in favor of peace." War, or better, the threat of war, had become a game of bluff. "Wars will no longer be fought," Riezler stated, "but calculated." Guns would no longer fire, "but have a voice in the negotiations." In a Europe divided between two antagonistic camps, the game of bluff (offensive diplomacy) could be played all the way up the escalatory ladder, stopping just short of war. But it was critical that the two antagonistic camps could at the flash point back down and avail themselves of a great power mediator – for Bethmann Hollweg, this meant Great Britain. Throughout the July Crisis, the chancellor planned to make use of the "British card."

Finally, playing directly against Riezler's and Bethmann Hollweg's model of the "calculated risk," was the military's concern with mobilization timetables, their plans allowing no pauses for negotiation. By 1914, the General Staff possessed only one contingency war plan – Schlieffen's notes for a short campaign in France. Germany had to be first to mobilize, first to take the field, and first to victory. Delay meant defeat.

That military-technocratic mindset was fully revealed on 1 August 1914 when the kaiser, falsely believing that Britain would stay out of the war, ordered Moltke to deploy the entire field army in the East. Moltke was flabbergasted. The "deployment of a million-man army," he lectured his Supreme War Lord, could not be "improvised." Any change in the *Große Aufmarsch* he had inherited from Schlieffen would cause chaos and result "in a disorderly heap of confused armed men without supplies" charging aimlessly toward the advancing Russians.

The Pressure Groups

Right-wing pressure groups by and large advocated bellicose policies before and during 1914. The Pan-German League, composed almost two-thirds of university-educated men of whom one-half were in public service, was a firm supporter of an aggressive foreign policy and of the need to back that policy with force, if necessary. Driven by social Darwinism and a militant, largely Protestant theology, the *Alldeutsche* repeatedly announced their willingness to sacrifice "blood and treasure" for the future of Reich and Volk. One of the League's leaders, Ernst Hasse, year after year assured his followers that war was imminent, and that the Pan-Germans were prepared "to manufacture a war threat" in case "Guillaume le timide" or the Reich's "weak and sleepy people" should lapse into a false sense of permanent peace.

The various veterans groups, formally organized into the Kyffhäuser Bund with its registered 2.8 million members by 1913, were perhaps the most servile of nationalistic Germans. Their leaders adored uncritically the Reich and its Hohenzollern masters. Born at "hour zero" on the battlefields of Gravelotte, Mars-la-Tour, and Sedan in 1870, the veterans groups saw themselves as "the kaiser's army in civilian frock." Parades, military tattoos, martial music, and battlefield recreations honed their rhetoric, if not their skills. In 1914 they rallied behind "Kaiser, Volk and Fatherland."

Germany's university professors, another influential group of opinion-makers, had long championed the national cause. The fact that professors yearned to don the reserve officer's tunic, that noted badge of honor, and that fraternities by and large had turned to conservatism, if not downright reaction, is well known. The German *civitas academica* supported the Hohenzollern Monarchy, founded the "Prussian school of history," and clamored for global expansion.

Of Germany's two major religions, Protestants most openly announced their pro-war convictions. The dominant features of Protestant theology by 1914 were "militarization of thought," growing acceptance of the "necessity of war" and willingness enthusiastically to participate therein, and preparing the flock for the "inevitable" war.

Many Protestant theologians depicted the July Crisis not only as a God-given time of national "awakening," but also as a new "German Pentecost." When war came in August 1914, Lutheran theologians celebrated it as a "holy war," as a great "educator and leveler" that would sweep away all that was "unjust, superficial and wrong."

Among Catholic theologians, the *Leitmotif* of July 1914 centered on the notion of a "just war." They depicted Germany, "the hearth of peace," as the "victim" of an evil armaments race. The Reich, "encircled" by a ring of hostile powers, had no choice but to defend itself. Catholic leaders did little to warn their flock about succumbing to the siren calls of war, but generally eschewed the extreme chauvinistic declarations of their Protestant brethren. In the end, they, too, rallied behind the official motto, "with God for Kaiser, Volk and Fatherland."

At another level, it is generally assumed that most captains of industry rallied to the flag. To be sure, armaments firms such as Krupp, Mauser, and Ehrhardt stood to gain from a war, but even here there exists a need for differentiation. While Alfred Hugenberg, chairman of the Board of Alfried Krupp, demanded a more "aggressive" German foreign policy – read expansion – Carl Duisberg, director-general of Friedrich Bayer & Co., favored a *rapprochement* with Great Britain. Again, while the influential Karl Helfferich, director of the Deutsche Bank, sought German expansion not by trade and investment but rather by military strength, his fellow director at the bank, Arthur von Gwinner, like Duisberg wanted Berlin to find a diplomatic "arrangement" with London.

Some captains of industry and banking even attempted to curb Wilhelm II's blustering rhetoric and expansionist aims. Hugo Stinnes, one of Germany's most dynamic entrepreneurs, hardly was in the camp of the "hawks" before 1914. When Heinrich Claß, head of the Pan-German League, demanded that Germany take advantage of the First Balkan War and launch a "preventive war" against the *entente*, Stinnes was not amused. After "3–4 years peaceful development," the Rhineland magnate lectured Claß, Germany would be "the undisputed economic master of Europe." Walther Rathenau, the chairman of General Electric (AEG), likewise counseled trade rather than war. Armament, to him, was a "negative" policy "grounded in fear, vanity, and megalomania," one conducted by "misguided princes, ambitious admirals, and inept diplomats." And just one week before the Sarajevo assassination, the Hamburg banker Max Warburg rejected Wilhelm II's bellicose query whether, in the face of the rapid pace of the

Russian rearmament program, "it would not be better to attack rather than to wait" until 1916–17. Warburg instead tendered the sage advice that there was no cause to draw the sword in the immediate future. "Germany becomes stronger with every year of peace. We can only gather rewards by biding our time."

But such sagacious counsel fell upon deaf ears. There is no record of a direct response to Gwinner, Ballin, Stinnes, or Rathenau on the part of the kaiser, chancellor, or foreign secretary. Nor is there any indication that their warnings against drawing the sword were discussed in depth by the Foreign Office or the General Staff. The "men of 1914" measured great power status not in terms of financial ledgers but rather in land and military might.

There were few direct links between the various Wilhelmian pressure groups and the Reich's small political and military elite. There is no question that men such as Bethmann Hollweg and Moltke were concerned with the views of public opinion-makers. But there is no evidence to suggest that they at any time during the July Crisis shaped their policies according to the perceived interests of those groups. Neither political leaders, nor eminent bankers, nor captains of heavy industry were consulted in the final considerations for war. Nor were Germany's academics, theologians, or veterans groups consulted.

Once having opted for war, the "men of 1914" certainly wanted to carry the broad public with them. And they wanted to be certain of the support of the labor movement and of its political arm, the Social Democratic Party (SPD). Thus, Bethmann Hollweg personally conducted the negotiations with its leaders during the July Crisis. The chancellor was delighted with the discussions and shelved plans to arrest the SPD's leaders at the start of war.

Finally, a recent survey of the "spirit of 1914" suggests that the lead articles of most German newspapers reveal neither a broad "war enthusiasm" nor a nation unified for war. Many historical accounts indicate that the "war euphoria" of August 1914 was most pronounced among students and the upper middle class; least among urban workers. The majority of Germans were willing to follow whatever course their government charted for them. Still, recent studies of Berlin, Darmstadt, Freiburg, Hamburg, Saarbrücken, and Wesel have shown that hundreds of thousands of workers – one scholar puts the figure at 100,000 in Berlin alone and at 750,000 throughout Germany – took part in peace demonstrations in late July. In short, available documentary evidence does not allow the conclusion that the "men of 1914" were responding to public opinion in deciding for war.

The Great Gambit

The Schlieffen plan with its inflexible timetable is regularly indicated as a major factor leading to the "great folly" of 1914. What, in fact, had the general committed to paper? In two famous memoranda of the winter of 1905–06, Schlieffen provided his final operational concept. The vast bulk ("hammer") of the German armies would assemble around Aachen, "punch" through the Maastricht Appendix and the Ardennes, and then "wheel" through Belgium around the French armies and fortresses to the south, before falling into the Seine basin in order to drive the disoriented French onto the "anvil" of the German forces anchored in Lorraine. A giant *Kesselschlacht*, or battle of envelopment and annihilation, would break the French Army. This 450-kilometer advance – truly a classic "best-case scenario" – was to be done in forty-two days from first mobilization. A single army corps was to fight a holding action in the East. Schlieffen simply assumed that Austria-Hungary would hold the Russians at bay long enough for his armies to defeat the French.

All was predicated on speed: "The offensive must never be allowed to come to a standstill." A delay of just seventy-two hours in railway mobilization and deployment could spell disaster. The German armies would have to force the pace of the war, never allowing the enemy to seize the initiative, but only to react – "The French Army must be annihilated." In its final version, the Schlieffen plan was little more than a staff college *tour de force*. At that, the document was permeated with hedge-words such as "if," "when," "perhaps," and "hopefully."

Schlieffen's great adventure was not without its critics. Quartermaster-General Ernst Köpke, when reviewing his chief's notes, had warned that France's numerical superiority in troops and its excellent network of fortresses had made a repeat of Sedan (1870) unlikely. "We cannot expect quick, decisive victories," General Köpke lectured Schlieffen. The war of the future would feature "a tedious and bloody crawling forward step-by-step," that is, "siege-style" warfare. He concluded ominously, "army and nation will slowly have to get used to these unpleasant perspectives if we wish to avoid a worrisome pessimism already at the outset of [the next] war,

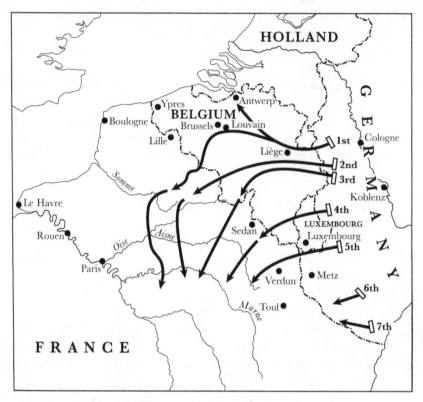

MAP 5. The German advance of August/September 1914

one that could lead to grave danger regarding its outcome." While Schlieffen found Köpke's critique convincing and could produce no counter-arguments, he declined to revise his *va banque* operations plan accordingly. Nor did he heed the warnings of the wily Field Marshal Gottfried von Haeseler, who warned that one could not simply "carry off the armed forces of a great power [France] like a cat in a sack."

But Schlieffen's critics lacked a viable alternative. Their vision (or fear) of a peoples' war lasting anywhere between seven and thirty years was unacceptable. The Second Reich was not the Third; total mobilization for total war was anathema to one and all. Thus, simply to reject Schlieffen's blueprint of a short war was to deny the very validity of what historian Gerhard Ritter called *Kriegshandwerk*. Put bluntly, to concede that the vaunted Prussian General Staff could no longer conduct short wars of annihilation was to admit that war had ceased to be a viable option by the start of the twentieth century.

In the final analysis, it is fair to state that the Schlieffen plan was little more than a blueprint for the opening operations in an uncertain campaign – a design for a *battle* of annihilation rather than a *war* of annihilation. War termination rested on two political propositions: a French government sufficiently strong to conclude peace, and a Russian regime willing to return to the *status quo ante bellum*. Perhaps realizing the highly questionable political nature of the plan, General von Moltke shortly before the war decided to avoid a violation of at least the Netherlands' neutrality; he canceled the planned march through the Dutch province of Limburg as no longer being a *military* necessity.

The Essence of Decision-Making

How and why, then, was the decision for war reached? Again, it is necessary to return to that small cadre of decision-makers surrounding Kaiser Wilhelm II. Many of them feared that the coming war would be a prolonged, bloody, exhausting, and possibly unwinnable undertaking. Yet, they opted for war in an almost exuberant manner. As General Karl von Wenninger, the Bavarian military plenipotentiary to Berlin, noted upon visiting the Prussian War Ministry, "Everywhere beaming faces, shaking of hands in the corridors; one congratulates one's self for having taken the hurdle." Perhaps what Wenninger noted can be attributed to "cognitive dissonance" – the joyous relief at the end of weeks of anxiety and uncertainty.

Of all the German decision-makers, General von Moltke harbored no illusions about the coming war. On 28 July 1914 he penned a secret "Evaluation of the Political Situation" for Bethmann Hollweg. Therein, Moltke spoke of the coming war as a "world war" – well before Europe's leaders had taken the fateful decisions for this eventuality. He foresaw "Europe's civilized nations" about to embark on a "mutual tearing to pieces" (*Zerfleischung*) of one another. An undefined "fate," Moltke argued, was about to unleash a war "that will destroy civilization in almost all of Europe for decades to come." Still, he saw no alternative but to launch the Schlieffen plan to provide Germany with a strategic advantage at the start of what he believed would be a long, hard war. On 29 July Moltke instructed Wilhelm II that Germany would "never hit it again so well as we do now with France's and Russia's expansion of their armies incomplete."

The arrival at Berlin on 5 July of the Austro-Hungarian special emissary, Count Alexander Hoyos, with a request for German backing of Vienna's planned actions against Serbia must be seen against this background. Around noon that day, Ambassador Count László Szögyény-Marich visited Kaiser Wilhelm II at Potsdam. Concurrently, Hoyos called on Under-Secretary Arthur Zimmermann (State Secretary von Jagow being on his honeymoon in Italy) at the Foreign Office. According to the ambassador's account of his meeting with Wilhelm II – the only record of the discussion at Potsdam – the kaiser encouraged a harsh policy vis-à-vis Serbia, "even if serious European complications" arose as a result. Wilhelm counseled Austria-Hungary "not to delay its action." Russia was unprepared for war. And even though its posture was sure to be "hostile," Germany "had been prepared for this for years." The kaiser's only caveat was that he be granted time to consult his chancellor.

At 5 p.m. that afternoon, Wilhelm II called Bethmann Hollweg, Zimmermann, War Minister von Falkenhayn, and Chief of the Military Cabinet Moriz von Lyncker to Potsdam. He told them of the "blank check" that he had just issued the Habsburg government, reaffirming that he would stand by the Viennese ally in case Russia were to intervene in an Austro-Serbian war. All present fully concurred, accepting the risk of Russian intervention leading to a general war. On 6 July Bethmann and Zimmermann formally conveyed Berlin's unequivocal support for Vienna to Szögyény and Hoyos.

Knowing that under the Constitution of 1871 a decision for war would require the consent of the Bundesrat, Zimmermann at once informed the Bavarians that Berlin saw the moment as "very propitious" for Vienna to launch a "campaign of revenge" against Serbia, "even given the danger of further entanglements." When the Bavarian plenipotentiary inquired what these "entanglements" might be, Zimmermann was perfectly candid: "War with Russia."

Thus, a small coterie of four decision-makers – Wilhelm II, Bethmann Hollweg, Zimmermann, Falkenhayn, and Lyncker – in a most offhand manner decided to escalate the crisis up to and including war. Even this can hardly be called a meeting of peers – the only voice that counted was that of the kaiser, in whose hands the "war powers" rested. Not until the next morning, just before departing for his annual cruise off Norway, did Wilhelm II get around to notifying the General Staff of this decision. Even then, he called to Potsdam not Moltke, who was on vacation, nor his deputy, Waldersee, but rather General

Hermann von Bertrab, a surveyor and cartographer who was not a member of the inner planning group at the General Staff. Unfortunately, the destruction of the General Staff records by Allied air raids in 1944 and 1945 does not allow insight into why Wilhelm chose a cartographer for such an important discussion. This notwithstanding, Bethmann Hollweg's mentor, Riezler, slyly summarized the decision of 5 July for a quick strike against Serbia as follows: "Fait accompli and then friendly [face] toward the entente; then we can sustain the shock [of war]."

But circumstances did not conform to Riezler's "model." As early as 7 July, Bethmann Hollweg realized that his room to maneuver was incredibly restricted. Any "action" against Serbia, he confided to Riezler, "can lead to a world war." Like Moltke, Bethmann Hollweg regarded "a war, regardless of how it ended," as anything but a forty-day march to Paris. The chancellor, in Riezler's words, equated armed conflict with "the overthrow of everything that exists." Zimmermann at the Foreign Office agreed with Austrian diplomats that an attack on Serbia meant a "European war . . . with a probability of 90 percent." In other words, the German Foreign Office regarded a "calculated risk" with only one chance in ten for peace to be acceptable. Leaders in Berlin fully expected a "hostile" Russian reaction to any Habsburg military play in the Balkans. Zimmermann's comment makes mockery of the "slide-into-war" theory later propounded by politicians and historians alike.

What to do? Bethmann Hollweg still felt secure that he held the winning hand – the "calculated risk," diplomatic bluff. Might this not be the last chance, he mused, to alter the strategic balance in the Balkans by exploiting the assassination and supporting an Austro-Hungarian strike against Serbia? Should the war come "out of the East," that is, if Germany appeared to be "fighting for Austria-Hungary and not Austr[ia]-Hungary for us," the Reich stood a very good chance "of winning it." But should Russia back down, Germany stood an equally good chance of having "maneuvered the entente into a parting of the ways." For almost three weeks these musings dominated his actions. And if all failed, he could still play the final card: an appeal to London to mediate the crisis at the eleventh hour.

Thus, Bethmann Hollweg escalated the game of bluff. From about 7 to 25 July, while Austria-Hungary was making the key decisions that led to war, Bethmann Hollweg adamantly refused all suggestions to involve Great Britain as a "mediator" in the Serbian matter. The time was still not ripe for this. Rather, he pressed Vienna to act against Belgrade, assuring the Austrians of Germany's full support. To act otherwise would cost the Reich "the last real ally." As well, Bethmann Hollweg was determined to show strength in the face of danger. To have abandoned Austria-Hungary in July 1914, he later wrote, would have been tantamount to "castration" on Germany's part. He doggedly pursued a policy that many historians have termed one of "deception." On 14 July Bethmann Hollweg informed Riezler that he would stay the course, even if it constituted "a leap into the dark." Indeed, Berlin escalated the calls for armed action against Serbia. On 25 July Ambassador Szögyény cabled Count Leopold Berchtold, the Habsburg foreign minister, that German leaders saw danger in delay; they advised Vienna "to press forward immediately [with war against Serbia] and to confront the world with a fait accompli."

It would be a classic case of academic overkill to retrace the petty bickering that began behind the scenes on 29 July concerning the proclamation of premobilization (the so-called "imminent danger of war"). This has been told and retold *ad nauseam*. Rather, it seems more profitable first to concentrate on Bethmann Hollweg's and Moltke's motivations, and second to examine the chaos and confusion at German headquarters. This is now possible due to a recently discovered diary fragment of War Minister von Falkenhayn, starting on 27 July 1914. The diary was given to the Reichsarchiv by Falkenhayn's widow in November 1927 and marked "confidential, not to be made public." It resurfaced in former East German archives after the "accession" of 1990.

Bethmann Hollweg, the central political figure of the July Crisis, revealed that he was no Bismarck. On 27 July he still imagined that he could manage the crisis. During a meeting with Wilhelm II and Moltke, to which Falkenhayn was not invited, chancellor and kaiser agreed "to see the matter through [to war] no matter what the cost." Bethmann Hollweg informed Riezler that he saw "a fate larger than human power" could control now descending over Europe – a shocking abdication of politics.

On 28 July Austria-Hungary commenced military operations against Serbia, whereupon Russia moved toward partial mobilization. Falkenhayn pressed for additional military measures. Moltke pushed hard for war: "We shall never hit it again so well as we do now." But Bethmann Hollweg could not decide. On the one hand, he deemed the time for negotiations with London still to be premature; on the other, he sought to rein in the military's war fever. Wilhelm II, the ultimate arbiter, at this point allowed that he "now no longer wanted war." A desperate Falkenhayn openly warned Wilhelm II that he had "lost control over events."

When news confirming Russian partial mobilization arrived in Berlin on 29 July, Bethmann Hollweg was the first to push the panic button. His one remaining hope was to pass responsibility for the coming European conflagration on to Russia. Thus, he dictated several telegrams for "Willy" to dispatch to his cousin "Nicky," Tsar Nicholas II, at St. Petersburg. Both rulers merely suggested that the other take the first steps to mediate the conflict; neither, apparently, was sincere.

The Russian partial mobilization also moved other senior decision-makers in Berlin. Falkenhayn and Moltke rushed to Bethmann Hollweg's residence, where the war minister demanded that the decree for premobilization be issued at once. Next, the two generals raced out to Potsdam, where they were later joined by the chancellor, to convince the kaiser of the urgency of the moment. Wilhelm II, having previously declared all threat of war to have dissipated with Serbia's cordial response to the Austrian ultimatum on 28 July, now undertook one of his customary about-faces and decided again in favor of war. "The ball that has started to roll," Falkenhayn stated in fatalistic terms, "can no longer be stopped." He reiterated the need to begin premobilization. But then, in an astounding turnaround, Bethmann Hollweg, now assisted by Moltke, urged caution and restraint.

Late that night, the two generals again visited the chancellor at Berlin to assess Russia's partial mobilization. Once again, Falkenhayn pushed for proclaiming a state of "imminent danger of war." Once again, Bethmann Hollweg and Moltke stood firm in their opposition, arguing that the Russian action "did not mean war." Both men wanted St. Petersburg to take the lead so that Russia could be depicted as being "responsible for the great debacle." In the end, Falkenhayn bowed to their wishes, declaring that "a few hours more or less" were of no importance to German premobilization.

In truth, Bethmann Hollweg had been less than forthcoming that day. After the generals departed, he decided to play his "trump" card. Shortly before midnight, the chancellor called the British ambassador to his residence. He assured Sir Edward Goschen that were Britain to remain neutral in the coming war, Germany would offer London a neutrality agreement, guarantee the independence of the Netherlands, and promise not to undertake "territorial gains at the expense of France."

Goschen, and later Secretary for Foreign Affairs Sir Edward Grey, rejected these proposals as "shameful."

The 30th of July, in Falkenhayn's words, was a day of "endless discussions." At a session of the Prussian Ministry of State, Bethmann Hollweg conceded that the "calculated risk" had blown up in his face; "the hope for England [was now] zero." Later he confessed that "all governments" simply had "lost control" of the July Crisis. "The stone has begun to roll." The seeming rationality of the "calculated risk" had yielded to the irrationality of a war *à outrance*. Later that evening, Bethmann Hollweg called Moltke and Falkenhayn to his residence – to launch a bitter debate with Moltke concerning personal responsibility "for the coming war." The generals seized the opportunity to convince the chancellor of the need to declare a state of "imminent danger of war," at the latest by midday, 31 July. Moltke now undertook another 180-degree turn and demanded war *"sans phrase,"* that is, without circumlocution. Falkenhayn was "at a loss" to explain Moltke's abrupt about-face.

The reason for the chief of the General Staff's sudden about-face became apparent on 31 July, another day of panic at Potsdam. That morning, Moltke received news from intelligence units in East Prussia that Russia appeared to be mobilizing its forces in Poland. But, there was no hard confirmation. "Unfortunately, Moltke very nervous," Falkenhayn noted in his diary. Finally, around noon, a telegram arrived from Ambassador Friedrich Count von Pourtalès in St. Petersburg stating that Russia had mobilized its entire army. Wilhelm II, in his constitutional capacity as Supreme War Lord, at once telephoned orders that a state of "imminent danger of war" existed. France and Russia were to be given ultimatums to declare their intentions.

The moment of decision finally was at hand. Falkenhayn arrived in the Star Chamber of the Neues Palais at Potsdam by 2 p.m. An intense discussion ensued, during which it was decided "to attribute the entire responsibility for war to Russia." Wilhelm II, in Falkenhayn's view, at long last rose to the occasion. "His bearing and his words are worthy of a German kaiser." Falkenhayn signed the decree declaring a state of "imminent danger of war." Moltke read an emotional appeal "To the German People." Later that night, after a last-minute plea by Tsar Nicholas II to preserve the peace, Falkenhayn visited Bethmann Hollweg and demanded that the order proclaiming German "war mobilization" be issued at once.

The first day of August brought yet another bizarre turn in "crisis management." Afraid that Germany might lose the psychological edge by declaring war on Russia first, Falkenhayn visited Foreign Secretary von Jagow (back in Berlin) and then Bethmann Hollweg to head off such a "foolish" declaration. "Answer: too late." Falkenhayn's last-minute attempt to bring Moltke and Tirpitz into the discussion was cut short by Wilhelm II's order that his political and military leaders prepare the "war mobilization" document and come to Potsdam at once. The order for "war mobilization" was signed at 5 p.m. on 1 August 1914. Then, a telegram arrived from London, wherein Ambassador von Lichnowsky suggested that Britain might remain neutral if Germany pledged "not to set foot on French territory." Another moment of chaos and recriminations ensued. Falkenhayn caught the moment thus:

> After excited exchanges between the chancellor and Moltke, I dictate the telegram of reply to Jagow on orders from the kaiser. Moltke telephones Trier that the 16th Division for the moment is not to march into Luxembourg. [Moltke] claims to be completely broken, because this decision by the kaiser shows that the latter still hopes for peace. I console Moltke.

The final turn in the July Crisis came around midnight, when another telegram arrived from Lichnowsky, this one stating that Britain's price for neutrality was the inviolability of Belgian territory. "It is decided," Falkenhayn recorded, "not to answer the 2. telegram." Moltke persuaded Wilhelm II to order the invasion of Luxembourg.

It is hard to escape the conclusion that the small political and military elite in whose hands the future of the German nation rested was utterly incapable of shouldering that responsibility. Far from conjuring up what Fritz Fischer called a "grab for world power," that elite was beset by doubts, petty bickering, confusion, and lack of vision. Their discussions at the end of July and the beginning of August centered only on managing the immediate crisis; there was no discussion of how that crisis related to the nation's future.

Falkenhayn's diary reinforces the suspicion that Berlin was a house without direction. Orders were issued, countermanded, reactivated. Wilhelm II and Moltke undertook radical, sometimes daily, shifts in their war policies. Each telegram from London and each piece of intelligence from East Prussia occasioned acrimonious debate and fundamental shifts in policy. Chaos and confusion rather than direction

and design were the hallmarks of German decision-making in July
1914.

Retrospect

Where does the debate concerning Germany's role in launching the
First World War stand? Almost four decades after Fritz Fischer first
put forth the explosive thesis that Germany had gone to war in 1914
as part of a bold "grab for world power," it seems incontrovertible
that this is stretching the evidence. Such an audacious "grab" would
have required careful planning, detailed preparation, and coordinated
action – in short, a firm and resolute monarch, a rational and efficient
government, and extensive detailed planning. Nothing of the kind can
be detected in what historian Stig Förster has called "the polychratic
chaos of the imperial system of government."

One could almost argue that in Berlin there existed *no* government
in control of events in 1914. There never took place a grand council
of state to decide the critical issue of war or peace in a rational, coordinated manner. Each branch of government pursued an independent
agenda. Wilhelm II failed abysmally in his assigned constitutional task
of coordinating German foreign and military policies. Basically, he was
incapable of decisive leadership. Five successive war scares in the prewar period had gone without the recourse to arms. What is striking
about Berlin during the July Crisis is the lack of government direction
and resolution.

Yet, Imperial Germany went to war. Why? Senior decision-makers
were convinced that time was running against them, and hence they
developed a "now-or-never" attitude toward a European war. Moltke,
looking back on July 1914, still expressed this mindset. First, he argued
that war had been a desirable option in 1914 – even if its outcome and
its duration could not be predicted. Next, he combined fatalism with
social Darwinism to suggest that Germany had gone to war simply to
"fulfill its preordained [*sic*] role in the development of the world." The
Reich could not "fulfill its role in civilization... without conflicts, as
time and again opposition has to be overcome; this can only be done
by way of war."

However one "gamed" the available options in the run-up to the
July Crisis of 1914 at Berlin, only the recourse to arms seemed to
offer a future that included Germany as one of the great powers. Put

differently, only the gamble of Schlieffen's grand concept remained. Thereby, Germany could hope to win a great opening battle in the initial campaign of the war and at best gain an advantage for the ensuing peace negotiations. To wait any longer entailed almost certain failure for the Schlieffen plan. Hence, the "strike-now-better-than-later" mentality that dominated Berlin during the July Crisis. In the process, Germany's decision-makers transformed Austria-Hungary's "localized" Balkan war into a general European war.

CHAPTER 5

Russia

Imperial Russia bore a special burden for the origin of the Great War. This was an *idée fixe* among educated citizens, especially among academics, for a half century after the outbreak of that war. During the July Crisis, German policy attempted to manage the unfolding of events in such a way as to make German mobilization appear to be the consequence of Russia's prior declaration. In the 1920s German, French, and British scholarship as well as diplomatic publications "documented" the crisis in terms that explained, or cautiously justified, its entry into the war. The interests of the young, militant Soviet regime, however, lay in discrediting the actions of its tsarist and bourgeois predecessors. Soviet central archives made public many of the most compromising historical documents they held on St. Petersburg's actions of the prewar period. A vast quantity of other documentation, however, remained hidden from independent examination until 1991.

The choices Russian statesmen and staff officers faced during the July Crisis were, paradoxically, simple and unaffected by decades of modernization, and yet clearly constrained by diplomatic and military choices made in preceding years. Statesmen, including Tsar Nicholas II, would struggle with the hour-by-hour development of the crisis, particularly after 24 July, without apparent reference to Russia's political and military crises of 1904–05, the Bosnian embarrassment of 1908, or the changes brought on by the Balkan Wars of 1912–13. Yet each of these points, and many others that preceded and accompanied them, constituted a matrix in which decision-making evolved in the Russian capital throughout the July Crisis.

There was no predetermined policy, either for or against war. Many feared war as much as they feared peace, and vice versa. Counsels were sharply divided. There existed pro- and anti-German elements within the leading civilian and military circles in Petersburg. Yet in the end, Russia's leaders, long known for their divisions and mutual hostilities, showed remarkable agreement in defining the national interest and the appropriate response – all favored a "tough" stand.

The Cast of 1914

Tsar Nicholas II headed Russia's decision-making coterie. He was poorly prepared for the role he assumed in 1894 at age 26. Nicholas confessed to a cousin on the day of his accession: "I am not pre-pared to be a Czar. I never wanted to become one. I know nothing of the business of ruling." This notwithstanding, he held unambiguous authoritarian preferences, accepting his "autocratic powers as divinely ordained and as intrinsically correct." Nicholas, as well as his wife Alexandra, felt ill at ease in Petersburg society and hence chose resi-dences "far away from the intrigues and bustle of Petersburg" – at the suburban palace of Tsarskoe Selo, at the Peterhof, at Nicholas' Polish hunting lodge, and at the spectacular Livadia Palace in the Crimea. This meant that for much of the year, the monarch was cut off from his ministers and senior military advisors.

While many scholars have described Nicholas as a "stupid man," this view was by no means universal. Sergei Witte, his first finance minister, wrote, "he has a quick mind and learns easily." Peter Bark, his last finance minister, claimed Nicholas possessed "remarkable intelligence." Unfortunately, they noted two other traits: "inconstancy and indecisiveness." Perhaps most importantly, the tsar–autocrat authorized his ministers and generals only grudgingly to exercise power independent of him. This was true in times of crisis or normalcy, the latter a rare circumstance during imperial Russia's final two decades. The isolation in which ministers and generals worked in St. Peters-burg, without reference to those of their colleagues who also had some responsibility for Russia's actions, hindered the operation of govern-ment as the July Crisis brought the empire closer to war.

Russia's humiliating defeat at the hands of Japan in 1905 brought about a radical change in governance. Nicholas' October 1905 Manifesto formed the constitutional basis for the Fundamental Laws,

enacted in May 1906, which posited various changes in the function-
ing of the state, touching civil rights, press freedom, police powers,
and the prerogatives of the new parliament, the Duma. But imperial
security and the war powers remained securely and solely in Nicholas'
hands. Under Article 4, the "Emperor of all the Russias" held "the
supreme autocratic power." Under Article 12, Nicholas had "supreme
control of all relations of the Russian Empire with foreign powers."
And under Article 13, he had the power to "declare war and conclude peace, as well as other treaties with foreign countries." Under a
reformed Council of Ministers, the ministers of war, navy, and foreign
affairs reported directly to the tsar, and they received instructions the
same way. The Duma's powers in the area of security were restricted
to approval of military budgets. It is fair to state that in the end, the
emperor (or those in whom he placed his confidence) made Russian
foreign policy and decided issues of war and peace. So it was in
July 1914.

The septuagenarian I. L. Goremykin, a conservative servitor, led
Nicholas' Council of Ministers on the eve of war. Historian Michael
Florinsky described Goremykin as "a cynical bureaucrat and a believer
in the comforting theory that except the will of the tsar, nothing mattered in Russia and that representative institutions and public opinion
were but 'nonsense' and 'idle talk'." Formerly head of Russia's police,
Goremykin believed that "the whole government is the tsar alone, and
what he will say is what we will execute, but as long as there is no clear
instruction from him we must wait and be patient." Passivity ensured
Goremykin would play little role during the July Crisis.

The man who controlled Russia's economy from 1906 to 1914,
Finance Minister V. N. Kokovtsov, was more powerful and important
to governmental deliberations. A brilliant bureaucratic in-fighter who
believed that the new Duma was an expendable element in government, he possessed Nicholas' complete confidence (*doverie*) but he
had no broad vision of Russia's needs. His major achievement before
the Great War was to bring the foreign debt into line with the means to
pay by following policies that helped spark rapid economic growth after
1907. In achieving that, he cut investment in security to a dangerously
low level.

S. D. Sazonov led the Foreign Ministry on the eve of the war. Rising
rapidly from minor diplomatic posts to be foreign minister in 1910,
Sazonov, in the words of historian Dominic Lieven, "had neither an
outstanding brain nor an equable temperament." He exercised his

post relatively cautiously for the half decade before 1914. Ill health restricted his effectiveness – as did his lack of a chancellery background, the traditional prerequisite to lead the Ministry.

Unexpectedly, Minister of Agriculture Alexander Krivoshein would play an important role during the July Crisis. An able administrator, Krivoshein oversaw a major land reform program that broke up communal village lands and sold them as individual holdings. On the eve of the Great War, he maneuvered his friend and client, Peter Bark, into the vital post of minister of finance. From early 1914 to summer 1915, Krivoshein, in the words of Lieven, was "the most powerful figure in the imperial government."

General V. A. Sukhomlinov, the minister of war, was Nicholas II's creature. His later reputation, shaped in the 1920s by military critics from both sides of Russia's Civil War, was of a shallow military thinker and the man who helped produce the disaster of Tannenberg in 1914. He was also a sturdy bureaucratic in-fighter who eventually brought the General Staff and War Ministry under his centralized leadership in the years before the outbreak of the Great War. The chief of General Staff, General N. N. Ianushkevich, knew little about core staff work such as mobilization planning. He was ill prepared for the challenges he faced in the third week of July 1914. His subordinate, General Iu. N. Danilov, on the other hand, epitomized the mobilization-planning technician par excellence. He strongly advocated centralized control of war planning and strategy formulation, and proved to be an important actor in War Ministry deliberations in July 1914.

These men came from the educated Russian nobility but, unlike their peers who managed landed estates, what mattered to the governing coterie during the denouement of the July Crisis was their shared experience of the preceding decade. They had together passed through Russia's military humiliation, revolutionary upheaval, and economic weakness after 1904. They believed that Russia's great power status would depend on its ability to counter or divert the Austro-German challenge in southeastern Europe.

The problem of compartmentalization, described earlier, limited communications between key decision-makers. Foreign Minister Sazonov, a rather excitable man, communicated only as necessary throughout the July Crisis with the emperor, with his ministerial colleagues, and with War Ministry counterparts. Danilov, the officer directly responsible for all mobilization preparations and intelligence collection, was on a staff ride in the Caucasus and returned to the capital only on 26 July, after some key decisions had been taken. Even then, Danilov operated with apparent detachment from both War Minister Sukhomlinov and Chief of General Staff Ianushkevich.

Military Reform

In the Russo-Japanese War, Russia suffered 400,000 casualties, lost two of its three fleets, and had seen its army repeatedly bloodied at the hands of "Asiatic inferiors." Former Finance Minister Witte concluded in 1907 that the war had "completely destroyed the entire economic organism of the country." From the point of view of national security, the most serious casualty was Russia's finances, and with the loss of that, its ability to repair and modernize its defenses.

Defeat often drives reform. To strengthen the influence and authority of the army's war planning apparatus, Nicholas II liberated the General Staff's war planning parts from War Ministry control, consolidated them as the Main Directorate of the General Staff (GUGSh), and subordinated this new organization to himself. He also created a Council of State Defense (GSO) to fashion a unified security policy for the empire. The new organization was supposed to reconcile competing strategies and the incompatible funding priorities they entailed, and to provide central leadership in matters of national security. GSO membership consisted of the war and navy ministers, the chiefs of the general and naval staffs, and the grand dukes who ran the main army inspectorates, under the chairmanship of the emperor's uncle, Nikolai Nikolaevich, an advocate of army modernization.

Russia's immediate security challenge was to restore its military forces. Refurbishment of the army, however, was constrained by three considerations. First, mutiny within the ranks that lasted through 1906 and tied down forces in the countryside somewhat longer, occupied large numbers of army units in unpleasant internal policing actions. Second, national bankruptcy brought on by the war allowed Finance Minister Kokovtsov to limit the War Ministry's spending as long as he thought Russia's fiscal liquidity was in danger. Third, Russia's alliance partner France demanded primary attention to its strategic objectives. Obviously, Russia needed a strategic consensus, approved by the tsar, on external threats.

The officers who led the General Staff after the Russo-Japanese War were divided between two groups. On one side were those who saw Germany and Austria-Hungary as the only serious security threat. On the other were officers who directed their attention toward Asia, who believed that Japan posed a more serious threat than any European power. Naturally, senior officers with responsibility for Russia's East Asian security joined those "westerners" in the officer corps who were converted to an eastern disposition by the recent humiliation in Manchuria. These tensions were not finally resolved until the strategic reorientation of 1911–12 and the military rebuilding programs of 1912–14.

The two orientations demanded quite different military tools. An active eastern policy required a large, modern, effective blue-water navy that would have to be able to face the Imperial Japanese Navy and squadrons from Germany, the United States, and Britain. Such an orientation would necessarily have run counter to Great Britain's and Japan's interests and would have brought Russia and the Central Powers onto better terms. The traditional western orientation, on the other hand, would demand a massive program of replacement and modernization of equipment, reorganization of field units, rapid and dense development of strategic railroad lines, and modernization of the citadel fortresses along the Vistula. In 1906 Russia's fundamental international alignments and relationships predicated only the latter, with Russia allied to France for confrontation with Germany. Each strategy had its price and the combined cost of reconstruction along both lines – new fleets and army rearmament – was beyond the capacity of the Russian state, economy, and people.

The GSO, formed to decide fundamental issues of national security such as these, was incapable of performing that role. Instead, it became the bureaucratic center of "interest group politics run amok," as historian William C. Fuller, Jr., has put it. Finance Minister Kokovtsov cleverly played off the GSO's priorities against other ministerial and General Staff agendas and blocked funding for any military reforms he thought too expensive. Under the reformist leadership of Nikolai Nikolaevich, GSO had the temerity to attempt to block the tsar's pet project, construction of a new navy, a split into which the Finance Ministry drove a very big wedge to prevent much spending until 1908. On the other hand, the Council vigorously culled the officer corps of dead wood: by 1907, some 7,000 "unsuitable and superannuated" officers had been pensioned off, making room for promotion of younger men whose Manchurian service had not discredited them.

The independent war planning apparatus (GUGSh) that Nicholas had set up in June 1905 proved to be a misguided reform as well. Separation of those elements from War Ministry control merely encouraged a breakdown in cooperation between them and caused pointless duplication of effort and unnecessary expense. The War Ministry, GUGSh, and the GSO were locked in a perpetual struggle for influence over matters of strategic importance. By the turn of 1909, both "reformist" institutions ceased operation: Nicholas disbanded the GSO and reincorporated GUGSh into the War Ministry. The appointment of Sukhomlinov, formerly commander of the Kiev Military District and a western-oriented officer, as war minister in early 1909 completed the postwar reorganization of strategy-making organizations.

Organizational paralysis in GUGSh and GSO reached a climax at precisely the time that Russia's relations with the Central Powers cast the entire basis for Imperial security – the 1893 Franco-Russian military agreement – into doubt. In September 1908 Foreign Minister A. P. Izvolskii was informed that Vienna intended to annex Bosnia-Herzegovina. At a secret meeting with his Austrian counterpart, Count Alois Aehrenthal, Izvolskii demanded as a *quid pro quo* that Austria-Hungary support Russia in revocation of the clauses of the 1878 Berlin Treaty, by which the Turkish Straits were closed to warships. But the plan blew up in October when Aehrenthal prematurely announced the annexation. Izvolskii now faced domestic outrage over his duplicitous dealings. In the Council of Ministers, the ministers of war, marine, finance, and interior denounced his initiative. A Russian threat of war to prevent the Austrian annexation was out of the question. And when Berlin cast its lot with Vienna, St. Petersburg lost whatever hopes it may have had of bullying its way into a graceful exit. Russia accepted Austria's new annexations.

This humiliation was a by-product of dysfunctional government: if Izvolskii had vetted his plan with council colleagues, he might have learned sooner of the army's precarious condition and the considerable risks his demarche entailed. Moreover, the Bosnian "retreat" reduced Russia's European policy alternatives to two. It could recognize German preeminence and come to terms with Berlin at the expense of its French alliance. Or it could cleave more closely to France (and Britain) in the expectation of nudging their policies toward the Balkans closer to its own. Petersburg explored first the Berlin course, then swung back to its alliance orientation.

Much has been speculated about Russia's "historic mission" in the Balkans. The Russian press then and historians since have attended closely to the pan-Slavic impetus behind Russian policy, suggesting that segments of Russian educated opinion embraced popular slogans about unity among Slavs in the face of the "German danger." But to assert that such opinion exercised influence over government policy toward the Balkans ignores the evidence of how policy was made in St. Petersburg. Even when influential personages with strong pan-Slavic ideas commanded imperial confidence, there was little they could do to direct the course of policy. Simply put, Russia was a toothless power after 1905, unable to raise the funds to rebuild its armed forces. That all changed with the beginning of an economic boom and resolution of the policy struggles that had occupied the War Ministry and foreign policy establishment.

The Great Program

The basic dilemma of Russian military planners was whether to concentrate against Japan or against Austria-Hungary and Germany. In 1908 General A. A. Palitsyn, chief of GUGSh, with the assistance of General M. V. Alekseev, the army's head of mobilization and intelligence, and Colonel S. K. Dobrorolskii, GUGSh's chief mobilization technician, crafted Mobilization Schedule No. 18. That plan held the army to strictly defensive dispositions during the first phase of war with the Central Powers, and shifted to active operations only when forces were fully mobilized and concentrated. Palitsyn argued to Nikolai Nikolaevich that the persistent danger in East Asia necessitated this fundamentally defensive strategy – and the transfer of 138 battalions from the western military districts to the central and eastern parts of the empire. This was hardly a strategic deployment designed to reassure Russia's ally, France.

Until about 1911, Russia's relations with France evolved little from the perspective of the two states' conventions. But when viewed through the reporting of Colonel V. P. Lazarev, the military attaché in Paris, a fundamental reorientation of Russia's strategic perspective was taking shape. As early as summer 1907, Lazarev reported "stubborn" French positions on various Baltic issues of interest to Russia. This reflected "if not the subscription, then at least the preparations for a convention and a plan of combined Anglo-French action in the event of war with Germany. Moreover, some signs point toward the conclusion that our agreement with France has been communicated to the English government." Lazarev's reports also noted "secret Anglo-French discussions" begun in April 1905 and continued January to March 1906 on the question of military cooperation between London and Paris. By late 1906, he continued, it was clear that the German army was not strong enough to carry off its planned swing through Belgium because "a British corps" would land on the Channel coast and threaten the German right flank. Palitsyn passed the military attaché's August 1907 report on these matters to Nicholas II.

Russia and France, in fact, began intensive exchanges of staff officers and intelligence information. The cooperation led, on 16 July 1912, to agreements formalizing Franco-Russian military and naval cooperation and coordination. The next month French military negotiators made their priority clear to the Russian side: strategic railroad construction from the Russian interior to the army's assembly points along the German frontier.

Although strategic railroads had preoccupied mobilization planners from 1868 onwards, by 1910 Russia could boast only ten lines from the interior to the Warsaw Military District. Only six of those were double tracked, which severely restricted the number of troop trains per day that could be moved to the border zone upon mobilization. France's concerns were justified, in view of its general knowledge of the Schlieffen plan. Yet by April 1913, Sukhomlinov could still tell Kokovtsov that he lacked 4,000 locomotives and 3,900 miles of track to meet Russia's and France's mobilization goals.

The bright forty-three-year-old staff planner, General Danilov, and Colonel Dobrorolskii consumed the intelligence information coming from their French counterparts. Danilov was a strong proponent of centralized control of war planning. He and Dobrorolskii concluded by late 1910 that Franco-British "coordination" in a war with Germany was virtually an accomplished fact. And they presumed a combined Russian-French-British alliance in the event of general war on the Continent and began reworking Russia's mobilization plans accordingly.

In March 1909 Sukhomlinov subordinated the independent General Staff to the War Ministry and elevated Danilov to quartermaster-general. Initially, Sukhomlinov and Danilov adopted parts of the Palitsyn plan to shift many regiments out of Poland to interior dispositions. Yet by 1910, a new Mobilization Schedule No. 19 placed greater emphasis on depth of deployment in the West and transfered

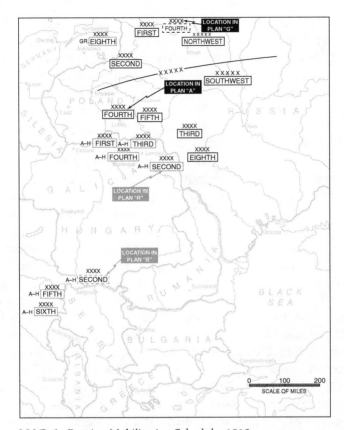

MAP 6. Russian Mobilization Schedule, 1910.

some 150,000 troops and almost 400 additional artillery pieces from Siberian military districts to the West. Mobilization in any future war with the Central Powers would occur in the Russian heartland and forces would then be transported for concentration and battle. This strategy could not satisfy France's persistent demand for Russian offensive action against Germany within two weeks of mobilization because Russia did not have the railroads to carry it out quickly. If Schedule No. 19 were implemented, Russia would be able to take the fight into Prussia on about M + 20. Russian statesmen soon felt the stinging reproof of the French press, politicians, and staff officers for their alleged appeasement of Germany and neglect of alliance obligations.

Sukhomlinov's Mobilization Schedule No. 19 anticipated concentration of the mass of Russia's active army in the relative safety of northern Belarus (east of the Bug River and north of the Pripet marshes).

There, it would be less exposed to disruption during the chaos of mobilization than if deployed along the Vistula River in Poland. After units from the general reserve arrived from central Russia, the force would drive northward into the open flank of an anticipated German offensive toward Petersburg. The risks were huge, for the new schedule could not account for the additional time needed to move units from the Volga River and Siberia back to the western part of European Russia. In that time, the war might already be lost.

In 1912 new and better intelligence about Anglo-French military coordination, intense lobbying by the commanders and planning staffs of the western military districts, as well as objections from defense circles in the Duma, led the General Staff to modify the strategic precepts of Schedule No. 19. With Russia entering a period of intense economic expansion and growth, Danilov felt sufficiently confident to favor a muscular strategy – "to go over to the offensive against the armed forces of Germany and Austria-Hungary with the objective of taking the war into their territory." Nicholas II signed the plan into effect in May 1912. Designated Mobilization Schedule No. 19 (Revised), the plan had two alternatives. Variant "A" envisaged massing against Austrian Galicia, Variant "G" against Germany. Under "A," two armies of twenty-nine divisions would attack into East Prussia to seize an "assembly area for future operations." At the same time, four armies (forty-five divisions) would fall on Galicia, strike across the Carpathian Mountains, and spread out across the Hungarian Plain. In contrast, under Variant "G" the armies on the northeast front almost doubled (to forty-three divisions) while the southwestern armies comprised thirty-one divisions, which would screen the rear of the advance into Prussia. The presumption of British subscription to the Franco-Russian alignment encouraged Russia to consider its strategic dilemmas in Central Europe resolved.

Events were to prove otherwise. In early 1912, naively encouraging an anti-Austrian defensive league among the Bulgarians, Serbs and later Greeks, Russia discovered that the alliance it had encouraged – the Balkan League – possessed aggressive appetites it could satisfy without reference to its sponsor. The League's members turned their military might against the Turks in October 1912 with great success in the First Balkan War. Unhappy with the division of spoils among themselves, Bulgaria turned on Serbia and Greece. Turkey and Romania then entered against Bulgaria and now, in the Second Balkan War, each took a piece of Sofia's recent gains.

These developments brought threats from Vienna, not least against Serbia whose forces had demonstrated vitality and capability on the battlefield. Vienna shifted five army corps to its border with Serbia in early 1913, prompting Sazonov and the General Staff to be concerned with Vienna's threatening attitude towards its neighbor, "upstart" Serbia. Moreover, the arrival in October 1913 of a German military mission to Turkey led by General Otto Liman von Sanders greatly troubled Petersburg. These developments, linked with Russia's economic recovery, resulted in a modest program of rearmament that allocated additional spending to the army and navy.

But the "Small Program" was doomed to a short shelf life. Reacting to the strategic reorientation of Schedule No. 19, War Minister Sukhomlinov in 1912 reversed some of its spending goals, such as demolition of fortresses. The War Ministry then launched an urgent examination of military reorganization and rearmament. The result was the "Great Program" of defense spending. Its approval by Nicholas II in October 1913 was merely a preliminary clue that the Russian government had finally put its house in order for the first time since the Russo-Japanese War. In 1912, with implementation of Mobilization Schedule No. 19 (Revised), Sukhomlinov responded halfway to the anxious appeals of the French General Staff for a return to Russia's traditional strategic dispositions that were tightly bound to the western frontier and focused on operations against East Prussia.

In the course of secret staff talks in 1912 and again in 1913, the Russians promised to attack Germany with 800,000 men fifteen days into a general mobilization. Chief of General Staff Ia. G. Zhilinskii went so far as to promise the same performance by M + 13 within another year (no matter how unconvincing such promises were, in view of the chronic shortcomings in strategic railroad network development in the western provinces). The Franco-Russian military accord was the only one of its kind in effect in Europe in 1914.

To carry out the revised mobilization plan, Russia also needed immediately a vast arsenal of new and reorganized field artillery, tactically more agile units, better organized logistical infrastructure, and, most importantly, a massive new program of strategic railroad construction to move units from central Russia to their concentration points in tsarist Poland. Much of this Sukhomlinov was promised with the Great Program.

In March 1913 Nicholas II agreed to immediate defense expenditures of 225 million rubles (181 million for artillery alone). In July he approved a five-year program just for artillery modernization and reorganization. Early in 1914 military reform received the infusion it needed for vast modernization: 433 million rubles. The Great Program consisted of funding in four principal areas:

1. 500,000 additional men (266,000 infantry, 126,000 gunners, and miscellaneous other technical troops).
2. Reorganization of unit mobilization by the creation of a "secret cadre" system by which a designated portion of the standing army would fall out of its peacetime units on M-Day to form the skeleton of 560 additional battalions.
3. A large-scale investment in all calibers of artillery including new heavy field batteries, to be completed by 1917.
4. A first, systematic investment in military aviation.

The Great Program marked the final triumph within the General Staff of the "Germany first" school. Berlin's seemingly aggressive behavior and Britain's quiet "commitment" to intervention convinced most Russian planners that they had little choice but to operate within the structure of their French obligations. But the Great Program was not intended to provide Russia a rapid victory; Germany and Austria-Hungary both continued to enjoy considerable advantage in the pace of their mobilization. As one insightful observer put it, "reorganization of troop units, recruitment of additional troops, provision of extra firepower – these were hardly the stuff of which dreams of military grandeur were made." Russian statesmen, including the tsar, knew in July 1914 that the program had not even begun (it had just been funded by the Duma weeks before), a fact that dampened any irrational enthusiasm for belligerency during the crisis. The knowledge that informed their decision-making was, instead, recollection of Austro-German coercion during the Bosnian crisis, acute awareness of Russia's military ill-preparedness, and the firm belief that Russia would no longer be seen as a great power if it allowed Serbia to be "chastised" by Vienna. Another salient consideration was the fear that the Turkish Straits would be controlled by the Triple Alliance.

The July Crisis

The Russian Council of Ministers under Premier Goremykin was well apprised of the unfolding crisis in the wake of the Sarajevo assassination on 28 June 1914 and settled on Russia's response at an early stage. From the start, the Council saw war as the "inevitable outcome." On 11 July Foreign Minister Sazonov reported to his colleagues on his ministry's estimation of the situation and the policy it proposed to follow. He placed responsibility squarely at Germany's doorstep for the danger, which he saw deepening in each report that arrived from Russia's missions in the European capitals. His and the government's knowledge of events rested also on intercepted foreign diplomatic cable traffic transmitted to or from embassies in St. Petersburg. Later, Sazonov described the impression that Vienna's strident response to the assassination crisis left on him:

> The moment had come when Russia, faced with the annihilation of Serbia, would lose all her authority if she did not declare herself the defender of a Slavonic nation threatened by powerful neighbors.... If Russia failed to fulfill her historic mission she would be considered a decadent State and would henceforth have to take second place among the powers.

Krivoshein, the influential conservative minister of agriculture, declared that "opinion" (public and parliamentary) would accept nothing short of bold action. Russian statesmen felt that their sovereign, Nicholas II, could now face the Germanic powers if Russia's vital interests demanded a showdown. Finally, the stability of Russia's internal order – its restive urban proletariat and the revolutionary cadres at work within it – would not be a threat to the regime in the event of war, thanks to a generally improving economy from 1910 onward. Three days later, Sazonov departed for his estate for a brief rest before the arrival in the Russian capital of France's President Raymond Poincaré and Premier René Viviani, expected on 20 July.

The Balkan crisis was apparently low on the agenda of points that the French intended to discuss. Nevertheless, by the end of the visit Sazonov and Viviani shared what they euphemistically termed a "perfect community of views" on the maintenance of peace in Europe. That nebulous expression in all likelihood meant that they had decided to take action against Vienna in case of a Habsburg attack on Serbia. Most importantly, the two powers solemnly affirmed the mutual obligations imposed by their alliance: France would stand by Russia against Austria-Hungary in the Balkan crisis. Unfortunately, the absence of precise documentation of the Franco-Russian discussions prevents more detailed analysis.

Austria's ultimatum to Serbia was delivered on 23 July, just after France's leaders departed Petersburg. The July Crisis was now an urgent concern, but Russia's leaders were poorly positioned for the development of an effective response toward Austria-Hungary and Germany. Key diplomats, including the ambassadors to Paris, Vienna, Berlin, and Belgrade, on whose diplomatic reports, intelligence collection activities, and foreign liaison the Foreign Ministry relied, were away from their posts on summer vacation. The chief of the General Staff's operations section, Quartermaster-General Danilov, and the Foreign Ministry's chief of the Near Eastern desk, Prince G. N. Trubetskoi, were also away from the Russian capital.

Foreign Minister Sazonov, hastily returned from his estate, was not surprised when the Habsburg ambassador, Count Friedrich Szápáry, presented him the formal text of the ultimatum Vienna had dispatched to Belgrade at 10 a.m. on 24 July. During the twenty-four hours preceding Austria's demarche, Sazonov had received six warning indicators about the turn Austrian policy was about to take. The Foreign Ministry's *camera noir* (its cryptographic section) provided two alerts that Vienna was on the brink of taking action. On 23 July Sazonov had read Count Szápáry's "secret" report to Austrian Foreign Minister Count Leopold Berchtold concerning the mood in Russia, as well as news from Szápáry's counterpart in Berlin on the German Foreign Ministry's position on the crisis.

From Russia's diplomatic agents in other capitals, Sazonov acquired further alarming news. His chargé in Vienna reported circulation there of a "sharp note" to be presented in Belgrade that day, underscored by Szápáry's urgent telephoned request to Sazonov on the evening of 23 July for an early appointment the next morning. From the Italian ambassador in Petersburg, Sazonov heard that Austria intended to present Serbia with "an unpleasant ultimatum" that very day. By cable that evening, from the Russian chargé in Belgrade, he learned that Vienna had, in fact, presented Belgrade with an ultimatum having a forty-eight hour deadline. Count V. N. Strandtmann in the Serbian capital cabled Petersburg that the Austrian minister had not only delivered the ultimatum, but had also verbally informed the Serbs that the Austro-Hungarian Empire intended to break off diplomatic relations if Serbia did not meet its demands within the mandated time. In other words, Russia's principal foreign policy decision-maker and the tsar's closest adviser were well informed from a variety of sources about the events precipitating the crisis.

When Szápáry informed Sazonov of the ultimatum's terms, Sazonov declared, "It's the European war!" – not because it came unexpectedly, but because the brash, undiplomatic bellicosity of Vienna's address to Belgrade signaled to him the extremity of Austria's position in the crisis. Sazonov understood that the ultimatum involved an enormous risk, one that Vienna was inexplicably willing to undertake. "You want to go to war with Serbia," he declared to Szápáry. In unusually forthright terms for a diplomat, he continued:

> I see what is going on. The German papers are adding fuel to the fire! You are setting fire to Europe. It is a great responsibility you are assuming, you will see what sort of an impression you will make in London and in Paris and perhaps elsewhere. It will be considered an unjustified aggression.

The Foreign Ministry hurriedly recalled all members of its chancellery and the Near East desk, while Sazonov began a cycle of meetings with Ambassadors Sir George Buchanan (Great Britain) and Maurice Paléologue (France). He knew that Russia was scarcely in a position to act militarily against Austria, even in response to aggression against Serbia. In the immediate term, Russia had little opportunity to begin preparations for a military crisis. The state's long-term plans for military modernization and rearmament remained years from completion, and the large-scale strategic railroad expansion would not approach completion until 1918.

Sazonov hoped that if the crisis could be drawn out, if Austrian action could be delayed, the other European powers might defuse the tensions. His goal was to achieve sufficient unity among the other powers to dissuade Vienna from pressing ahead with its demands in Belgrade. He made this clear to the foreign ambassadors in Petersburg, appealing directly to Buchanan to activate Britain's influence in Berlin and Vienna for moderation of the Austrian ultimatum, and, foremost, to extend the deadline. Although Sazonov said that the Russian government had yet to consider whether an Austrian invasion of Serbia constituted a *casus belli*, Buchanan sensed that France and Russia together intended to stay the course – with or without Britain's cooperation. Put differently, Russia was prepared to block with military means any Habsburg offensive against Serbia while France prepared to meet the expected German attack.

Late that same morning, Foreign Minister Berchtold assured the Russian chargé, Prince N. A. Kudashev, that Vienna understood the consequences of a policy of humiliation toward Serbia – "repercussions" from Russia – and declared the matter one of balance of power and dynastic politics. Kudashev asked what Austria intended to do in the event that Serbia failed to comply with the ultimatum. Berchtold replied that the Habsburg Mission would depart Belgrade – to which Kudashev declared, "*Alors! C'est la guerre!*" and reported the exchange to St. Petersburg.

In St. Petersburg, the Council of Ministers met for two hours that Friday afternoon, 24 July. Nicholas II personally led the Council in full session to advise him and to discuss Russia's response. This it did on the grave diplomatic and political issues that Sarajevo presented – but completely in ignorance of what Russia's mobilization planners could deliver. Dominic Lieven's assessment – that Nicholas "preferred heads of departments to confine themselves to their own specific spheres and that he regarded foreign affairs as being peculiarly the business of himself and those to whom he chose to turn for advice" – summarized the tsar's notion of proper ministerial government.

The Council of Ministers under Goremykin proposed five resolutions for Nicholas' consideration, to defuse the crisis and to protect Russia's interests:

1. that the great powers be involved in examination of the conspiracy surrounding the assassination at Sarajevo;
2. that Serbia's fate be entrusted to the great powers;
3. that Nicholas II authorize declaration of mobilization in four military districts and the Baltic, based on the subsequent unfolding of events;
4. that the War Ministry build up material stockpiles in preparation for a possible mobilization; and
5. that Russia take steps immediately to reduce its sums of exchange on deposit in Germany and Austria-Hungary.

According to the minutes of the meeting, the *partial* mobilization, against Austria-Hungary, would achieve two objectives. First, it would send an unmistakable signal to Vienna that Russia's "verbal protest" would be backed with steel. Second, it would send pacific signals to Berlin because Russian reservists would not be mobilized within any military district adjacent to Germany. Nicholas approved the preparations for this partial mobilization and directed War Minister Sukhomlinov and Chief of General Staff Ianushkevich to begin those the next day. The tsar also had the resolutions transmitted to the Serbian ambassador for relay immediately to Belgrade.

Shortly before noon on Saturday, 25 July, Nicholas approved the Council of Ministers' proposal for partial mobilization, affecting 1.1 million men in the Odessa, Kiev, Moscow, and Kazan military districts and in the Black and Baltic Sea fleets. He also declared that, if Austro-Hungarian troops violated Serbia's borders, Russia would declare mobilization and war preparations would begin. Even then, he stated, it would proceed only in the districts adjacent to Austria. Russia would in any case enter the "period preparatory to war" during the night of 25–26 July. All troops would return to winter quarter from leave or furlough, and all fortresses on the western frontier would transition to a war footing.

Ianushkevich ordered his planners (still without Danilov's leadership) to activate plans for the transition to "the period prior to mobilization," a military phase of the "period preparatory to war." This required officers to return to their regiments from leave and instantly converted all "probationary" General Staff officers to permanent status. He next prepared the draft declaration of partial mobilization for the tsar's signature.

Neither the war minister nor his chief of General Staff had any background in the details of mobilization planning. Neither was familiar with the intricacies of Russia's mobilization schedule or the assumptions on which it had developed. Neither understood the relative inflexibility of Russia's mobilization plan and thus the limitations on their choices in ordering partial mobilization. Neither anticipated the stridency of the professional staff's technical arguments *against* partial mobilization when it learned of their recommendation to the tsar. In fact, the mobilization experts in the General Staff greeted the tsar's order for the extemporization of a partial effort with horror.

General Danilov, head of mobilization planning, had viewed war with the Dual Monarchy as the trigger for German mobilization. Thus, partial mobilization, regardless of any usefulness it might serve as a "diplomatic telegraph," threatened to paralyze Russia's war fighting ability *when* (rather than *if*) Germany declared mobilization. Furthermore, Schedule No. 19 (Rev.) comprised a single, integrated, general mobilization; parts could not be pried off and jettisoned. To carry out Nicholas' order would have required the preparation of an entirely new schedule that addressed only select military districts – and with no assurance that the partial measure would "fit" with Schedule No. 19 (Rev.), should Germany subsequently take offense and the tsar have to declare general mobilization.

The final act of the drama began on 28 July when Austria-Hungary declared war on Serbia. The General Staff technicians believed general mobilization was essential, and thus the urgency of advising Nicholas of the implications of a partial mobilization became acute. The following day, 29 July, Petersburg learned that Austria's gunboats had bombarded Belgrade. Count Friedrich von Pourtalès, Germany's ambassador to Petersburg, warned that if Russia did not cease and reverse all military activity immediately, Germany would mobilize. Sazonov, already doubting the wisdom of partial mobilization before that threat, wrote: "As we cannot fulfill Germany's desires, it remains for us to speed up our armament and count on the true inevitability of war." On 30 July Sazonov, Sukhomlinov, and Ianushkevich agreed to urge Nicholas unequivocally to declare general mobilization.

Nicholas sustained the hope that through direct communications with his German cousin, Wilhelm II, the emperors together could eliminate the disagreements into which their respective governments had seemingly locked them. Even at that crucial moment, Sazonov, Sukhomlinov, and Ianushkevich believed that even *general* mobilization by no means implied war with both Vienna and Berlin. The slow pace of Russia's shift to a wartime footing – twelve to sixteen weeks – in their view offered extensive room for maneuver and negotiation. Danilov later wrote that, in principle, a declaration of general mobilization affected only the empire's ability to defend itself and to place its forces in readiness.

Powerful as the military imperative for mobilization might have appeared, it did not convince Nicholas II on 30 July when, in a series of meetings with Sazonov and others, he labored long over the decision. Nicholas refused to take any of the urgent telephone calls from the General Staff that morning as he mulled over a telegram from his cousin: the kaiser declared that the decision for European war rested solely on Nicholas' shoulders! Wilhelm II assured him that he would not be able to hold back events if Nicholas' government took unilateral military steps.

That afternoon, Nicholas' ministers urged him to act. Sazonov noted that Berlin had demanded "from us a capitulation to the Central Powers, for which Russia would never forgive the Sovereign, and which would cover the good name of the Russian people with shame." Krivoshein argued that Russia was not the weakened state of 1908, but could again assert itself with confidence as a great power. Krivoshein's strong conservative position, balancing considerations of strategic danger and domestic stability, gave him *de facto* leadership of the Council, eclipsing Goremykin whose deferential views of Council authority would lead to continued inaction.

Sazonov knew of Berlin's diplomatic threats to Paris of the previous day and communicated this news to Nicholas. When confronted with this, his German cousin's apparent deception, Nicholas II agreed to order general mobilization. Sazonov immediately called Ianushkevich with the imperial order – and told him to smash his telephone, to forestall any imperial second thoughts. The order went into effect on 31 July; Germany declared war the following day.

Conclusion

Did Russia's leaders have a realistic grasp of the implications of their mobilization? Did they comprehend the nature of Germany's policy sufficiently clearly to choose the best course for Imperial Russia? An important distinction should be noted: Russia mobilized; Germany declared war. Neither Russia's entry into war with Germany, nor the empire's eventual collapse from within, were over-determined by the political, economic, and social crises facing the country before 1914. Nor was military defeat preordained. At the beginning of 1915, much of Austrian Galicia as well as part of East Prussia were in Russian hands. Even a year into the war, Russia's military prospects, if not sanguine, were far from bleak, in spite of setbacks. The German army had advanced no more than a few score kilometers from the East Prussian border and had not reached the Bug River. Even after the disastrous loss in the 1915 Gorlice campaign and even in December 1917, when Germany extracted a punitive armistice from Russia's new Bolshevik regime, the front still had yet to reach the Russian core.

The conservative statesman Petr Durnovo from the Ministry of the Interior had written directly to Nicholas in February 1914 of the danger Russia faced if it confronted Germany. He declared that, "in the event of defeat, the possibility of which in a struggle with a foe like Germany cannot be overlooked, social revolution in its most extreme form is inevitable." His prediction reveals just how little understanding Russia's statesmen had of the quarter from which danger to the dynasty and state would come. The government's gross inability to govern through the usual means available to a "well-ordered state" in times of either peace or war meant that its enemies, external or internal, would ultimately profit as crises turned to chaos.

CHAPTER 6

France

France's long-standing hostility toward, and fear of, Germany led to the Dual Alliance with Russia, and the *entente cordiale* with Great Britain. These provided the framework for Germany's diplomatic isolation. After 1911, as war seemed more and more likely, French financial support for a massive Russian military program scheduled to be completed in 1917 gave Germany's military leaders reason to fight sooner rather than later. In the immediate crisis of July 1914, with French support assured, Russia mobilized against Austria-Hungary and Germany, Germany declared war, and the Austro-Serbian conflict was turned into a European war.

In many respects, the French government's goal in July 1914 was to avoid making decisions. For any action taken in that highly incendiary situation could contribute to igniting a conflagration that France did not want and for which it did not wish to be responsible. Against this motive for inaction, however, were the countervailing imperatives of the Franco-Russian alliance. Crucially, France had to avoid arousing Russian fears that French support was in any sense uncertain. To treat support for Russia as a matter for decision was to imply that France had the option of abandoning its ally and, conversely, that Russia was free to abandon France. In short, France's leaders had to adhere wholeheartedly to the alliance and to act as if the nation had no options at all.

Concern for foreign and domestic opinion also weighed in against visible decision-making. It was important to the French leaders that both the British government and its own people recognize that France was being dragged by Austria-Hungary and Germany into an unwanted war. Discussions of whether or how much to assist Russia would give the impression that France had more choices than it chose to admit. Not only was the most important French decision preordained, but France's leaders denied that there was even a decision to be made.

The Cast of 1914

Constitutionally, the key figure in July 1914 should have been Premier and Foreign Minister René Viviani. But Viviani's selection as premier was a by-product of the contentious general election of May 1914, fought largely over the 1913 three-year military service law and proposals for a progressive income tax. The elections returned more than 260 Radicals and 100 Socialists, obliging an unhappy President Raymond Poincaré to look to the Left for the next premier. The president bowed to general pressure to select the independent ex-socialist, who promised not to overturn the three-year military service law. Advertised by Viviani as "an elegant mosaic," the resulting Cabinet was a motley collection united only by a willingness to serve and an agreement not to give up the three-year law, at least not too precipitously.

Although often portrayed as a moderate counterweight to the bellicose Poincaré, Viviani was actually incapable of maintaining a policy of his own. He began his first premiership with a shaky Cabinet and unprepared for his foreign affairs portfolio. Poincaré noted Viviani's "complete ignorance of foreign affairs" and as late as July 1914 "spent the four-day voyage to Kronstadt giving foreign affairs lessons to Viviani." During the trip to Russia, the premier was incapacitated by nervous strain and abdicated his role to Poincaré, whose diaries suggest that he was not at all loath to assume control of the negotiations. Once war started, Viviani moved quickly from the stage, on 3 August yielding the Foreign Ministry to Gaston Doumergue.

While Viviani was too weak to handle the considerable powers of the premiership, Poincaré's authority reflected his personal resolve rather than his limited constitutional power. He had previously arranged cabinets so as to extend his own influence, especially over foreign affairs. Beginning with his election to the presidency in January 1913, Poincaré insisted on dictating foreign policy to the Cabinet. As well, he conducted foreign policy directly by communicating with foreign ambassadors. And he chose Viviani as premier because he was suitably pliable.

After the war, Poincaré would exploit the formal weakness of his office in denying his responsibility for the events of 1914, but his complaints of "helplessness and isolation" were much exaggerated. He had shaped the Viviani cabinet so as to maximize his own control over French policy. During the period between his return from Russia and the outbreak of war, Poincaré chaired virtually constant Cabinet meetings, keeping a firm hand on the smallest elements of French policy.

Because Poincaré was the Frenchman best placed to make key decisions in July 1914, his politics demand attention. Standard descriptions of Poincaré as a conservative Lorrainer and bipartisan vituperation terming him a "warmonger" misrepresent the Moderate Republican. Typically for a man on the right side of the Republican Center, Poincaré was anticlerical but not antireligious, nationalist but not bellicose, a defender of property rights, free markets, and small government. No ideologue, he was a practical politician willing to work with any true Frenchman but adamant in defending France from the Socialist Left, the Catholic Right, and, of course, Germany.

Though often treated as *revanchist*, this native Lorrainer's policy toward Germany was pragmatically defensive. Poincaré's famous warning about the German "menace" and his calls for rectification of past injuries inflicted by the Germans were not cries for war but rejection of the appeasement proposals of Joseph Caillaux and Jules Cambon. Poincaré objected to concessions to Germany because he believed that conciliation would not work. In his diary for March 1914, he described France's posture toward Germany as "no longer a question of revenge, it is a question of threat." He believed that it was possible to deal with Germany on specific issues, but that moving too close to Germany would be dangerous and costly. It was dangerous because such a move would unnerve Russia and undermine the Dual Alliance. It was costly because Germany would sell her friendship only for colonial concessions.

Moreover, boyhood memories of the Franco-Prussian War left Poincaré with no desire for conflict. Though a champion of military preparedness, Poincaré, "despite his ardent patriotism and his ancestral links with the lost provinces, found the idea of war repulsive." Under his presidency, "The grand designs of French foreign policy continued to be motivated by the need to strengthen France's position on the international stage through reinforcing her militarily, through tightening the links of the Triple Entente, and through refusing any penetration of the alliance systems."

Central to this deterrence was solidarity of the Russo-French alliance. Signed while Poincaré was serving as minister of education in his first cabinet, the Franco-Russian pact was one of the foundations of his political world. The Russians had no doubt about his convictions. Ambassador Alexander Izvolskii from Paris reported to Foreign Minister Sergei Sazonov after Poincaré's inauguration: "Russia can count, not only on the armed co-operation of France in the case provided for in the Franco-Russian agreement, but on her most vigourous and effective diplomatic assistance in all the enterprises of the Russian government on behalf of those States."

This pro-Russian orientation notwithstanding, not even the Germans viewed Poincaré as bellicose. His first stint as premier in January 1912 met with general approval in Berlin. Apparently, Germany respected the man who described his own policy as based on "a sincerely pacific spirit, courteous and frank relations, inspired by a mutual respect of interests and dignity." Poincaré's election to the presidency in the tense diplomatic atmosphere of 1913 likewise aroused no concern in Germany.

Still, Poincaré's reputation for bellicosity stemmed from his exhortations for military preparedness, his warnings about the German threat, his Lorraine background, and campaign slanders from elements of the French Left about "Poincaré la Guerre." Such political invective hides the more important point that the Socialists, though ever alert to opportunities to charge nationalists with warmongering, helped Poincaré to win the presidency by failing to throw their support behind the Radical Party's candidate, Caillaux. Historian J. F. V. Keiger tellingly observes, "at no point between 1912 and 1914 did the left-wing Radicals even accuse him of being a warmonger, let alone oppose his candidacy on those grounds."

Aside from the president and premier–foreign minister, the minister of war had the greatest role in decisions of war and peace. Few of the thirty-one French war ministers from 1871 made much of a mark, but ex-soldier Adolphe Messimy of the Radical Party was better than most. As war minister in Caillaux's Cabinet from July 1911 to January 1912, Messimy was responsible for the ouster of defensive-minded Chief of Staff General Victor Michel. Reacquiring the portfolio in the Viviani government of June 1914, he authorized all French military measures during the July Crisis and proved willing to act unilaterally during Poincaré's and Viviani's absence in Russia. Upon the French leaders' return from Russia, however, Messimy fell into line behind Poincaré. Later, Messimy took credit for the decision to shift three corps to defend Paris, and, consequently, for making possible the "miracle of the Marne."

The power of the professional diplomats in the Quai d'Orsay (the Foreign Ministry) and of the ambassadors in foreign capitals to push their own varied agendas should not be overlooked. The Quai d'Orsay was generally anti-German, but the ambassadors operated independent fiefdoms. Paul Cambon, who served as ambassador to the Court of Saint James's from 1898 to 1920, had far more influence than any foreign minister over Franco-British relations. His brother Jules, who was France's ambassador to Berlin from 1907 to 1914, sought to nourish the Russian alliance and to support German interests overseas, "in areas likely to divert her gaze from the European continent and from the French Empire."

The role of the French ambassador to St. Petersburg in the July Crisis will be discussed later. Still, it is useful here to mention one extraordinary attempt by a French ambassador to dictate national policy. On 5 June 1914 Ambassador Maurice Paléologue returned from St. Petersburg to announce that he would resign his post if the proposed Viviani Cabinet failed to retain the three-year military service law.

The only other claimant to an important role in the decision-making process in 1914 was the French Army, or, more precisely, Chief of Staff General Joseph Joffre, its sole spokesman. Joffre's denial that the army could guarantee victory was enough to prevent France from going to war in 1911. His insistence on mobilization insured that France could not stay out of war in 1914. Although Joffre's opinions mattered greatly, on the issue of whether France would fight, he remained subject to War Minister Messimy and the Cabinet as a whole. On the different but critically important question of how France should conduct military operations against Germany, Joffre's was the decisive voice.

The navy, incidentally, had no voice in French policy. Two strong navy ministers, Vice Admiral Augustin Boué de Lapeyrère and Théophile Delcassé, oversaw naval improvements from 1909 to 1913. But their successor, Armand Gauthier, historian Gordon Wright reports, "had shown incompetence, even negligence, and was replaced on 3 August on 'health grounds'."

Absent from this list of key actors in 1914 are many of the "usual suspects" – military leaders, arms manufacturers, press lords, pressure groups – those who, presumably, represent the forces of militarism, capitalism, and nationalism and are often blamed for the outbreak of the Great War. None of these, however, had a role in French decision-making in 1914 nor influenced the men who did. Only one of them, the military leaders, had clearly identifiable opinions on foreign policy.

Some French officers published opinions more bellicose than the army's official position. There was a faction that welcomed war with Germany as an opportunity to restore its honor and regain France's lost provinces. In John Cairn's words, "Sure that war was both imminent and in the long run desirable [the soldiers] struggled to combat all internal weakness and to place France in a material and psychological position where she would be able and ready to choose the most favorable moment to fight for her life, her honor, and the restoration of her former greatness."

These men, however, were a minority even within the army, and their domestic agenda tended to discredit their foreign policy. Their struggle was not against Germany alone but also against the internal weaknesses of France – socialism, pacifism, and parliamentary government. General Guillaume Bonnal, an extreme proponent of these views, proclaimed that war would "deliver Alsace-Lorraine from the Germans and France from the 'parliamentary yoke'." However much such men welcomed war in 1914, they had no influence over the parliamentary system they detested.

As for the notorious "merchants of death," arms manufacturers had little power in a country where most munitions contracts went to government arsenals. David Stevenson's exhaustive study of arms races before World War I offers not the slightest suggestion that French manufacturers urged their government to go to war.

The War Powers

Before discussing the "war powers" question, it should be pointed out that France's government made few decisions in July 1914. The Senate and Chamber of Deputies began their summer recess on 15 July 1914 and reconvened only on 4 August – after the German declaration of war. President Poincaré, Premier–Foreign Minister Viviani, and Pierre Jacquin de Margerie, political director in the Foreign Ministry, put themselves out of the action by embarking on a long-planned visit to St. Petersburg. At sea from 16 July until their arrival in Russia on 20 July, they were again in touch only by radio during the return voyage of 24–29 July. In the absence of Viviani, the responsibilities of government fell to the inexperienced Minister of Justice Jean Baptiste Bienvenu-Martin.

Still, even decisions not to decide require decision-making procedures. The general interpretation of the Third Republic's ambiguous constitution is that power rested with the two legislative assemblies, either of which could oust a government by rejecting essential legislation. Sitting together, the Senate and the Chamber of Deputies chose the Republic's president. According to the Constitution of 1875, the president had the power to "dispose of the armed forces," to "negotiate and ratify treaties," and in case of emergency to "declare war." But the lawmakers of 1875 had built in a system of checks and balances on the president's powers: his direction of the armed forces required that a minister countersign every presidential order; and his power both to negotiate treaties and to declare war required the previous consent of the two chambers.

This formal constitutional framework of checks and balances notwithstanding, the French Senate never developed its constitutionally privileged position to ratify treaties or to declare war analogous to the American Senate (discussed in Chapter 11). Instead, it concentrated its efforts on domestic affairs, on the award of patronage and contracts. In the sixty-year history of the Third Republic, according to constitutional expert Frederick L. Schuman, the French parliament "never once voted a formal declaration of war upon the recommendation of the Cabinet." And thus it was on 3 August 1914: the Cabinet simply informed the two houses that war already existed due to German aggressive acts, and the patriotic chambers readily voted the necessary war credits with no discussion of war or peace and with no formal declaration of war.

In fact, the day-to-day governance of France fell to the Council of Ministers (in English, the "cabinet"). The chief voices in the Council were its president (the "prime minister" or "premier") and the foreign minister. Crucially, the Council had the authority to mobilize the armed forces. Since the ministers served at the sufferance of the legislative assemblies, policy conflicts, which might have remained largely submerged in a presidential system, resulted in frequent reshuffling of ministerial portfolios. "Between 1907 and 1914," one scholar stated, "there were nine Ministers of Foreign Affairs, eight Ministers of Finances, seven Ministers of the Navy, nine War Ministers and twelve Presidents of the Council." The Council's deliberations were secret, no minutes were kept, and it reached decisions by consensus rather than votes.

The Public Mood

The argument that the French people as a whole desired war rests on superficial assumptions about the persistence of French *revanchism* and misunderstandings of the significance of President Poincaré's election by the French parliament. As the memory of the Franco-Prussian War faded, ever fewer Frenchmen yearned to die for the return of the "lost provinces" while the inhabitants of Alsace-Lorraine came to accept German rule. A contemporary analyst stated that "the very idea of war had disappeared from the popular mind" and that the French people believed war to be impossible. A recent study of French policy bluntly asserts that by 1911, "France had not only renounced revenge but even begun to believe that there would never be another war." Although Germany claimed to fear French *revanchism*, Ambassador Wilhelm von Schoen's reports from Paris reveal that he knew better. Secretary of State for Foreign Affairs Gottlieb von Jagow as late as 18 July 1914 denied that France was "anxious for war at the present time."

Swayed by reported national manifestations of "sacrificial joy" in July 1914, some historians have projected backwards an exaggerated French desire for war. The method is suspect, for such manifestations may have been less a reflection of genuine feeling than an emotional defense against fear and despair. Long before Jean-Jacques Becker's demolition of the fiction that most Frenchmen marched to war with zeal and optimism, Paul de la Gorce pointed out that "songs and warlike slogans helped to make the moment of leave-taking bearable" and that "in the villages ... there was no crowd, no band, no popular enthusiasm to hide the simple truth that the men were going."

Although the years before the war in France, as elsewhere in Europe, saw a substantial outpouring of romantic, nationalist prose exalting the morally pure and mystical experience of battle for *la patrie*, the militarism often identified as endemic in European populations had little hold on French policy-makers and even less on the general population.

For every nationalist intellectual declaiming in Paris about the virtues of self-abnegation, heroism, and war, there were thousands of Frenchmen in the provinces tending their gardens.

To be sure, the rhetoric of France's leaders was anti-German, their specific policies supporting such an interpretation. To the extent that the Russian alliance, colonial *rapprochement* with Britain, and efforts to reconcile her Russian ally with her new British friend strengthened France, they naturally aroused German resentment. The very existence of the *entente cordiale* angered Germany's francophobic elements, and French actions sometimes seemed to vindicate German paranoia. France on the eve of the Great War was a country little interested in current international events but fearful of potential calamities.

The July Crisis

The assassination of the Austrian archduke aroused little interest in a country that was deeply engrossed with the consequences of a much more interesting murder. Frenchmen cared much less about the European response to Gavrilo Princep's deed than about the fate of Madame Caillaux, wife of Radical leader Caillaux, for emptying a revolver into *La Figaro*'s editor Gaston Calmette. Mme. Caillaux's trial from 20 to 29 July, which overshadowed the Austrian ultimatum to Serbia and Poincaré's state visit to St. Petersburg, constituted France's "July Crisis." But as Becker put it, "one may suspect that Mme Caillaux's trial did not divert public opinion from the crisis; rather public opinion, largely unconscious of the danger, had no reason to shift its attention from the trial."

Generally speaking, France had no reliable strategy for avoiding war in July 1914. It could only hope to deter Germany by manifesting military readiness and maintaining the Russian alliance. This had to be deterrence "in a low key," however, as the need to maintain national unity militated against threatening language. A key to understanding French actions in 1914 is the passage in General Joffre's *Mémoires* noting,

> one can affirm that the Russian General Staff's certainty about our offensive plans and our commitment to the clauses of the military agreement, a certainty reinforced at every contact with our General Staff, strongly contributed to leading the Russian General Staff to intensify its effort.

If it had sensed on our part any less firmness, there is no doubt that our
allies would have been more cautious at the beginning of the war.

Reassuring the Russians was crucial for French security, but so too
was avoiding talk likely to generate public antiwar sentiment. On this
score, the government was fortunate. French voters, who had recently
returned a Socialist and Radical Socialist majority to the Chambre
des Deputés, could trust Viviani's government to take all reasonable
measures to avoid war. When war came, the public saw it as "forced
upon a peaceable Republic as a result of German aggression."

France's security depended on its military convention with Russia.
This was perhaps the only instance in 1914 of an alliance with clear
obligations and firm commitments. In August 1911 Joffre had sent
General Auguste Dubail to St. Petersburg. The staff talks resulted in
an agreement that Russia would launch an offensive by the sixteenth
day of the war and expect to engage five or six German corps. By
1912, Poincaré and Joffre had wrung from Y. G. Zhilinskii, the Russian
chief of staff, an agreement that Russia and France would mobilize in
response to German mobilization without waiting for consultation. In
sum, the most important decision that France had to make during the
July Crisis was effectively determined by the urgent need for alliance
solidarity.

France's prewar ambassadorial appointment in St. Petersburg
reinforced its military commitment to the alliance. Ambassador
Paléologue's journal attests that Premier Doumergue had told him
in January 1914, "The safety of France will depend on the energy and
promptness with which we shall know how to push [our allies] into
the fight." Paléologue's promises to Foreign Minister Sazonov on 25
and 28 July 1914 of "unequivocal French support" were entirely in
line with Poincaré's admonition to the Austrian envoy in St. Petersburg on 21 July that France would support Russia and Russia support
Serbia.

Historians who see a conflict between, on the one hand, Viviani's
telegram of 27 August about "neglecting no effort to resolve the conflict" and actions "in the interest of the general peace," and, on the
other, the assurances offered Russia by the ambassador on 28 August,
treat Paléologue as a loose cannon, whose Germanophobia led him
to exceed his authority. That interpretation, however, misconstrues
both the intent and the authorship of "Viviani's" communications.
By 27 August, Viviani's nerves had given out. Any telegram sent over

his name contains the views of Poincaré. More to the point, it is difficult to believe that after several days of personal contact with the ambassador in St. Petersburg, the French leaders would have relied on ship-to-shore radio to communicate the nuances of their foreign policy. Surely, messages about conflict resolution and peace sent by such insecure means were intended for international consumption, not to undermine promises of unequivocal support given privately in St. Petersburg. That such messages were sent, effectively, by Poincaré is even more revealing as, unlike Viviani, Poincaré has never been described as irresolute in 1914. In Keiger's summary, "to have held Russia back from entering the war, had that been possible, would have allowed Austria-Hungary to regain some of her prestige, while seriously reducing that of Russia, thus altering the balance between Triple Entente and Triple Alliance to the disadvantage of the former."

We would be better able to understand the role of Franco-Russian relations in the events of July 1914 if the substance of the St. Petersburg conversations were known, but official document collections and the personal papers of the participants are equally devoid of pertinent material. The unusual silence suggests a concerted effort at concealment. Because France could not be seen to be encouraging Russian action against Austria, the absence of evidence about the talks reinforces the theory that Poincaré's message to the tsar was one of alliance solidarity. Nothing frightened France more than facing the German Army alone, and thus her leaders worked to bind Russia to her obligations.

Preventing war through a display of alliance strength was probably more hope than policy, but the Poincaré-Viviani mission took no military measures to insure against a failure of deterrence. The meetings in St. Petersburg appear to have been purely political, with no discussion of how to fight a war against the Germanic powers. In the absence of military conversations, the Russian military attaché quite reasonably asked Joffre on 28 July whether France would mobilize against Germany if Germany moved against Russia alone. Poincaré and Viviani had avoided the issue because war planning would have betokened political failure and, perhaps, encouraged Russia to act rashly. When the French leaders landed at Dunkirk on 29 July, both still believed that war would be avoided.

The contrast between French promises of support and the absence of concrete plans made Russia nervous. Understandably, Russia asked what France would do if deterrence failed. And when Premier Viviani announced that France would not "neglect any effort toward a solution of the conflict in the interests of universal peace," this so worried Russia that it briefly suspended mobilization. As late as 31 July, President Poincaré tried to avert war by appealing to King George V to convince Germany "that the *entente cordiale* would be affirmed, in case of need, even to the extent of taking the field side by side."

France's relationship with Great Britain was even more awkward than that with Russia. French diplomacy took British support for granted; its military plans assumed the presence of British troops on Joffre's left flank and of the Royal Navy to defend the Channel. Although the British government refused to commit itself to continental operations, Director of Military Operations General Sir Henry Wilson drew up contingency plans as if British intervention were certain. But no formal political agreements backed these assumptions, and, if France was loath to plead for guarantees, Britain's Liberal government refused to abandon its traditional diplomatic "free hand" by offering them. In the absence of formal political agreements between the two states, France could only avoid actions embarrassing to Britain and trust that London would fulfill its informal commitments.

Army leaders were the only elite in France that favored war, this as a means to restoring the nation's lost glory. But the need to impress friends and foes alike with French martial virtues does not explain the almost somnolent manner in which the French Army moved from peace to war. While the government denied the need to make any decisions, the army acted as if all relevant decisions had already been taken and as if their plans and premises required no further examination.

Initially, French military leaders seem to have been as oblivious as the rest of the country to the diplomatic crisis of summer 1914. The highest military coordinating agency, the Conseil Supérieure de la Guerre, devoted its meeting of 21 July to general issues such as France's defensive fortifications and artillery construction programs. Commander-in-chief-designate Joffre admitted to being distracted by the rumblings of war but not to the extent that the Council changed its agenda.

Only on the evening of 24 July did War Minister Messimy share with Joffre his concern that "we will perhaps have to go to war." Learning on 25 July that Messimy had ordered generals and unit commanders to their posts, Joffre asked the minister the next day for permission to execute the entire contents of the *Instruction sur la préparation à la mobilisation*. In particular, Joffre wanted to cancel troop movements and leaves and to recall officers and troops from leave or furlough. While agreeing to all of the other measures, the Cabinet refused until late on 27 July to stir up public concern by curtailing agricultural furloughs. That day, Joffre concluded that war was imminent. He asked the minister of war to "insist of the Russian government by every possible means" that its army undertake the promised offensive in East Prussia.

On 28 July Joffre learned from the minister of war that Jules Cambon had apprised the Quai d'Orsay of German preliminary steps toward mobilization as early as 21 July! Believing France to be "headed straight for war" and that Germany had achieved a week's head start, Joffre asked Messimy for permission to establish the *couverture* (frontier covering force), but Messimy preferred to await Poincaré and Viviani's return to Paris the next day. Thus, it was without political authorization that Joffre told the Russian military attaché (A. A. Ignatiev) of France's "full and active readiness faithfully to execute her responsibilities as an ally." Only on 30 July did the Cabinet finally authorize deployment of the *couverture* – and only to the extent that it could be accomplished without movement by railway, calling up reservists, or requisitioning horses. Moreover, to avoid unintentional contact with German troops, no French soldiers were to come within 10 kilometers of the border.

Convinced that war was imminent, Joffre continued to insist on the need to deploy the complete frontier covering force – reservists, horses, and all. In a strongly worded note, he warned his government that "beginning this evening, every twenty-four-hour delay in calling up the reservists and sending the orders relating to the *couverture* will translate into a withdrawal of our areas of concentration. That is to say that we will have initially to abandon part of our territory, perhaps fifteen to twenty kilometers for every day of delay." By 9 p.m., when Joffre received permission to establish the *couverture*, Russia had ordered general mobilization. Joffre insisted that France follow suit.

It is clear that in July 1914 Joffre advised escalation to higher levels of military alert. Hesitation, to him, would not prevent war but would alarm the Russians, encourage the Germans, concede the edge in a race to mobilize, and undermine the reputations of the French Army and its commander-in-chief. In any case, the important decision, the formulation of the French war plan, had already been made.

When Joffre assumed the combined posts of chief of staff and commander-in-chief-designate of the French Army in 1911, he identified as a major strategic concern "the need to defend against a German violation of Belgium" and noted that Germany was more likely to violate Belgium neutrality than not. He had little faith in the army's defensive Plan XVI and was encouraged by President Armand Fallières' repudiation of defensive thinking. "French soldiers," Fallières announced, were temperamentally suited to the offensive and "would advance on the enemy without hesitation." In short order, Joffre shaped a new Plan XVII, which called for the army to advance against the foe – strategically, operationally, and tactically. As the regulations of 1912 specified, "The French Army, reviving its old traditions, no longer admits for the conduct of operations any other law than that of the offensive."

The Conseil Supérieur de la Guerre authorized Plan XVII on 18 April 1913 and the minister of war approved it on 2 May 1913; it was completed in May 1914. The plan placed the bulk of the French Army in the northeast theater with small forces screening the Alpine and Pyrenean frontiers. The northeastern force comprised five armies: First Army around Epinal, Second Army in the Toul-Nancy region, Third Army opposite Metz, Fifth Army farthest north from Hirson to St. Menehould, and Fourth Army in reserve near Bar-le-Duc. In the event of war, these armies would attack into Alsace and Lorraine, avoiding the political and geographical obstacles imposed by Belgium and Luxembourg, respectively. Given the German operations plan to invade northeastern France via Belgium, Joffre thus badly misplaced his army to counter the anticipated German thrust. Hand-in-hand with the new offensive doctrine, France in July 1913 expanded male military service from two to three years, thereby increasing the ratio of active to reserve troops and enhancing the army's offensive capabilities. Still, the *Loi des Trois Ans* merely added an extra year to obligatory male conscription and the sweeping victory of the Left in the 1914 elections virtually assured that it would be amended shortly.

It is interesting to analyze how Joffre handled the mounting evidence that the plan would not work because Germany had different intentions. He appears to have adopted two techniques – ignoring unfavorable evidence and refusing to calculate the likely outcomes of his planned detailed course of action. First, with Joffre's fixation on the offensively oriented Plan XVII, he sent staff officers to Belgium and Luxembourg to assess the suitability of the territory for a French attack. The report was unfavorable. Thus, the ill-fated Lorraine offensive has to be understood as a decision by a general who preferred for reasons of doctrine and alliance policy to attack in the wrong place rather than not to attack at all.

Second, having determined that Belgium was not a good place for an offensive campaign, the last thing he wanted to hear was that the German Army intended to fight there. He persuaded himself, therefore, that Germany lacked the manpower to move west of the Meuse unless reserve troops combined with active ones. Faced with mounting evidence, including reports from French, British, and Russian military observers, that the Germans intended to move west of the Meuse, Joffre looked more skeptically at the intelligence reports than at his own premises. The dismissal of evidence about German intentions in Belgium was characteristic of his decision-making process: instead of basing his strategic decisions on intelligence, Joffre interpreted his intelligence according to its repercussions for his strategy. Plan XVII was useless against a German sweep through Belgium, but the obvious alternative, a defensive deployment designed to react to several contingencies, contradicted Joffre's public commitment to a short war. Rather than deciding on the best strategy, Joffre acted as if Plan XVII were the only possibility.

Making matters worse, Plan VXII had no operational specifics. It dictated only French deployment with the later moves to be devised as needed. Joffre explained the omissions on the grounds that "it was impossible [to] define a specific maneuver plan in advance; one had to take into consideration all of the unknowns which complicated the problem." He would not commit to a specific line of advance until German intentions had become clear. Given that the transport and supply of huge modern armies cannot be improvised, Joffre's insouciance is astonishing. It was as if he had elevated to the operational level Colonel Louis de Grandmaison's famous dictum, "it is more important to develop a conquering state of mind than to cavil about tactics." Shockingly, Joffre did not share his strategic premises with France's civilian leaders. How else can one explain Poincaré's diary entry for 3 July 1914: "We are expecting, of course, a German attack through Belgium, as our High Command has always predicted"?

In the final analysis, the army, like the government, put its trust in the Franco-Russian alliance. In his *Mémoires*, Joffre took pains to explain this confidence. There had been regular staff talks between the two armies. He and Grand Duke Nikolai Nikolaevich had developed a personal friendship at their first meeting in France in September 1912. The grand duke's subsequent hospitality to Joffre during the

Russian maneuvers of August 1913 had far exceeded obligatory courtesy. Over the period of three weeks, Nikolai and Joffre had "numerous conversations" about the importance of a rapid Russian offensive and, Joffre reports, he had assured his ally that "it was essential to bring relief to our front at any price." Available evidence does not, however, show that the two men coordinated the opening movements in any future war, although both were well aware of the general contours of the Schlieffen plan.

Still, the wartime actions of the grand duke, then commander-in-chief of the Russian Army, vindicated Joffre's trust. Nikolai advanced his forces on the fifteenth day after mobilization, six weeks before his reserves were fully deployed. In a telegram received by Joffre on 7 August, Nikolai announced that his headquarters would fly the tricolor alongside his personal flag.

Unfortunately, the same level of trust did not exist between army and government. The Foreign Ministry refused to share diplomatic plans with either the General Staff or the War Ministry. Thus, the Quai d'Orsay "guarded its information jealously and simply refused to communicate information [to other agencies] it considered incompetent." Thanks to the Foreign Ministry's failure to inform military leaders about the Franco-Italian convention of 1902, for a period of seven years the army unnecessarily stationed two corps to deal with a nonexistent Italian threat. The War Ministry, showing a similar concern, kept from the Foreign Ministry the details of the Franco-British staff talks.

Joffre believed that the army ought to be briefed on foreign policy *before* drafting its war plans, but Premier Caillaux was "unwilling" to share his government's views. At a meeting of the Conseil Supérieur de la Guerre on 11 October 1911, at which Joffre and President Fallières requested diplomatic guidance during the military planning process, Caillaux, vigorously seconded by Foreign Minister Justin de Selves, literally told Joffre to "shut up." Obviously, the Quai d'Orsay was not about to defer to the General Staff on matters of high diplomacy. And while Joffre succeeded in getting several Foreign Ministry assessments of other countries' likely policies, France's civilian authorities gave him no clear statement on such issues as their attitudes toward the problem of Belgian neutrality and Britain's expected contribution to any French military effort.

Equally notorious disputes occurred in the realm of intelligence, where vital information was squandered as ammunition in intramural conflicts. The Foreign Ministry's *cabinet noir* had broken the German diplomatic code and routinely decrypted Berlin's telegrams. But in 1911, Foreign Minister de Selves, believing that Caillaux was using the decrypts to deal secretly with the Germans, began a smear campaign against him. Astonishingly, Caillaux called on the German chargé d'affaires and asked to see the originals of the decrypted telegrams! The Germans immediately changed their codes and France lost "her single most valuable source of foreign intelligence." Conflicts between the Sureté Générale and the Quai d'Orsay and between the War Ministry and its own cryptography section further impeded French intelligence assessment.

Cooperation fell short even within the General Staff, whose Second (intelligence) and Third (operations) Bureaus showed no greater fraternity than did the War and Foreign Ministries. Far from exchanging intelligence and planning information in a mutual effort to improve both, the two bureaus appeared driven to thwart one another. As a British liaison officer, Sir Edward Spears, lamented, "Who will ever know what harm was done by the often unconscious adoption of a thesis by the 3ème Bureau just because the opposition point of view was advanced by the 2ème."

Conclusion

French diplomatic decisions mattered rather little in July 1914. Almost regardless of what it did, France would be dragged into an unwanted war. But the decision-making process remains important. To the extent that French choices had any impact at all, its support for Russia made war more likely rather than less. Worried about its alliances and military conventions, France feared that any hesitation would erode its understandings with Russia and Great Britain. In this atmosphere of uncertainty and fear ("nothing firm from St. Petersburg, nothing firm from London"), French leaders did not weigh alternatives but desperately held onto the one dangerous option that brought them greatest assurance. Supporting Russia risked war, but it also brought hopes of alliance solidarity, firmer military agreements, and a more effective defense against Germany.

Soldiers working under different circumstances also found themselves constrained to a single, desperate course of action. Compared to the confusing world of politics and diplomacy, that of the military planners was relatively straightforward. Friendly military assets were quantifiable. Relatively good information was available about German capabilities and intentions. Even if French military leaders did not confront the implications of the Schlieffen plan, they should have recognized the dangers inherent in their inflexible commitment to Plan XVII. They refused to take advantage of the greater predictability of their world. As committed as their political masters to the Russian alliance, they could not put that alliance at risk by reconsidering the military assumptions behind the promised offensive. Fear of the probable answers – and of their impact on French alliance policy – discouraged questions. Joffre had remarked in 1913 that "fear is the beginning of wisdom." It is hard to say whether in 1914 France felt too little fear or too much. Whatever the case, Paul Cambon summarized accurately when he pointed to the impotence of French policy in late July 1914: "The situation is very serious and we cannot see any way of controlling effects."

CHAPTER 7

Great Britain

The First World War was by far the bloodiest conflict in Britain's history. Yet for all the war's prominence in national consciousness, the debate on its origins has been desultory and muted. The British feel that they have little need to reproach themselves over the war's causation. Indeed, few historians have accused Britain of having instigated the war.

To be sure, that history is not without controversy. In the 1930s David Lloyd George in his memoirs suggested that Sir Edward Grey, the British secretary of state for Foreign Affairs, was culpable for failing to deter German aggression. In other words, Grey might have faced Germany down had he categorically declared, in July 1914, Great Britain's readiness to go to war if France were attacked. But such an allegation of reluctance to threaten force is hardly damning; it is surely more reasonable to attribute blame to those statesmen whose readiness to employ violence, as seen in previous chapters, was all too great.

There was another difficulty: Grey could not issue such a declaration in July – because a majority of the Cabinet, including Lloyd George, opposed intervention. A declaration by Grey would probably have brought down the government and that, for the moment at least, would have removed the deterrent threat.

Any assessment of Great Britain's part in the origins of the First World War must address several basic questions. Who made the decision to enter the war and why? Where did the "war powers" lie? By what process was the decision for war reached? What was the background to that critical decision? And finally, a question fueled by recent counterfactual musings: should Britain, despite its agreements with France and Russia, have kept out of the war?

Decision-Makers July 1914

With strict constitutional propriety, Prime Minister Herbert Henry Asquith's Liberal Cabinet made the decision for war. The House of Commons could have stopped British intervention by bringing the government down, but the leaders of both major parties, Liberals and Unionists, favored intervention. Members of Parliament followed their leaders. The prime mover, as will be shown, was Foreign Secretary Grey who, from the outset, was supported by First Lord of the Admiralty Winston S. Churchill.

The most important voice, of course, was that of the prime minister. Asquith belonged to a small group of "Efficients" and "Liberal Imperialists" within the Liberal Party. He and his followers pursued a program of national efficiency, imperialism and reform in the hope of thereby increasing their national support and reestablishing the Liberals as a "patriotic" party. Although with only limited influence in Parliament and in local boroughs, this group would gain in importance in the run-up to 1914 as the Liberals set out on a massive program of social reform (women's suffrage, labor, Irish Home Rule). A consummate master of the art of evading difficult decisions, especially with regard to foreign policy, Asquith was happy to leave that area with his foreign secretary and senior officials at the Foreign Office. In July 1914 Asquith was far from enthusiastic about intervention but trusted Grey's judgment in foreign policy.

A landed aristocrat, Grey longed for the solitude of casting for stippled trout in the River Itchen near Winchester. When forced to be on business in London, he sought refuge by playing billiards at Brooks's. Like Asquith a member of the "Liberal Imperialist" branch of the party, Grey was convinced of the need to maintain a balance of power on the Continent. He believed strongly in the long-term German threat to British interests. Thus, Grey most deviously had not informed his colleagues in the Cabinet back in 1911 that he had, quite on his own, authorized "military conversations" with the French General Staff. He was the staunchest supporter of the *entente* in London. In February 1906 Grey wrote:

> If there is a war between France and Germany, it will be very difficult for us to keep out of it. The *Entente* and still more the constant and emphatic demonstrations ... of affection (official, naval, political, commercial and in the Press) have created in France a belief that we shall support them in war. ... If this expectation is disappointed the French will never forgive us. ... On the other hand the prospect of a European war and of our being involved in it is horrible.

Grey's reading of these matters would not change, in essentials, between February 1906 and August 1914.

Grey eventually attracted two supporters in the Cabinet: Churchill and Lloyd George, the chancellor of the Exchequer. Both had joined the Asquith Cabinet in April 1908 and both believed, like Grey, that Germany posed a threat to British interests. Churchill depicted the Royal Navy as Britain's "crown jewels," and he yearned to "seek out, hunt down, and destroy" the rival German fleet. On 5 August 1914 tears streamed down his face as Asquith announced that Britain was at war with Germany. Lloyd George, initially a member of the nonin-terventionist faction in the divided Cabinet, rallied in support of Grey when Germany invaded Belgium – an affront to this self-proclaimed Welsh champion of small nations.

It is fair to ask: what part did King George V play in the British decision for war? Until a late stage in the crisis, the king's instincts were pacific and neutralist – like those of most of his ministers and the majority of his people. By 4 August, however, George V had concluded that German behavior had made British involvement inevitable. As he later told the American ambassador, "My God Mr. Page, what else could we do?" Under Britain's unwritten constitutional system of 1914, it would have been almost impossible for a British monarch to prevent a declaration of war by a prime minister supported by the bulk of the Cabinet and the great majority in the House of Commons.

In striking contrast to what occurred in Austria-Hungary, Russia, and Germany, military men had little direct influence on the government's handling of the crisis. It is true that there had been intermittent staff talks with the French since 1906. It is also true that by late summer 1911 the General Staff had worked out plans for the dispatch of six infantry divisions and a cavalry division to support France. But informal staff talks do not amount to a binding commitment.

During late July and early August 1914 the Cabinet certainly did not speak and act as if it believed Britain was committed by promises made by army officers. It did not consult the service chiefs. General Henry Wilson recorded on 28 July, "no military opinion has been asked for by this Cabinet, who are deciding on a question of war." Indeed, for much of the critical period from 23 July to 4 August, the leaders of the General Staff were not even officially informed of the Cabinet's deliberations. On 2 August Field Marshal Sir John French is reported to have telephoned Lord Riddell of the Newspaper Proprietors' Association and asked, "Can you tell me old chap, whether we are going to be in this war? If so, are we going to put an army on the Continent and, if we are, who is going to command it?" Far from considering itself bound to enter the war by General Staff contingency plans, the Cabinet decided to send the expeditionary force to the Continent only two days after Britain entered the war.

Nor did senior civil servants play a significant role in the decision, except, perhaps, by helping to shape Grey's outlook in the years preceding the crisis. Grey appears to have told senior Foreign Office officials very little of what he was thinking in late July and early August 1914. His moves were so obscure that Sir Eyre Crowe, Grey's assistant under-secretary, considered him cowardly and indecisive when he was actually straining every nerve to secure British support for France.

What of the role of industry and finance? As two of Britain's most eminent economic historians have shown, British industrialists exerted relatively little influence on the nation's policy-making elite. The class of "gentlemanly capitalists" – the great financiers of the City of London – in 1914 was terrified of war, believing that a major European conflict would lead to economic ruin. Whatever triggered the British declaration of war in 1914, it was not the wishes of the nation's "finance capitalists."

The "War Powers"

Where, then, did the "war powers" lie? Under Britain's unwritten constitutional system, the right to make foreign policy and to declare war was part of the royal prerogative – the power of the crown to act independently of Parliament. By custom and precedent, however, the monarch's ministers and in particular the prime minister were expected to exercise the powers on the monarch's behalf.

The position of prime minister was critical to the British system of government. A politician became prime minister by being invited to form a government by the monarch. The individual selected would then form a Cabinet, which would have collective responsibility for the government's acts. The monarch was obliged to pick a party leader capable of leading a majority in the House of Commons, for without such backing, it was virtually impossible to govern.

A British government with the committed support of both Houses of Parliament (Commons and Lords) had, in accordance with the doctrine known as the "sovereignty of Parliament," almost unlimited political and legal power. The government was not obliged to submit a decision to go to war to a Commons vote. But if the Commons disapproved of being taken into a war, members could demand a "confidence motion." If the Commons voted that it had no confidence in the government, the latter was obliged (by constitutional convention) to resign, or at least to hold a General Election without delay. The popularly elected chamber had the "power of the purse." No government could wage war without spending public money, and the Commons had to approve that expenditure. It would be a political disaster for a prime minister to deliberately lead the country into war without being certain of gaining that support.

It was critical for any prime minister to preserve his party's cohesion in the Cabinet. Simply a group of the most important government ministers, its members were normally drawn from both Houses of Parliament. Its size and composition were up to the prime minister. The British Cabinet, like its counterpart in France, did business in a very informal way. Minutes were not taken – historians are dependent on contemporary letters and diaries for knowledge of what was said. There were no formal votes. The prime minister would try to achieve consensus behind major policies. If a minister felt he could not accept responsibility for a policy adopted, he was free to resign, indeed honor-bound to do so. Yet the resignation of a high proportion of cabinet ministers at the same time on the same issue would bring a political crisis. The prime minister would be entitled to replace those who resigned, but he might not be able to do so without fracturing his party and jeopardizing his all-important Commons majority. That crisis might last several weeks, thus postponing any decision with regard to intervention. This was a prospect that confronted Asquith in late July–August 1914.

Asquith's Liberal Party was in power in the Commons in 1914. Liberals, for the most part, had serious doubts about the morality of imperialism and, moreover, were reluctant to spend heavily on the armed forces. They were allied to an emerging Labour Party representing trade union and working-class interests. The Unionist Party, led in 1914 by Andrew Bonar Law, was formed from a marriage between the Conservatives and the Liberal Unionists. It controlled the House of Lords. Most Unionists were proud of the empire and willing to spend money on the armed forces. The clearest division between the parties was over Ireland. The Liberals, allied to the Irish Nationalist Party in the Commons, wanted to give Ireland "Home Rule." The Unionist Party wished to preserve the union between Great Britain and Ireland, or at least to exclude the northeast of Ireland, known as Ulster, from the provisions of the Home Rule Bill. When the July crisis started, a major domestic struggle over Home Rule had been fought for several months.

In fact, Ireland was on the brink of civil war. Paramilitary groups on both sides of the Home Rule issue had armed themselves and were actively training. The Unionist Party had strong links with the Ulster Volunteer Force – a paramilitary group in the northern part of the country. The bulk of British Army officers were Unionists and some had felt sufficiently disaffected to mount an officers' mutiny known as the "Curragh Incident" in March 1914. And when war came on the Continent, General Sir William Birdwood of the Army Department perhaps put the generals' case best: "*What* a piece of real luck this war has been as regards Ireland – just averted Civil War and when it is over we may all be tired of fighting."

The Run-up to 1914

Great Britain's position in the world depended critically on a balance of power on the Continent. It was important that no single state be in a position to sever or seriously constrain its trade with the Continent, still less to offer a serious threat to the home islands or the empire. Lord Salisbury, the British statesmen with the greatest experience in foreign policy, continued to believe until the turn of the century that it was possible to protect the national interest by reliance on economic and naval strength, combined with astute diplomacy, without entering into long-term commitments to other powers.

But a direct challenge was emerging from across the North Sea. Kaiser Wilhelm II's government was following a new course in foreign policy. Never very clearly defined, *Weltpolitik* broadly meant trying to expand Germany's possessions and influence, especially in the world outside Europe, by way of a massive naval expansion program. This was bound to cause concern for British policymakers, who were beginning to sense what Paul Kennedy has called "overstrain" and were trying to reduce risks by making deals with other powers.

Thus, in 1902 Lord Lansdowne had concluded a treaty with an emerging power. From the British point of view, the aims of the Anglo-Japanese alliance were to limit Russian expansion in China and to prevent the Royal Navy in the Far East being overwhelmed by a Franco-Russian naval combination. This formal alliance contained obligations to support a foreign power with armed forces in some circumstances. Many contemporaries therefore saw it as a radical departure in British foreign policy.

The Russo-Japanese War, beginning in February 1904 with a Japanese attack on Port Arthur, further alarmed Britain as it entailed a possible clash with France, Russia's ally. Neither Lansdowne nor Théophile Delcassé, his French opposite, wished to see that, and in April 1904 the two concluded an Anglo-French *entente*. In essence an agreement on colonies, spheres of interest and fishing rights, it committed neither partner to military action. But by lowering the potential for conflict in several parts of the world, it dramatically reduced Britain's strategic problems. Specifically, it allowed the Royal Navy to withdraw its major surface units from East Asia and to concentrate them at home against Germany.

The next episode in the division of Europe into two armed camps came with the signature of an Anglo-Russian *entente* in August 1907. The French were fortunate in the choice of the new British foreign secretary, Grey, who in February 1906 had announced: "An *entente* between Russia, France and ourselves would be absolutely secure. If it is necessary to check Germany it could then be done." As with the Anglo-French *entente*, the Anglo-Russian agreement was also a settlement of spheres of influence (in Persia, Afghanistan and Tibet), and again there was no obligation for either power to provide military support to the other. But again, it sent a clear signal to Berlin that London was willing to reach accords with colonial rivals in the face of the German threat.

Still, during the last two years of peace, it appeared that Britain's relations with Germany were improving. By 1912, Admiral Alfred von Tirpitz, head of the German navy, was forced to scale down his building program. Various conflicts involving the Ottoman Empire were also resolved. During the Balkan crises of 1912 and 1913, Grey worked with the Germans to prevent a clash between Austria-Hungary and Russia that might have brought on a general European war. And in June 1914 Britain and Germany arrived at a wide-ranging agreement concerning their economic interests in Mesopotamia. Thus, for the British government, the assassination of Archduke Franz Ferdinand on 28 June 1914 was set against the background of generally improving Anglo-German relations. Few informed persons in Britain, therefore, believed that the assassination might result in war.

The July Crisis

In these circumstances the reaction of the Asquith Cabinet to the European crisis that followed the Sarajevo assassinations unsurprisingly was rather slow and, until very late, quite ineffectual. First and foremost, Grey appears to have been slow to realize the danger of the situation. Vienna's initial response to the assassinations seemed to him "neither alarmist nor extreme." Thus, he set out to work with Berlin "as far as might be possible" to defuse the crisis – without, however, moving away from Paris and St. Petersburg. But on 23 July, when the Austrian ambassador in London informed him of the text of Vienna's ultimatum to Serbia, Grey finally grasped the imminent danger of European war. He was further encouraged in his new reading of the seriousness of the situation on 28 July when the Germans rejected his proposals for mediation. And there was an even more important obstacle, a deeply divided Cabinet. A small minority was prepared to take a committed stand beside France and Russia – to the point of war if necessary – to preserve the balance of power on the Continent. But as late as 1 August, the majority of ministers would not commit themselves to war.

On the afternoon of 24 July Grey first alerted the Cabinet to the risk of a European war. It had spent most of a lengthy meeting trying to stave off civil war in Ireland. The Cabinet, in Churchill's famous phrase, "toiled around the muddy fields of [the Irish counties of] Fermanagh and Tyrone" without reaching any definite conclusion. The meeting was about to break up when, again in Churchill's words, "the quiet grave tones of Sir Edward Grey's voice" were heard reading the Austrian note to Serbia:

> This note was clearly an ultimatum; but it was an ultimatum such as had never been penned in modern times. As the reading proceeded it seemed absolutely impossible that any State in the world could accept it,

or that any acceptance, however abject would satisfy the aggressor. The parishes of Fermanagh and Tyrone faded back into the mists and squalls of Ireland, and a strange light began immediately, but by perceptible gradations, to fall and grow upon the map of Europe.

As stated above, Grey was initially inclined to take a hopeful view of German intentions, in part because of the cordial relationship that he enjoyed with Ambassador Prince Karl Max von Lichnowsky. On 24 July Lichnowsky reported to Berlin a conversation in which Grey stated: "The danger of a European war, should Austria invade Serbian territory would become immediate. The results of such a war between . . . Russia, Austria-Hungary, Germany and France . . . would be absolutely incalculable." That formulation gave German policy-makers hope that the British would stay out of any war that resulted. It is inconceivable that Grey intended to give that impression. During his meeting with Lichnowsky that 24 July, Grey seems to have been thinking aloud – a dangerous thing to do at the best of times.

Over the next couple of days Grey came under pressure from the Russians and the French openly to declare Britain's position in the event of a European war. By 26 July, Grey appears to have made up his mind what the British position should be – though he could not be sure that the Cabinet would follow his advice. Sir Arthur Nicolson, permanent under-secretary at the Foreign Office, and Sir William Tyrell, Grey's private secretary, had strong words with Lichnowsky that evening. On 27 July Grey informed Lichnowsky that, in the event of a European war, Britain would align itself with France and Russia. Lichnowsky relayed this message to Berlin.

But a different reading of British intentions reduced the impact of Lichnowsky's communication. Prince Henry of Prussia, Wilhelm's younger brother, had been yachting at Cowes. Before returning home, on 26 July he briefly called at Buckingham Palace and discussed the crisis with George V. Shortly after his arrival at Kiel on 28 July, Henry wrote to the kaiser, quoting the king as saying: "We shall try all we can to keep out of this and shall remain neutral." Wilhelm II seized on this second-hand assurance; the word of a monarch was good enough for him!

At a Cabinet meeting on 29 July Grey presented his view of the European situation. He tried to persuade his colleagues to make a commitment to support Belgium and France in the event of an attack by Germany, and he argued that the Treaty of London of 1839 obliged

Great Britain to defend Belgian neutrality. Though supported by the prime minister, Asquith, and the first lord of the Admiralty, Churchill, Grey met strong resistance from the majority. Most ministers rejected the view that Britain was obliged to defend Belgian neutrality by force of arms. The Cabinet would not commit itself in advance to any course of action in any particular set of circumstances; it merely decided not to decide.

Later that day Grey, in a desperately weak position, played for time. He confided to the French ambassador, Paul Cambon, that the Cabinet had not yet decided what to do in the event of a Franco-German war. The ultimate British decision, Grey averred, might depend on whether the Germans violated Belgian neutrality – as well as on the state of public opinion in Britain. Next, he reassured Lichnowsky yet again that if Germany became involved in a war with France, it would not be possible for the British government "to stand aside and wait for any length of time." The kaiser dismissed this as bluff.

On the evening of 29 July Theobald von Bethmann Hollweg, the German chancellor, approached Sir Edward Goschen, the British ambassador in Berlin, with an offer: if the British remained neutral, the Germans would restore Belgian integrity after the war and would annex no French territory except colonies. Grey was driven to fury by what he regarded as a shameless attempt on the part of Germany "to buy our neutrality." He rejected the overture the next day, informing his colleagues of Bethmann's approach on 1 August. It brought little response even though it clearly indicated Germany's intention to attack France.

In the absence of formal minutes and formal votes, our knowledge of what was said at the critical cabinet meetings, and of the positions that individuals adopted at different stages in the debate, is incomplete. It is possible, however, to assess from contemporary diaries and letters that on Friday, 31 July, the Cabinet was divided into three unequal groups. The largest group, those still undecided, seems to have consisted of six ministers, including Asquith and Lloyd George as well as Herbert Samuel, president of the Local Board of Trade. The second group of five, those favoring an immediate declaration of neutrality, included John Morley, secretary of state for India, and Sir John Simon, the attorney general. Only Grey and Churchill, the third group, were in favor of intervention in a European war.

Furious, Grey threatened to resign if "an out-and-out uncompromising policy of non-intervention" were adopted. Asquith feared the immediate breakup of the Cabinet, an option that was avoided only by putting off any decision. Grey secured the Cabinet's agreement to ask both Paris and Berlin to give a guarantee that they would respect Belgian neutrality. A positive reply from the French arrived at 2:15 a.m. on 1 August. The Germans replied that they could give no such assurance. To do so, they said, would reveal details of their war plans.

On the morning of 1 August Grey's position was still desperately weak. The majority of the Cabinet wished to stay out of the war at virtually any price, arguing that the Austro-Serbian-Russian dispute involved no vital British interest. Grey that morning suggested to Lichnowsky that if Germany did not attack France, Britain would remain neutral. Lichnowsky leapt at this offer, guaranteeing, on his own authority, that Germany would not attack France. Perhaps unsure of the worth of Lichnowsky's guarantee, Grey did not pass it on to the Cabinet.

At a meeting commencing about midday on 1 August, the Cabinet heard the responses of the French and German governments. Despite the German refusal to offer a guarantee of Belgian neutrality, the majority of the Cabinet remained opposed to any intervention in the European crisis. In the end, Grey again had to threaten resignation to head off a negative decision. As a *quid pro quo*, he and Asquith agreed that the British Expeditionary Force would not be sent to France. Lichnowsky passed this tepid British warning on Belgian neutrality to the German Foreign Office that evening.

With Lichnowsky's previous suggestion of possible British neutrality in hand, Wilhelm II at 7:02 p.m. on 1 August dispatched a telegram to George V, assuring the king that Germany would not attack France if France remained neutral and if France's neutrality were "guaranteed by the British Fleet and Army." Grey was summoned to Buckingham Palace later that Saturday evening to help frame a reply. He drafted this in pencil on a scrap of paper. "I think," replied the king to the kaiser, "there must be some misunderstanding of a suggestion that passed in friendly conversation between Prince Lichnowsky and Sir Edward Grey." Neither the British nor the Germans pursued the scheme of Franco-German nonaggression after 1 August.

Saturday, 1 August, was a critical date in the crisis. That evening news reached London that Germany had declared war on Russia, and that Germany and France had begun to mobilize their armies. It seemed to Grey that a German invasion of Belgium and France was only a matter of time. The British Army had "war gamed" such a possibility ever since 1905 and Grey knew about and had sanctioned unofficial conversations with the French Army to deal with such a contingency. But he planned to intervene by land only if Germany attacked France. By 1 August, that scenario had become realistic. Thus, at some point on Saturday evening, Grey decided to confront the neutralists in the Cabinet the next morning and to carry out his threat to resign if they opted for neutrality. His hand was strengthened on 2 August when Bonar Law, leader of the Unionist Party, and Lansdowne, the Unionist spokesman on foreign policy, offered Asquith "unhesitating support" for any measures the government considered necessary to support France and Russia. Still, Asquith opined, "a good 3/4 of our own [Liberal] party in the House of Commons are for absolute non-interference at any price."

Grey finally put his cards on the table at two cabinet meetings on Sunday, 2 August. He was "outraged," he stated, "by the way in which Germany and Austria...had put aside all attempts at accommodation," all the while marching "steadily towards war." He wanted the Cabinet to declare in favor of intervention. But the majority still was not ready to do this. The most that Grey could obtain was agreement to inform the French that if the German fleet undertook hostile operations against French coasts or shipping, the Royal Navy would give France all the protection in its power. Even this modest concession required Grey's threat of resignation and insistence by Asquith that he would go if Grey did.

That the bulk of the Cabinet held together through the crisis appears to have been due in great measure to the efforts of Herbert Samuel, one of the "undecideds," who thought the imminent war would be "the most horrible catastrophe since the abominations of the Napoleonic time, and in many respects worse." Samuel wished to place "the onus of provoking any [British] intervention on Germany." Two sets of circumstances would justify Britain declaring war: a German naval descent on the north coast of France, and a German threat to Belgium. Britain had recognized Belgium's independence and neutrality by treaty in 1839 and thus had some responsibility for protecting that country – though not perhaps an automatic obligation to go to war in its defense.

Samuel pressed his case at the two cabinet meetings of 2 August. He hoped to hold the Cabinet together, for, if it split, the result would be either a Unionist government or a coalition government; both would take Britain into the war. Asquith also drove this point home when, at one of the cabinet meetings, he read Bonar Law's letter of support for intervention.

Perhaps because Samuel's formula seemed to remove some of the burden of decision from individual ministers and perhaps also because it offered the prospect of the government holding together and remaining in office, the majority ultimately went along with it. At their evening meeting on 2 August ministers heard that the Germans had violated Luxembourg's neutrality. Grey was now authorized to tell the House of Commons that if the Germans substantially violated Belgian neutrality, Britain would act. It appeared that in such an eventuality most of the Cabinet would stay together. Samuel cherished hopes that:

> Germany will neither send her fleet down the Channel nor invade Belgium, and we shall be able to keep England at peace while rendering France the greatest of services – the protection of her north coasts from the sea and the protection of her 150 miles of frontier with Belgium. If we achieve this without firing a shot, we shall have accomplished a brilliant stroke of policy. . . . If we do not accomplish it, it will be an action of Germany's, and not of ours which will cause the failure and my conscience will be easy in embarking on the war.

Most major Liberal newspapers were neutralist up to the end of July, and popular opinion was at best uncertain. But from the beginning of August, there were indications that public opinion, at least in London, seemed to be shifting in favor of intervention – seeing the Germans as aggressors. An antiwar demonstration held in Trafalgar Square on the afternoon of 2 August received little support. With the benefit of hindsight, Lloyd George relates in his memoirs that pro-war feeling was on the rise in the capital:

> I shall never forget the warlike crowds that thronged Whitehall and poured into Downing Street, whilst the Cabinet was deliberating on the alternatives of peace or war. . . . On Monday afternoon I walked with Mr. Asquith to the House of Commons to hear Grey's famous speech. The crowd was so dense that . . . had it not been for police assistance we could not have walked a yard. . . . It was distinctly a pro-war demonstration.

The apparent late shift in popular sentiment in London may have influenced Asquith. He had noted on 31 July, "our actions must depend upon the course of events including the Belgian question and the direction of public opinion here." But there can be little doubt that an attachment to office caused others who abhorred war to remain in a war government. Resignation would not have helped the careers of ambitious politicians like Samuel and Simon. And there was always an interventionist Unionist government waiting in the wings.

The British Cabinet entered the war with great reluctance and a deep sense of dread. By the time it met at 11 a.m. on 3 August, Germany had demanded free passage for its troops through Belgium. The Belgians decided to resist. The atmosphere in London was highly charged. As Samuel put it: "The Cabinet was very moving. Most of us could hardly speak at all for emotion.... The world is on the verge of a great catastrophe." Simon and Beauchamp tendered their resignations, adding to those of Burns and Morley the previous day. But Asquith and Lloyd George ultimately prevailed upon Simon and Beauchamp to remain.

At 3 p.m. that same afternoon Grey delivered a momentous speech to the House of Commons. He argued the importance of defending Belgian neutrality and asked whether it would be in Britain's interest for France to be "in a struggle of life and death, beaten to her knees, [losing] her position as a great Power... subordinate to the power of one greater than herself." Would it be tolerable for "the whole of the West of Europe opposite to us... [to be] under the domination of a single Power?" He argued that if Britain allowed the violation of Belgium and the subjugation of France, "our moral position would be such as have lost us all respect."

A further cabinet meeting on the evening of 3 August decided to dispatch a message to the German government, asking it to withdraw its demand to march through Belgium. A moderately worded telegram was sent only at 9:30 the next morning; Grey's tardiness in this respect was never adequately explained.

The Cabinet received definite reports of German violation of Belgian neutrality on 4 August. Asquith and Grey decided to issue an ultimatum, to expire at midnight Berlin time (11 p.m. London time). If the Germans had not announced their intention to desist by that time, the British "would be obliged to take all steps in their power necessary to uphold the neutrality of Belgium."

After receiving the British ultimatum, Ambassador Goschen at about 7 p.m. delivered the note to Gottlieb von Jagow. The German foreign secretary made it clear that there was no chance of withdrawal from Belgium. Goschen next went to see Bethmann Hollweg, who,

intensely irritated and emotional, made his famous remark about the
British going to war for a "scrap of paper." The chancellor recorded
that Goschen was in tears at the end of the interview.

By that time – the afternoon of 4 August – Asquith had announced
the ultimatum to the House of Commons. It accepted the news "very
calmly and with good deal of dignity and we got through all the business by half-past four." The Germans sent no reply to the British
ultimatum. On the night of 4–5 August the Foreign Office delivered
the British declaration of war to Lichnowsky. When the British public
awoke on the morning of Wednesday, 5 August, the nation was at war.

Conclusion

Who made the decision for war and who exercised the "war powers"?
Clearly, the Asquith Cabinet made that decision, however indecisive
and tortuous the process may have been. The House of Commons in
turn gave its assent to the prime minister's decision to intervene in the
European war. Neither soldiers nor sailors, press lords nor financial
barons determined British policy in 1914. The "war powers" rested
under the unwritten British constitutional system with the Cabinet
in general and with the prime minister and his foreign secretary in
particular. King George V acted in a constitutional manner when he
left the nation's fate in the government's hands.

What was the background to war? Britain felt threatened by the ambitious, often aggressive, crude, and incompetent conduct of German
foreign policy under Wilhelm II. The Anglo-German antagonism,
combined with perceived imperial "overstrain," prompted London to
abandon splendid isolation in favor of *ententes* with France and Russia.
In Grey's mind, at least, the *entente* became part of a system of maintaining a balance of power on the Continent and thus keeping Germany
in check.

Might the British Cabinet have prevented a European war if it had
acted more decisively during the crisis? That is conceivable. But Lloyd
George's attempt to blame Grey for British ineffectiveness during the
crisis is a piece of the grossest hypocrisy, a shameful accusation by
one who, for all his undoubted talents, was to bring much shame on
British public life. By 24 July Grey was fully aware of the gravity of the
situation. From that point onward the slow British response stemmed
from the extreme reluctance of the Cabinet to follow Grey's advice and

to take a strong line with Germany. Without the committed support of the majority of the Cabinet, any British action could only be regarded as bluff. If the Asquith government had fallen over this issue, the resulting crisis would have postponed any British response. The consequences could have been either no troops sent to the Continent or, more likely, a delay in their arrival.

Grey's decision for intervention in the European war of 1914, ultimately supported, from a mixture of motives, by the great majority of his cabinet colleagues, was rational in the circumstances of the time. It was entered into with a deep sense of foreboding in the belief that any other course would have been potentially even more damaging than war to Britain's national interests.

Should Great Britain have remained neutral? Two historians, Niall Ferguson and John Charmley, have suggested that Britain should have adopted a policy of neutrality. Even after a German victory, Ferguson imagines Britain living quite amicably with a German-dominated "Kaiser's European Union." Such speculation rests on an (unfounded) belief that Germany's leaders, had their armed forces won the war, would never have developed grandiose war aims in Europe, leading to continental hegemony.

A final question: how did Britain's decision to intervene affect the European war in general and the Battle of the Marne specifically? The preceding chapters have detailed how an Austro-Serbian war escalated by way of decisions made in Berlin, Paris, and St. Petersburg into a continental European war with major actions on both eastern and western fronts. Surely, it is one of the many ironies of 1914 that the British intervention, however tortuous in nature, helped defeat the Schlieffen plan and thereby turn the anticipated "short war" into a long-term conflagration. For by stumbling into the "gap" that had developed between the German First and Second Armies north of the Marne early in September 1914, British cavalry helped the French Army make its historic decision to stand on that river. On 9 September the Germans retreated behind the Aisne River. Events in East Asia and in the Near and Middle East thereafter extended the war further, far beyond its European center.

CHAPTER 8

Japan; The Ottoman Empire

As the armies of the Triple Alliance and the Triple Entente went off to war, governments in Asia and Asia Minor met to consider the possibility of their participation. Since 1902, Japan had an alliance with Great Britain, one that committed it to "strict neutrality" in case Great Britain became "involved in war with another Power." What leaders in Tokyo saw as the great "confusion" in Europe could spell opportunity for Japan to assert itself as the "chief nation of the Orient." Foreign Minister Katō Takaaki and a handful of his closest advisors single-handedly took the government into the war.

And in Constantinople, a handful of Young Turk leaders, Enver Bey, Talât Bey, Ahmed Cemal Pasha, and Helil Bey, decided that alliance with Germany would best serve their nation's interests. Germany became their last and unavoidable choice – to establish their economic independence, to abolish the Anglo-French financial "capitulations," and to secure their crumbling empire.

Japan

The Japanese Cabinet decided on war against Germany on 8 August, just four days after Britain cut ties with Berlin. Why did Japan, so far from the principal theater of conflict, declare war on Germany? Elder statesman Inoue Kaoru spoke of the outbreak of war in Europe as "divine aid," this based on his sense of widespread exhilaration in Tokyo. Just as British Prime Minister David Lloyd George hailed the chance to rediscover "the great peaks" of "Honour, Duty,

Patriotism," Japanese adventurer Ioki Ryōzō praised the "awakening" of the Japanese from their petty political battles, worship of money, "anti-state nihilism," "naturalism," and "vulgar sensualism." This was the opportunity, Ioki proclaimed, for a return to "simplicity and purity."

Antecedents

Japanese statesmen looked fondly upon an earlier age, when Japan transformed itself, moving from a backward feudalism to join the ranks of the great powers. During the reign of the Meiji emperor (1868–1912), a select group of low-ranking samurai had transformed a disparate coalition of over 270 semi-autonomous feudal domains into a modern, unified nation–state, complete with the trappings of a world power: constitutional government, a modern army and navy, and an empire. By 1895, when Japan's armed forces defeated China, the former cultural and political hegemon of Asia, foreign observers hailed Japan as the Continent's pioneer of progress. After its surprising victory over Imperial Russia in 1905, Tokyo's statesmen proclaimed to the world the spectacular consummation of a "New Japan."

Three developments raised serious concerns about the future of the empire after the Russo-Japanese War. First was the outbreak of revolution in China. The Cabinet of Prince Saionji Kinmochi tried to mediate a settlement to produce in Beijing a constitutional monarchy along Japanese lines, and then watched in astonishment as Chinese General Yuan Shikai accepted the mediation of Britain and founded a republic on the model of the United States. Having explicitly rejected republican rule for their own state in 1889, Japanese statesmen were appalled. It was, warned Terauchi Masatake, the governor general of Korea, a "serious matter for Japan's National Polity."

Soon after this evidence of Japan's waning influence on the Continent, the emperor passed away. Baron Makino Nobuaki sensed a deep "anxiety" in the nation following the emperor's death "as it hit home that a shadow was descending on an exalted age." And no sooner had the throngs of mourners dispersed from their vigil outside the Imperial Palace, than Japan faced the most serious crisis of its short history of constitutional government. Early in December 1912 War Minister Uehara Yusaku resigned over the Cabinet's refusal to fund a long-awaited expansion for the army. When the elder statesmen (*genrō*) nominated one of their own, Katsura Tarō, to succeed Saionji, Japan's politicians cried foul. In February 1913 a coalition of political parties brought down an oligarchic cabinet for the first time in the history of modern Japan. Field Marshal Yamagata Aritomo deplored the tragic "confusion of public sentiment" brought on by the Taishō political crisis.

On the eve of the Great War, then, Japan seemed to have lost its luster as the "pioneer of progress in the Orient." Abroad, it had failed to inspire China to emulate its constitutional monarchy. At home, the political unity so highly touted by Japan's preeminent statesmen in 1907 appeared fragmented beyond recognition.

When Japanese policymakers and opinion leaders learned of general mobilizations in Europe, they responded with a sense of relief and enthusiasm. The August 1914 "confusion" in Europe was widely viewed as providing the opportunity to advance Japan's "larger" continental ambitions. Yoshino Sakuzō, soon to gain celebrity as the preeminent champion of democracy, saw it as "absolutely the most opportune moment" to advance Japan's standing in China. And Marquis Inoue Kaoru welcomed the "solidarity of national unity" that a renewed drive for influence on the Continent would bring.

While Japanese enthusiasm over war in Europe focused on the opportunity to consolidate its interests in Asia, this did not necessarily translate into an immediate call for war against Germany. Foreign Minister Katō Takaaki, the man most responsible for Japanese belligerence, noted that Japan was not obligated under the Anglo-Japanese alliance to join in the fray. Some members of the Cabinet, in fact, hoped to prevent the spread of hostilities to Asia. And the traditional wielders of state power in Japan, the four remaining elder statesmen, worried about potential Japanese losses in a military engagement with Germany. The outcome of a war between Britain and Germany was, in August 1914, by no means certain. Most Japanese military experts and members of the Imperial Army, in fact, gave Germany a better than even chance of victory in Europe.

Germany was a late-comer among Europe's imperialists in Asia and the Pacific having only modest holdings in the area and those without adequate defenses. Two German missionaries had been killed in China in November 1897. Sensing a "splendid opportunity," Kaiser Wilhelm sent forces that occupied Jiaozhou Bay and the port of Qingdao on the Shandong peninsula. In 1898, following the Spanish-American War, Germany purchased three groups of Pacific islands, the Carolines,

Marianas, and Marshalls, from Spain. In August of 1914, given the manifest superiority of the British navy, those possessions were virtually indefensible. The events in Europe now provided Japan with its "splendid opportunity." For Japan's governing elites, Qingdao was the object of greatest interest. For them, Shandong was an easy "stepping stone" to China.

The Decision-Makers

Under the February 1889 Imperial Constitution, all sovereign powers resided in the "sacred and inviolable" emperor (Article 3). He exercised "supreme command of the army and navy" (Article 11) and had the power to "declare war, make peace, and conclude treaties" (Article 13). There was, however, a striking disparity between the constitutional statements and the reality of Japan's governance. Taishō, who assumed the throne in 1912 on the death of his father, Emperor Meiji, "was sickly as a child and later mentally deranged . . . After 1912, the emperor was more and more removed from decision-making and was relegated to an almost purely symbolic role in government." The governance of Japan, accordingly, rested largely with those individuals having direct ties to the emperor, those that could be said to be acting on his behalf: the Imperial Cabinet, Imperial Diet (parliament), Imperial Army and Navy, Imperial Courts, and the Privy Council. A decision for war was made through consultation among some combination of imperial advisers – the genrō (elder statesmen), Cabinet, military leaders and/or Privy Council. At the very least, a declaration of war required a cabinet decision and formal sanction by the emperor.

The Japanese decision for war followed only the bare minimum requirements for consultation. On 1 August Foreign Minister Katō Takaaki instructed the Japanese ambassador to London, Inoue Katsunosuke, to sound out British Foreign Secretary Sir Edward Grey about Britain's proposed response to developments in Europe. Grey said he considered it unlikely that the Anglo-Japanese alliance would be invoked if Britain became involved in the war. Two days later, Katō summoned the British ambassador to Japan, Sir Conyngham Greene, to offer Japanese assistance in the event of a German attack on Hong Kong or of other acts of aggression in Asia. The following morning, Prime Minister Ōkuma Shigenobu called an extraordinary cabinet session to clarify Japanese policy on possible hostilities in Asia. In the midst of the meeting, a messenger from Ambassador

Greene presented Katō with a telegram from Grey outlining Britain's expectation of Japanese aid if Germany attacked Hong Kong or the British concession of Wei-hai-wei in Shandong. In response, the Cabinet agreed to take "all means necessary" to aid Britain in the event that war spread to East Asia. Katō informed Ambassador Greene that afternoon of the Cabinet's decision and added that the Japanese Second Battle Fleet, comprising four large cruisers, was lying ready at Sasebo naval base "for immediate action if required."

The formal British request for assistance came in the afternoon of 7 August. Katō responded by presenting an outline of Japan's official response to Prime Minister Ōkuma, who organized another extraordinary cabinet session for 8 p.m. that evening. After four hours of debate, the Cabinet decided on war with Germany. The following morning, the foreign minister informed the emperor of the decision at the latter's summer escape at Nikkō, north of Tokyo. A special *genrō*-cabinet conference that evening (8 August) delivered the sanction of Japan's elder statesmen. One week later, on 15 August, a second *genrō*-cabinet conference, this time in the presence of the emperor, approved an ultimatum, drafted by Katō and three of his closest advisers, demanding Germany transfer her Jiaozhou concession to Japan.

The Japanese decision for war resulted largely from the initiative and efforts of one man, Foreign Minister Katō Takaaki. He seized the initiative, set the direction, and, effectively, presented the elder statesmen and army leadership with a fait accompli. According to those present at the 7 August cabinet meeting, the foreign minister "deflected all doubts, solved all questions and, in every way, decided upon war with Germany on his own."

Katō's coup came at the expense of Japan's established elite, most importantly its elder statesmen. They had wielded enormous influence in the first two decades of the new cabinet system from 1885, occupying most cabinet posts and directing the nation's domestic and foreign policies. But due to age and dwindling numbers, they increasingly yielded to younger statesmen after the Russo-Japanese War. In August 1914 the four remaining *genrō* – Inoue Kaoru, Matsukata Masayoshi, Ōyama Iwao and Yamagata Aritomo – were all septuagenarians. Only Yamagata remained a formidable political force by virtue of his leadership of an extensive network of supporters in the civilian and army bureaucracies.

In fact, Katō could easily hold his own against potential political rivals. At 54, he was in his prime and already a seasoned veteran of

foreign affairs and Japanese bureaucratic politics. As a career bureaucrat in the Foreign Ministry, Katō had served twice in Britain and
he had enjoyed three brief stints as foreign minister. Katō developed
a reputation at an early age for not suffering fools gladly. As foreign
minister, he had always insisted upon pursuing an agenda free from
the interference of extra-cabinet elites such as the elder statesmen. In
April 1913 Katō's political importance was secured when he became
president of the second largest political party in the Imperial Diet, the
Rikken Dōshikai (Constitutional Association of Friends).

In addition to being foreign minister and president of the Dōshikai
Party, Katō had significant help from members of the Cabinet in his
effort to outmaneuver his military–bureaucratic rivals. Prime Minister
Ōkuma at age 74 was past his prime and eager to cede the policy
initiative to Katō. As well, Katō had handpicked most of the Cabinet,
including Minister of Agriculture and Commerce Ōura Kanetake and
Minister of Justice Ozaki Yukio. Beyond that, Katō could count on
the support of two service ministers: Minister of War Oka Ichinosuke
and Navy Minister Yashiro Rokurō. And while Katō had handed the
Imperial Army a fait accompli with the cabinet decision for war on
8 August, he most likely had coordinated his activities with Yashiro
and the Imperial Navy.

The Decision for War

The basic question remains: why did Katō bring about the Japanese
decision for war? One part of the answer involves the volatile arena of
Japanese domestic politics. By the beginning of the twentieth century,
the elder statesmen had begun to relax their grip on power, and Japan
faced a formidable question: who would govern in their stead? This
was the fundamental issue of the Taishō political crisis, which brought
the end of oligarchic rule and its replacement by a coalition of political
parties. As the Meiji era yielded to Taishō (1912–26), the question of
the basic character of Japanese politics came to a head. Did the small
circle of samurai from the Satsuma and Chōshū domains retain the
right to rule the nation? Or, as the liberal journalist Ishibashi Tanzan
argued, was the "greatest enterprise" of the Meiji years to be "the
implementation of democratic reform in all political, legal and social
systems and thought?" At the outbreak of war in 1914, the Meiji ruling
circle struggled desperately to repair their waning political authority

and looked upon the "European war" as a chance to rouse the nation united behind their command. Conversely, the victors of the Taishō crisis – party politicians – welcomed the opportunity of war to further their efforts to consolidate representative government. One of Foreign Minister Katō's reasons for the choice of war was to influence the domestic struggle, that is, to redefine the Japanese nation.

There was a second reason, an external component, to Katō's calculus for war. Like most of his contemporaries, he viewed the war in Europe as an opportunity to extend Japan's influence in China. More generally, one source declares his "fervent diplomatic wish [was] to strengthen Japan's position in Asia." In doing so, he sought to emulate Great Britain, the grandfather of modern empires. For, if Katō's conception of the Japanese polity was progressive, the diplomatic component was traditional. He readily subscribed not only to British parliamentarism but also to the British imperial worldview.

Katō was an early advocate of the Anglo-Japanese alliance of 1902. For him, the key to Japan's world standing remained in steadily expanding economic privileges in China and continued association with the world's greatest naval power and largest commercial presence on the Asian continent. As he told the Cabinet on 7 August, participation in the war made sense "from the alliance friendship from which Britain's request derives."

This version of Japanese intent in August 1914 may surprise students of British policy in East Asia. For, as Peter Lowe and Ian Nish have shown, Anglo-Japanese tensions began to flare in the wake of the Chinese revolution. They intensified at the outbreak of war in Europe when London, surprised by the alacrity with which Japan responded to its request for assistance, withdrew its invitation only four days later. The subsequent diplomatic tussle over the scale of Japanese involvement in the war was "the first major dispute between allies" and had a decidedly negative effect upon mutual confidence. Many British leaders later saw this episode as the beginning of a pattern of Japanese behavior: far from aiding the Allied cause in the war, they aimed simply to profit at the expense of the European powers' interests in Asia.

That Katō's actions of August 1914 rested on his devotion to the Anglo-Japanese alliance may best be seen by considering the aims of his greatest political rival, Yamagata Aritomo, the most powerful of the four founders of Meiji Japan who remained in 1914. Like many of his contemporaries, Yamagata viewed the war as an ideal opportunity to expand Japanese influence in China. In August 1914 he described the

European war as a "golden opportunity" to correct past missteps in China and develop an "inseparable spirit" between Tokyo and Beijing. And like Katō, Yamagata envisioned a domestic political benefit to war in Europe. Put differently, he and fellow *genrō* Marquis Inoue Kaoru viewed the "European War" as "a rare occasion" to "turn the calamities of domestic and foreign policies into fortunes." They urged Prime Minister Ōkuma to seize the opportunity to effect "national unity" immediately through close cooperation with themselves. They hoped, in other words, for a renaissance of *genrō* power.

While Yamagata welcomed Japanese expansion in China, he had grave misgivings about Katō's worldview. If Katō followed the conservative pattern of great power behavior in China since the latter nineteenth century, Yamagata anticipated the unbridled expansionism of a subsequent age. Where Katō considered Japan as one among many powers competing for interests in China, the elder statesman increasingly rejected any limits to Japan's continental presence. His 15 August memo to the Cabinet, in fact, called upon China to accede to "mutual reliance" in economic matters. The field marshal hoped to replicate in China the protectorate that Japan had established in Korea only a decade earlier. He urged Prime Minister Ōkuma to have Beijing consult Tokyo on all political and economic problems involving foreign countries.

Yamagata had less interest in the alliance politics of the nineteenth century than in what would become the ideological foundations of Japanese expansionism in the 1930s: pan-Asianism. In place of the alliance with Britain that facilitated Japan's victory in the Russo-Japanese War, he increasingly considered only one policy practical for Japanese survival: an "inseparable spirit" with China, with which Japan shared the "same color and culture." Such intimate ties would guarantee Japanese independence in an eventual "contest between the yellow and white races."

At the outbreak of war in Europe, Yamagata's sympathies lay with Britain's primary enemy, Germany. His daughter lived in Germany, married to the Japanese ambassador in Berlin. Yamagata confidently predicted victory for the Central Powers by a 60:40 margin. The British, after all, fought half-heartedly, "as if fighting for someone else's sake," and the French placed priority on minimizing casualties. "I would like to see [British Foreign Secretary Edward] Grey's face," Yamagata sneered in August 1914, "as the German army poises to march on Paris."

These sharp differences of opinion over Germany and the Anglo-Japanese alliance raise questions about Katō's motives for declaring war against Germany. Given the declining enthusiasm for the Anglo-Japanese alliance and glorification of German prowess among other influential circles in Japan, the speed and decisiveness with which the foreign minister responded to London's request for assistance take on added significance. That Katō chose to pursue his domestic and foreign policy aims through a declaration of war rather than through direct negotiations with China stemmed primarily from his desire to halt the growing movement in Tokyo to abandon the Anglo-Japanese alliance.

To push the logic even further, one might speculate that Katō mobilized like a "force of lightening" in August 1914 to forestall a contrary move among the Japanese leadership. In fact, Baron Gotō Shinpei, a bitter rival, had proposed a German-Japanese alliance after the Chinese revolution – a "golden opportunity" to shift Japanese sights from the declining Britain, which was increasingly plagued by "decrepitude," to "approach" the most rapidly rising power in Europe, Germany. General Tanaka Giichi, a future vice chief of the Army General Staff and a protégé of army patriarch Yamagata Aritomo, on the eve of the Great War had urged a political alliance with Germany to "contain Russia on her Western border."

There is evidence that Japanese generals welcomed the prospect of military action on the Asian continent, even at the expense of their former instructors. They considered the war a golden opportunity to expand their area of operations in China and to bolster their waning political fortunes at home. After the fall of Qingdao in November 1914, General Terauchi Masatake urged that Japanese troops should "share the responsibility" of public peace in China with Beijing. Vice Chief of the Army General Staff Akashi Motojirō called for an immediate attack on the German concession at Jiaozhou. Otherwise, Russia would seize the territory after her victory over Berlin. At home, Terauchi hoped that the war would enable Japanese policymakers to "redirect internal discord outward" particularly away from the heated parliamentary debate over taxes, which threatened army prospects for expansion.

The plans of Japanese generals for expansion during the war went well beyond the bounds of great power behavior in China. Like Field Marshal Yamagata, General Tanaka described the war in Europe as a "race war," and envisioned at the center of Japanese diplomacy not the Anglo-Japanese alliance but "intimate" Sino-Japanese relations.

General Terauchi saw his strategy for taking advantage of the war as an "Asian Monroe Doctrine," and spoke of Japan's particular racial and cultural affinity with China. The European war was a "race war":

From our perspective as Asians, it is a war between Christians and, if we borrow their words, heathen peoples. Although we will not insist upon excluding Europeans and Americans, it is proper to inform the Westerners that, up to a point, Asia should be under the control of Asians.

Terauchi hoped to restrain the "haughtiness" of the Europeans and establish Japanese international authority. "Eventually all of Asia," he urged, "should be under the control of our Emperor."

Given such expansive visions of Japanese power within the Imperial Army, Katō feared that as soon as hostilities began the army would run away with the wartime agenda, that it would pull the nation into a wildly ambitious scheme of territorial expansion in China. The fact that Katō decided to join the war despite this danger again testifies to his complete commitment to the Anglo-Japanese alliance. Once it was decided to join Britain in the war against Germany, Katō painstakingly maneuvered to minimize army involvement in Japanese war aims.

The Imperial Navy posed much less of a threat to Katō in August 1914. On 3 August the Naval General Staff adopted a plan of operations for the Japan Sea and called for an assault on Qingdao, in concert with the army, aimed at "permanently extinguishing Germany's power in Asia and eliminating its ambition." But Navy Minister Yashiro was far more cautious. During the joint *genrō*-cabinet conference of 8 August he advised that Japan refrain from belligerency. Five days later, he urged the Cabinet to postpone a declaration of war and, instead, to send an ultimatum to Germany to restore Qingdao to China and withdraw the German fleet from the China Sea. But beyond the expulsion of the German fleet, naval leaders perceived few advantages to military action in East Asia. It was the Cabinet that authorized a limited occupation of the German Caroline, Mariana, and Marshall islands, and it was Foreign Minister Katō who later informed the British that Japan desired to maintain the islands in perpetuity.

Finally, what was the role of the media (and possibly public opinion) in the Japanese decision to enter the "European war"? Generally speaking, the national media echoed the government's enthusiasm for war. On 19 August the liberal *Tokyo Asahi shinbun* hailed the prospect of a brand new continental mission. "Imperial [Japanese] subjects," it declared, "will not be the only ones to rejoice over the warning to deliver Jiaozhou to the Empire and the extinguishing of German ambitions." Likewise, the *Ōsaka Mainichi shinbun* revealed rapidly expanding imperial ambitions. On 11 August it urged a Japanese takeover of the "source of evil in the Far East," German-occupied Jiaozhou. The following day it spoke of "a critical period in which Japan, as a member of the Anglo-Japanese alliance, must assume the responsibility of protecting Anglo-Japanese interests east of India." The message of 13 August was that "this might be the time for Japan, as an independent empire in the Far East, to press for what we believe necessary for self-defense, regardless of our alliance with Britain."

Widespread celebration marked the fall of the German fortress at Qingdao in November 1914. The *Ōsaka Mainichi shinbun* talked of "sowing the seeds" that would ensure the future "luxuriant growth" of Shandong province according to Japanese wishes. And the *Tokyo Asahi shinbun* welcomed the prospect of increased trade with China, especially in Shandong, where goods would now travel inland "after inspection by Japanese [customs officers] and along railroads run by Japanese."

Conclusion

The Japanese decision to declare war on Germany was the work of one man, Foreign Minister Katō Takaaki. The Cabinet's swift decision on 8 August had two principal aims. The first was to effect the outcome of a turbulent domestic debate over Japan's governance. The second was to enhance Japan's position in Asia, the easiest option being to eject the vulnerable Germans. This was achieved in less than four months when Qingdao fell in November 1914. At the same time Japan seized all of the Carolines, the Marianas (except Guam), and the Marshall Islands. Foreign Minister Katō Takaaki had insisted on Japanese participation in the war "upon the broad foundation of the Anglo-Japanese alliance" but that alliance did not obligate Japan's participation. British leaders subsequently asked Japan's leaders for assistance in fighting the European conflict. In mid-April 1917, Japan sent eight modern *Kaba* class destroyers and the cruiser *Akashi* to the Mediterranean where they did excellent convoy duty. Early in 1918, the Allies asked that more destroyers be sent but, arguing "possible German raids" from Wilhelmshaven, the request was refused.

The Ottoman Empire

Among the countries that entered the Great War before the end of 1914, the Ottoman (or Turkish) Empire was destined to play a major role in shaping its course and eventual outcome. Despite its economic backwardness and financial penury, this polyglot state of about 22 million people put up a remarkable war effort against the *entente* powers and forced them to divert large numbers of troops and significant naval forces to the newly opened Turkish theaters of war, thus reducing Allied pressure on Germany and her Austro-Hungarian ally for long periods of time. Moreover, by barring Allied shipping through the Black Sea Straits, Ottoman armed forces contributed in a major way to Russia's supply shortages and thereby hastened the collapse of the Tsarist regime in 1917. In the end, of course, the Ottoman Empire collapsed under the strains and stresses of the Great War.

Antecedents

Often derided as "the Sick Man of Europe," the tricontinental Ottoman Empire, under pressure from reformist army officers and various other Young Turk groups, had been transformed into a constitutional monarchy during the summer of 1908. After the suppression of a counter-revolutionary coup in April 1909, Sultan Abdülhamid II had been removed from the throne and replaced by his brother Reşad, who would henceforth preside over the empire as Mehmed V with very clearly defined limitations of his powers. In the Ottoman Chamber of Deputies, elected during the fall of 1908, the party with the largest number of seats was the so-called Committee of Union and Progress (C.U.P.), an organization that had its headquarters in Salonica. While it was strong in the legislature and usually quite well represented in the Cabinet, the C.U.P.'s political influence varied considerably during the next four years, and it was only in 1913 that it gained absolute power in the country.

In December 1876 the Ottoman Empire had, under the influence of Mithat Pasha, promulgated the first constitution in any Islamic country. It gave full executive power to the sultan, to whom ministers were individually responsible. But Sultan Abdülhamid used the Ottoman-Russian War the following year as an excuse to end the First Constitutional Period. The Second Constitutional Period, revived in

July 1908, proved to be equally short lived. Wars with Italy (1911–12) and with several of the Balkans states (1912–13) transformed a budding democratic environment into a single-party autocracy, in whose hands the war powers rested. Thus, the decision to join the Great War was in the hands of a small faction of the C.U.P. Party's upper echelons.

The so-called "Young Turk" state was baptized in war. In September 1911 the Kingdom of Italy invaded the sultan's Tripolitanian provinces (today's Libya). The small Ottoman garrisons in the region, backed by thousands of native tribesmen, successfully prevented the invaders from penetrating into the interior of the country, but that did not deter the Italian government from proclaiming its annexation on 5 November. Mehmed Said Pasha, an experienced elder statesman, sent to Libya several energetic staff officers, including one of the heroes of the 1908 revolt, Major Enver Bey, who had previously served as military attaché at the Ottoman embassy in Berlin.

While the Turks were busy dealing with the Italians, several Balkan states (Montenegro, Bulgaria, Serbia, and Greece) in October 1912 declared war on the sultan's realm. The numerically inferior Ottoman armies were defeated in a number of pitched battles, losing control of Macedonia, Epirus, Albania, and most of Thrace. When the Ottoman government, now headed by another elderly statesman, Mehmed Kâmil Pasha, agreed to make major territorial concessions during peace talks in London early in 1913, a group of nationalist officers with close ties to the C.U.P. decided to stage another coup d'état. Headed by Enver Bey, they stormed into the grand vizier's office on 23 January and forced him and his Cabinet to resign. While Mahmud Şevket Pasha, a senior army general with only loose ties to the Committee of Union and Progress, became the new grand vizier (and minister of war), several other important portfolios were taken over by prominent C.U.P. figures, including Prince Said Halim Pasha (Foreign Ministry).

Less than five months after his appointment as grand vizier, Şevket Pasha was assassinated on his way to the Porte. Under heavy pressure from the C.U.P., Sultan Mehmed V agreed to make Prince Said Halim Pasha the new grand vizier. Wealthy, intelligent, and well educated, this Egyptian-born grandee had risen rather rapidly in the councils of the C.U.P. But during his long tenure as grand vizier (until February 1917) his colleagues both in the party and in the Cabinet often ignored his views.

The Decision-Makers

By far the strongest and most talented member of Said Halim's new
Cabinet was a former postal official, Mehmed Talât Bey. A veteran
of underground work against Abdülhamid's regime, Talât since 1908
had held important posts both in the government and in the party; as
minister of the interior he would keep a close eye on the grand vizier
and eventually, in 1917, succeed him. In December 1913 General
Ahmed Cemal Pasha, another senior figure in the C.U.P., joined the
Cabinet as minister of public works; in January 1914 Enver Bey joined
the Cabinet as minister of war. Barely 32 years old, Enver Pasha (as
he would henceforth be known) shortly thereafter married one of the
sultan's nieces.

It has often been claimed that from early 1914 on the Ottoman
Empire was run by a triumvirate composed of Enver, Talât, and Cemal
(who switched from Public Works to the Navy Ministry in March
of that year), but that generalization is misleading. There is ample
evidence to support the conclusion that both before and during the
Great War the Central Committee of the C.U.P., the *Merkezi Umuni*,
remained the principal policy-making body in the empire, and that no
government minister could take action on any major matter without
gaining support from a majority of the committee's members. These
men share a great deal of responsibility for the foreign and domestic
policies of Prince Said Halim's Cabinet.

From August 1914 on, the C.U.P. leadership increased its power
within the empire as well as its capabilities for covert action abroad
through the establishment of a "Special Organization" (*Teskilâti
Mahsusa*). As well, the C.U.P. made excellent use of the press to generate support for its policies. Among the newspapers directly under
the control of the party, the *Tanin* was probably the most widely read.
Its editor, Hüseyin Cahit (Yalçin), was both a brilliant journalist and
a man of action, serving simultaneously in the Chamber of Deputies
and as the Ottoman delegate on the council of the Public Debt Administration (an agency representing foreign creditors with extensive
control over the Porte's tax revenues).

In addition to its heavy indebtedness to foreign bondholders, the
Ottoman Empire on the eve of World War I faced numerous other
structural problems. Foreign companies mostly owned its transporta-
tion system, underdeveloped as it was. The same was true with regard
to public utilities and several other sectors of the economy. To patriotic

Ottomans, another cause for resentment was the refusal of various foreign governments to allow the abrogation of the "capitulations," a series of commercial treaties going back to the sixteenth century that granted a number of privileges to certain categories of foreigners.

Having lost numerous territories in both Europe and Africa between 1911 and the spring of 1913, the Ottoman government in May of that year decided that its military establishment needed major changes, and that German army officers should supervise these reforms. After lengthy discussions with Berlin, agreement was reached on the size and functions of the new mission, and in mid-December 1913 the first contingent of the German reformers arrived in Istanbul. Headed by a recently ennobled cavalry general, Otto Liman von Sanders, the mission was reinforced during the following four months and had roughly seventy members scattered all over the empire by July 1914.

To the Russian government especially, the dispatch of this military mission looked like a major increase of German power and influence in the Ottoman Empire. But such fears were unjustified. While Liman and his subordinates were busy training and upgrading the Ottoman officer corps and certain "model" regiments, the Porte established contact with the member states of the Triple Entente, probing their willingness to finance the revival of Ottoman strength and even their inclination to conclude an alliance with Turkey. In February 1914 the Ottoman government formally conceded to Russia the authority to "supervise" reforms in the Armenian-populated provinces of eastern Anatolia. Three months later the powerful minister of the interior, Talât Bey, led an Ottoman delegation to the tsar's summer palace in the Crimea, where he proposed a Russo-Turkish alliance to the Russian foreign minister, Sergei Sazonov. The latter was quite skeptical about the offer and nothing further developed.

In the first half of July the Ottoman navy minister, General Cemal Pasha, went to Paris for political talks. In a meeting with Pierre de Margerie, a senior official of the French Foreign Ministry, Cemal pointed out that the Ottoman government was willing to establish closer relations with the *entente*, but expected some help in return on the status of the Aegean islands seized by Greece during the Balkan War. Since René Viviani, the French premier and foreign minister, was about to leave Paris for a state visit to St. Petersburg, Cemal's invitation brought no response.

As for Great Britain, the C.U.P. regime continued the policy adopted by previous governments, particularly by maintaining close ties in naval matters with that country. Aside from employing a large British naval mission under Rear Admiral Sir Arthur H. Limpus for the improvement of the sultan's fleet, the Porte also had several warships on order in British shipyards.

The July Crisis

Since the Porte's various overtures to the *entente* had produced no tangible results, the C.U.P. regime in the latter part of July 1914 approached the German government with an offer of closer ties. As Enver Pasha informed the German ambassador in Istanbul, Hans Baron von Wangenheim, on 22 July, the Ottoman Empire needed "support from one of the Great Power groups." While a minority of his C.U.P. associates "favored an alliance with Russia and France" because the Triple Entente was stronger in the Mediterranean than the German-led Triple Alliance, Enver, as well as Prince Said Halim, Talât, Halil Bey (Mentese) (the president of the Chamber of Deputies), and a majority in the party's central committee preferred to link up with the Reich. With remarkable frankness, Enver further explained that their option was based on two considerations: they did not like the risk of having the Ottoman Empire become "Russia's vassal," and they were also convinced that Germany and her allies were militarily stronger than the *entente* powers and would prevail in the war.

Although Wangenheim reacted rather coolly to Enver's offer, Kaiser Wilhelm II ruled two days later that in view of the tense international situation, the Ottoman interest in a closer connection with the Triple Alliance should be accommodated. During the next few days, negotiations regarding the scope and nature of the proposed Ottoman alignment with the Reich were initiated in Istanbul, and on 28 July a formal Ottoman alliance proposal was presented to Berlin. After some modifications, German Chancellor Theobald von Bethmann Hollweg advised Wangenheim on the evening of 31 July that he was authorized to sign the treaty *if* he was sure that the Turks could, and would, "undertake some action against Russia" that was more than a mere gesture. The ambassador the next day invited both Enver Pasha and General Liman to his office to review the plans and capabilities of the Ottoman Army. The three men eventually agreed that the Ottoman divisions in eastern Anatolia would initially adopt a defensive posture while the bulk of the army would be deployed in Thrace for a joint offensive with the Bulgarians against southern Russia or, possibly, for action against Greece.

Even though this "plan" was rather vague on several key issues – neither Bulgaria's willingness to cooperate nor Romania's willingness to allow Ottoman and/or Bulgarian troops to march through its territory was as yet known – Wangenheim decided to proceed with the treaty. On the afternoon of 2 August he and Prince Said Halim signed the document on behalf of their respective governments, though both were fully aware that it would take a long time, at least four weeks, to complete the mobilization and deployment of the Ottoman Army. Within the next twenty-four hours the Porte ordered general mobilization, but it also issued a declaration of Ottoman neutrality in the rapidly expanding European war.

Reflecting the haste with which the alliance had been cobbled together, the treaty called for the Ottoman Empire's intervention on Germany's side if the latter became involved in hostilities with Russia in connection with the Austro-Serbian conflict – a contingency that, of course, had already become a reality by 2 August. Other clauses of the treaty stipulated that Liman's military mission was to have "an effective influence on the general direction" of the Ottoman Army, that the Reich would help to protect the territorial integrity of the sultan's realm, and that this "secret" treaty would remain in effect beyond the year 1918 unless it was renounced by either party.

On 5 August, two days after the Porte had issued its declaration of neutrality, Enver Pasha told the Russian military attaché in Istanbul that the recently ordered mobilization of the Ottoman Army was not directed against Russia. The Porte was prepared to thin out its troops along the Transcaucasian border with Russia and to use its forces instead to neutralize "this or that Balkan State which might intend to move against Russia." Ottoman troops might even become available to assist other Balkan countries "against Austria," provided that the Russians helped the Porte to regain possession of the Aegean islands (from Greece) and of Western Thrace (from Bulgaria).

Enver Pasha's overture to the Russians, which he repeated a few days later, may seem rather strange at first sight, but it made sense. First, his statement provided a cover for the planned concentration of Ottoman troops in eastern Thrace. Second, a negative response from the Russian government would strengthen the case against those

C.U.P. elements, in both the Central Committee and the Cabinet, who still leaned toward an alignment with the *entente*. Even in the unlikely event that St. Petersburg proved willing to meet Enver's conditions, the move would greatly enhance the Porte's bargaining position vis-à-vis Berlin.

That the C.U.P. regime was in a bargaining mood was first brought home to the Germans at one o'clock in the morning of 6 August, when Prince Said Halim summoned Wangenheim to his office. The Cabinet, the grand vizier allowed, had just decided "unanimously" to open the Dardanelles to both the German Mediterranean Squadron (the battle cruiser *Goeben* and the light cruiser *Breslau*) and any Austro-Hungarian warships that might accompany them, while the Ottoman Empire would maintain its neutral status. Well aware of the precarious situation in which the two German cruisers found themselves at that time, the grand vizier then asked Wangenheim whether he was prepared to pledge Germany's acceptance of the following six proposals:

1. assistance in the abolition of the capitulations.
2. support in regard to the indispensable understandings with Romania and Bulgaria, for which Turkey would secure a fair agreement with Bulgaria with reference to possible spoils of war.
3. no peace unless Turkish territories (which may be occupied by its enemies in the course of the war) are evacuated.
4. return of the Aegean islands should Greece enter the war and be defeated by Turkey.
5. a small correction of Turkey's eastern border, which shall place it in direct contact with the Muslims of Russia.
6. an appropriate war indemnity.

Fearful lest he endanger the rescue of the German cruisers by "protracted discussions," Wangenheim immediately accepted the grand vizier's proposals and later in the day confirmed the agreement in writing. As he subsequently pointed out to his superiors in Berlin, most of the promises he had made would come into play only if the Central Powers won the war "decisively." The German government thereupon formally approved the deal.

The agreement of 6 August marked a definite improvement in the Porte's diplomatic position. Unlike the alliance treaty signed four days earlier, the new accord formally assured the Ottoman Empire of certain tangible gains after victory once it entered the war on Germany's side.

On 9 August, while Wangenheim and other Germans in Istanbul were impatiently waiting for the arrival of the *Goeben* and *Breslau*, the grand vizier politely informed the ambassador that the Bucharest government had proposed the conclusion of an Ottoman-Greek-Romanian "neutrality pact," and that under certain circumstances the Porte might decide to enter into such an arrangement. In that case, he added, the secret alliance with Germany would "of course remain in effect," though it would be necessary to convert the *Goeben* into an Ottoman ship "by means of a fictitious sale."

As soon as these propositions became known in Berlin, Bethmann Hollweg wired back to Istanbul that none of them was acceptable, and that every effort should be made to bring both the Ottoman Empire and Bulgaria into the war. That demand was highly unrealistic, for by this time the governments of both states had ample reasons to postpone any overt action. The entry of the British Empire into the war as well as Italy's and Romania's refusal to fight on the side of the Central Powers had visibly shifted the power balance in the Mediterranean and the Balkans; both Istanbul and Sofia were receiving strong warnings from the *entente* not to do anything foolhardy.

Contrary to Berlin's expectation, the arrival of the German Mediterranean Squadron at the Dardanelles on the afternoon of 10 August did not immediately strengthen its hand vis-à-vis the Porte. Although Enver Pasha authorized the Dardanelles command to admit the German cruisers into the Straits, Prince Said Halim soon thereafter made it clear to Wangenheim that he, and the rest of the Cabinet, objected to the squadron's "premature" arrival. No progress had been made in lining up the Bulgarians, and if the *entente* decided to declare war because of the cruisers' presence in the Straits, Bulgaria might "exploit Turkey's engagement elsewhere and march on Constantinople." After prolonged arguments with Wangenheim, the grand vizier eventually offered the following "compromise": while the two cruisers would be allowed to stay in some "remote spot" in the Sea of Marmara, the Porte would insist on turning them into Ottoman property through a fictitious purchase.

Before Berlin had time to react to this proposal, the Porte issued a public statement that the two German cruisers had been bought "for eighty million Marks." A few days later, on 16 August, a solemn ceremony was staged near the Golden Horn, during which Cemal Pasha officially welcomed the ships, and their crews, into the sultan's navy. The *Goeben* was formally renamed *Yavuz Sultan Selim*, the

Breslau became the *Midilli*, all German sailors donned fezzes, and the squadron's leader, Rear Admiral Wilhelm Souchon, was officially entrusted with command of the entire Ottoman fleet.

Public opinion in the Ottoman Empire was elated over the "acquisition" of the two ships, all the more so since earlier in the month two dreadnoughts that had been ordered from British shipyards (and already paid for) had been requisitioned by the Royal Navy. However, both Wangenheim and his Austro-Hungarian colleague in Istanbul, Johann Margrave von Pallavicini, recognized that the Ottoman Empire was simply not ready for war, and they so informed their superiors in Berlin and Vienna.

Admiral Souchon and a number of other Germans quickly came to the conclusion that the Dardanelles defenses were in woeful shape, thus making Ottoman intervention far too risky for the time being. To remedy that situation, Berlin agreed to send roughly 700 sailors and coast defense specialists to Turkey. Headed by Admiral Guido von Usedom, these men arrived at the Straits at the beginning of September and began their remedial tasks.

On 8 September, to the complete surprise of its allies, the Porte announced to the world that it had decided to abrogate the capitulatory privileges of all foreign powers. Intent on placating hostile reactions from the neutral world, Wangenheim and Pallavicini joined the ambassadors of the *entente* bloc (and of Italy) in signing a formal note of protest against the Porte's resort to unilateral action. Simultaneously, they advised the grand vizier that the Central Powers would not really press the issue. On 1 October the Porte began to implement its program, raising the hitherto foreign-controlled customs duties and closing all foreign post offices in the empire. Most of the other capitulatory privileges were canceled shortly thereafter.

On 14 September Enver Pasha authorized Admiral Souchon to take his ships into the Black Sea and to open fire on any Russian vessels he might encounter. But before Souchon could act, the grand vizier arranged a showdown on the issue in the Cabinet. He emerged triumphant and Enver eventually had to withdraw his directive. Frustrated on the Black Sea front, Enver bided his time for about a week and then struck his next blow, ordering the Dardanelles closed to all foreign ships, effective 26 September. While the grand vizier assured *entente* governments that the waterway would be reopened as soon as Britain and France withdrew their warships from the vicinity of the Dardanelles, Talât on 2 October made it clear to Wangenheim that the Straits would remain closed, *entente* protests and threats notwithstanding.

A few days later Enver Pasha advised the German ambassador that both Talât and Halil Bey had moved closer to his own position – intervention in the near future – as had the "overwhelming" majority of the C.U.P. Central Committee. Cemal Pasha was leaning toward intervention, Enver stated, but more needed to be done to obtain his unconditional support. Ottoman entry into the war might come as soon as mid-October, provided that Germany furnished adequate gold supplies without delay.

The Porte had first requested a gold loan of five million Turkish Pounds in late September, but so far Berlin had insisted that 95 percent of that amount could only be paid out *after* the Turks had become involved in the war. In order to expedite matters, Enver, accompanied by Talât, Halil, and Cemal, called on Wangenheim on 11 October for a strategy conference. The upshot of their meeting was that they would send Souchon's ships into action against the Russians as soon as at least 40 percent of the gold had arrived in the capital; if the grand vizier refused to sanction intervention, he would be induced to resign.

In response to these pledges, Berlin on the next day dispatched one million Turkish Pounds in gold coins on a special train. Routed through Austria-Hungary, Romania, and Bulgaria, the shipment reached Istanbul on the evening of 16 October. A second shipment, dispatched on the following day, arrived in the Ottoman capital on 21 October, despite Russian diplomatic efforts in Bucharest to block its transit through Romania.

Once the gold had arrived, Enver transmitted an action plan to German imperial headquarters: hostilities would be opened by naval action against the Russians in the Black Sea while the bulk of the Ottoman Army would remain assembled in Thrace for future joint operations with the Bulgarians against Serbia and/or Russia. The latter operation, though, depended on Romania's cooperation, something that was quite unlikely, as the Porte knew all too well. An advance against Egypt (which the Germans had urged on Enver since August) would require at least six more weeks to prepare and involve at most two Ottoman corps.

On 24 October Enver Pasha, in his newly acquired role as "deputy commander-in-chief," issued a directive to Admiral Souchon to take the Ottoman fleet into the Black Sea and attack the Russian fleet if a "suitable opportunity" presented itself. Navy Minister Cemal Pasha dispatched a secret order to senior Ottoman officers of the fleet that the German admiral was to receive their support. On 27 October the Ottoman fleet steamed out of the Bosporus. Once the ships were at sea, Souchon informed senior German and Ottoman officers under his command that they were on a mission of war, and ordered an *immediate* assault on the enemy's ports. His decision made sense from an operational point of view. Early on 29 October several ports and other targets on the Russian coast were shelled, mines were dropped in major shipping lanes, and some Russian ships were sunk. But it produced needless political embarrassment for Enver and his colleagues in the Cabinet, all of whom had expected a less provocative initiation of hostilities (a manufactured "incident").

The news of Souchon's raid provoked a major crisis in the Ottoman Cabinet as well as heated debates in the Central Committee of the C.U.P. While many details of the ensuing power struggle are still obscure, it is clear that Prince Said Halim put up a valiant effort to prevent further hostile acts; that he was backed energetically by the finance minister, Cavid Bey; that several other ministers threatened to resign in protest; and that the anti-interventionist members of the Central Committee argued vigorously against Enver Pasha's policies. After almost four days of wrangling, the interventionists came out on top, but only after making a number of concessions. One of these was the dispatch of a conciliatory note to Petersburg (on 1 November); another was an appeal to Berlin to agree to a revision of the alliance treaty, particularly by lengthening and broadening the guarantees Germany had given to the Porte. On 2 November the Russian government formally declared war on the Ottoman Empire.

Conclusion

The decision of the most influential members of the C.U.P. regime in July 1914 to throw in their lot with Germany and their intervention in the Great War three months later sealed the fate of the empire. Contrary to the hopes of its proponents, the alliance with the Reich aligned the Ottoman Empire with a power bloc that was materially weaker than the opposing side and would ultimately lose the war. It is small wonder, then, that for many years thereafter the official Turkish view of the C.U.P. regime would be highly critical, depicting Enver Pasha and his interventionist colleagues as reckless adventurers or even servile helpmates of German imperialism. Recently, these harsh verdicts have been replaced by more moderate judgments. It is widely held today that most of the men who took the sultan's realm into the Great War were patriots, albeit misguided ones.

Suggestions that the C.U.P. regime entered that war to promote the "modernization" of the Ottoman Empire and to enhance its status as a "European" state seem rather far-fetched. Indeed, if the Ottoman interventionists agreed on anything, it was that their country should regain some of its lost territories and expand further into Transcaucasia, the Caspian region, and beyond. Most of them also hoped that participation in the war would facilitate the administrative "centralization" of the sultan's realm, particularly by whittling down the remaining privileges of its various ethnic and religious minorities. In the case of the Armenian communities in the eastern provinces of the empire, that policy would be implemented in 1915 with a degree of ruthlessness that shocked the world. The "Greek Problem," on the other hand, would only be solved in the aftermath of the Greco-Turkish War (1919–22), when Athens and Ankara agreed on a major population exchange between the two countries. As for the "Kurdish Question," it is still very much an issue today.

CHAPTER 9

Bulgaria, Romania, and Greece

With Montenegro and Serbia engaged in the First World War from its outbreak, three other Balkan countries, Bulgaria, Romania, and Greece, hovered on the periphery. Because, like Italy, all three desired to realize their nationalist aspirations at the expense of their neighbors, they could not ignore the opportunities presented by the war; affiliation with the Triple Entente or the Central Powers promised substantial benefits. Before acting, each Balkan nation had to determine which side offered the greatest gains and the most likely chance of victory. Conversely, the two warring alliance systems (Triple Alliance and Triple Entente) looked to their possible advantage in the Balkans.

These three nations like their Serbian neighbor, devoted much energy and treasure toward the establishment of large national states based on historical and ethnic claims. Bulgaria fought Serbia successfully to this end in 1885; Greece fought the Ottoman Empire unsuccessfully in 1897. In the Balkan Wars of 1912–13 all three countries participated to further their nationalist aims. The victories of Greece and Romania, and the defeat of Bulgaria, only intensified nationalist strivings. In the aftermath of the Balkan Wars, Greece and Romania sought to expand their gains; the Bulgarians to obtain revenge and to restore their national aspirations.

Since 1895, Bulgaria enjoyed the patronage of Russia. From 1882, Romania had a formal alliance with Austria-Hungary, and through that arrangement with Germany and Italy. Moreover, its ruler, King Carol I, was from the Sigmaringen branch of the Hohenzollern family and thus closely related to Kaiser Wilhelm II of Germany. Greece lacked the direct support of any great power, but after the marriage in 1889 of Crown Prince Constantine to Sophia Hohenzollern, the sister of Wilhelm II, Germany developed a benevolent attitude – which increased after Constantine's accession to the throne in 1913.

Bulgaria

Bulgaria possessed similar political and social structures to those of Serbia. The monarch lacked a secure throne. Tsar Ferdinand, née Coburg, was the scion of an Austro-German house and the grandson of Louis Philippe of France; he came to Bulgaria after an army putsch in 1886 deposed his popular predecessor, Alexander Battenberg. The distinctly unmilitary Ferdinand was commander-in-chief of the Bulgarian Army, but he did not completely dominate it. Real power was wielded by a small group of military and political leaders close to the throne, aided and abetted by a largely foreign-educated middle class elite. As in Serbia, secret societies advocated direct action in pursuit of national aspirations. The Supreme Macedonian Committee (Supremist) was formed in 1895; it advocated the annexation of Macedonia and received political and material support from the Bulgarian Army. Through the Supremists, the Bulgarian government and military attempted to influence the Macedonian movement. A competing society, the Internal Macedonian Revolutionary Organization (IMRO), formed in 1893, operated relatively independently of the Sofia government. Its members advocated autonomy for Macedonia within a Balkan federation with the slogan "Macedonia for the Macedonians." This idea, of course, threatened the goal of a "greater Bulgaria."

The identification of the vast majority of the population – the peasant masses – with the national ideal was by no means certain. Bulgarian peasants, like those in Serbia, were mainly owners of small plots of land and they (like the peasants of Greece, Romania, and Serbia) had little influence on policy. Their perceptions of national interests were essentially unknown. Clearly, the idea of "Greater Bulgaria" (or "Greater Greece," or "Greater Romania") did not mesmerize everyone. Just before the outbreak of the First Balkan War, the Bulgarian Agrarian Party leader Aleksandŭr Stamboliski eloquently stated his opposition to the impending conflict: "We are not seeking war with Turkey, because we know how the horrible consequences are borne by working peasants, who fill the barracks and who will sacrifice the most capable of their children on the battlefield." Nevertheless, the Bulgarian peasantry, like that of the other Balkan states, responded to the government's call to arms in 1912, 1913, and 1915 with stolid acquiescence.

Bulgaria's national aspirations centered on Macedonia, an area of extremely mixed population. The Slavic element predominated, but Albanians, Turks, Roma, Vlachs, Greeks, and others also live there. The only issue was whether to accomplish this with or without Russian assistance. Russophiles contended that Russian help offered the best opportunity to restore a "Greater Bulgaria." Russophobes, on the other hand, increasingly perceived the Triple Alliance powers, especially Austria-Hungary, as Bulgaria's great power sponsors. The terms Russophile and Russophobe were not official party designations; they simply signified the orientation of virtually all Bulgarian politicians.

Greece and Serbia rejected Bulgaria's claims to Macedonia; all three states supported guerilla units, which battled Ottoman authorities as well as each other. The Romanians laid claim to the lands of the Vlach minority, whose language is closely related to their own. Political violence was frequent. In 1895 Macedonians assassinated former Prime Minister Stefan Stambulov because he had been too friendly to the Ottomans. After the failure of a Macedonian uprising in 1903, these groups fragmented further into competitive factions. Neither the Supremists nor the IMRO could claim supremacy. The volatile mix was revealed in August 1912, when a bomb exploded in the Macedonian marketplace of Kochana, prompting vengeful Turks to massacre more than 100 Macedonians. The "Kochana incident" clearly demonstrated the ability of nongovernmental organizations to preempt policy.

In the First Balkan War, the Bulgarians, allied with the Serbs since March 1912, achieved great victories over Ottoman armies in Thrace. The conquest of the main goal of Bulgarian aspirations, Macedonia, was left to Serbia. When the Serbs refused to abide by the terms of the alliance and evacuate Macedonia in spring 1913, the Bulgarians prepared to fight their erstwhile allies. Unable to reach a settlement with the Serbs, Ivan Geshov, the architect of the Balkan League, resigned as Bulgarian prime minister. Stoyan Danev, a zealous Russophile, replaced him. Danev later remembered: "I would suffer the consequences for what might happen if [Serbia] snipped off part of Macedonia. I did not intend to yield, because we had signed the agreement of 1912. At last we had to act."

Reluctantly, Russian Foreign Minister Sergei Sazonov agreed on 15 June 1913 to uphold his government's promise to arbitrate the Bulgarian-Serbian dispute. Meanwhile, the situation in Bulgaria became critical. The peasant soldiers of the Bulgarian Army, who had been at arms since the previous autumn, were becoming restive. They were exhausted and wanted to go home. The Bulgarian commander, General Mihail Savov, demanded that the government either fight the Serbs for Macedonia or allow the army to disperse. Under this pressure, Danev insisted that the Russians act within a week. But before Russian arbitration could proceed, fighting began in Macedonia.

A limited Bulgarian attack against Serbian troops on 29 June precipitated the Second Balkan War. General Savov later justified this by insisting: "In the first days of June everyone, with only rare exception, was for the war, because no one, given the partition of Macedonia, wanted to *sign the death warrant of the national ideal*." Macedonian bands threatened Ferdinand and Danev with assassination if Bulgaria agreed to Russian arbitration. The Bulgarian attack on Serbian positions demonstrated the ability of the military and the nationalist societies to dictate policy. The position of the Sofia government in June 1913 was not unlike that of the Belgrade government in June 1914. In both cases, the government had to assume responsibility for actions taken by more aggressive elements within the military establishment. The difference was that in 1913 the Bulgarian attack was directed against two other Balkan states, while in 1914 the Serbian terrorist action had as its target a great power, Austria-Hungary.

The result of General Savov's orders was war with Greece and Serbia. Serbian and Greek armies deflected Bulgarian attacks and counterattacked. Worse still, on 11 July 1913 the Romanian Army crossed the Danube and moved into Bulgaria in hopes of seizing (southern) Dobrudzha. At the same time, the Ottoman Army, perceiving the opportunity, took Adrianople. The invasion of Romanian forces from the north and Ottoman forces from the southeast ensured a catastrophic defeat for Bulgaria. Danev's Russophile government resigned in the face of the Russians' refusal to help their Bulgarian clients. A Russophobe government, led by Vasil Radoslavov, replaced it and immediately sued for peace. The subsequent peace treaties of Bucharest and Constantinople deprived Bulgaria of most of Macedonia as well as southern Dobrudzha and eastern Thrace.

The Balkan Wars, begun in such glory, had ended in catastrophe for Bulgaria. Its armies had decisively defeated the former Ottoman masters, only to falter against its onetime Greek and Serbian allies. For Bulgaria, the peace of 1913 was an unmitigated disaster. One member of the Bulgarian delegation, General Ivan Fichev, later wrote: "This day must be the day of the deepest sorrow of the Bulgarian nation." Despite the sacrifice of so many Bulgarian lives and so much material, the Bulgarians saw Macedonia partitioned between Greece and Serbia.

Equally important, Bulgarian leaders now had confirmation that Russia no longer protected their interests. Prime Minister Radoslavov explained this to Alexander Savinski, Russian minister to Sofia in January 1914. "At Bucharest, we clearly realized that Russia had turned away from us; ... therefore we find ourselves in our present melancholy position." The Russophobe Radoslavov government now looked to the Triple Alliance for support.

The assassination of Archduke Franz Ferdinand in June 1914 aroused the apprehensions of Tsar Ferdinand, who feared that Macedonian or Serbian secret societies might make an attempt on his life. While Ferdinand's concerns were exaggerated, they demonstrated his appreciation of the power wielded by the Macedonian secret societies.

The threat of European war that summer presented Bulgaria with a clash of loyalties as well as an opportunity to revise the Treaty of Bucharest. General Franz Conrad von Hötzendorf, the chief of the Austro-Hungarian General Staff, urged the Bulgarians to attack Serbia, insisting on 29 July that "there is no more favorable moment than today." Yet many Bulgarians remained strong Russophiles. At the outbreak of the war, the Bulgarian minister in St. Petersburg, General Radko Dimitriev, resigned his post to accept a commission in the Russian Army. Other Bulgarians also volunteered to serve in the Russian Army. A political ally of Radoslavov explained the dilemma for Bulgaria at the beginning of the war this way: "Our natural place was with Russia. Yet after ... the Bucharest Peace Treaty, how could Bulgaria take Serbia's side?"

At first, Radoslavov maintained Bulgaria's neutrality, insisting that the country needed time to recover from the Balkan Wars. But in an effort to obtain Macedonia, Bulgaria negotiated with both warring alliances. Although favoring the Central Powers, Radoslavov wavered according to their fortunes on the battlefield. After the Russian capture of the Austro-Hungarian fortress of Przemysl and the Anglo-French landings at the Dardanelles in the spring of 1915, he expressed interest in cooperating with the *entente*. On 29 May 1915 the *entente* promised Bulgaria most of Macedonia and eastern Thrace, but the offer came too late. The Russians were in retreat in Galicia and the British remained stuck on the beaches at Gallipoli. As one Bulgarian historian has noted, "the Russophile policy was deeply wounded" by the Russian defeats that spring and summer.

The Central Powers saw their chance and promised Bulgaria all of Macedonia. Radoslavov accepted the offer, declaring that Bulgaria "cannot and will not be denied its historical and ethnographic rights. It cannot be without Macedonia, for which it has shed so much blood." A German promise to participate in an attack on Serbia was the decisive factor in persuading Ferdinand and Radoslavov to join the Central Powers. Such a powerful ally was certain to crush Serbia and deliver Macedonia. Ferdinand, in his Manifesto to the Bulgarian People of 14/15 October 1915, announced Bulgaria's entry into the war: "Both warring sides recognize the great injustice, which was inflicted upon us by the division of Macedonia. And both warring sides are agreed that the greater part of it needs to belong to Bulgaria." With this assertion, Bulgaria began the third of four unsuccessful wars for Macedonia over a period of thirty years.

The Bulgarian decision to intervene on the side of the Central Powers appeared justified at the time. Berlin and Vienna promised Sofia the immediate annexation of all of Serbian-held Macedonia. Bulgarian troops had only to take it. With the Central Powers winning the war, the time seemed propitious to act. Over the next two to three years, Bulgarian forces, in tandem with their new allies, overran Serbia, Montenegro, Macedonia, and Romania. Ultimately, Bulgarian arms failed again. The armistice of 29 September 1918 brought an exhausted Bulgaria further territorial losses.

Romania

Bulgaria's entry into the war on the side of the Central Powers left Romania surrounded by belligerents, all of whom had reason to regard it with suspicion and antipathy. Over the previous three years, Romania had been a faithless ally to Austria-Hungary, a covetous irredentist to Russia, and a treacherous opportunist to Bulgaria. Those unneighborly attitudes imperiled Romania's position on the Balkan Peninsula.

The acquisition of southern Dobrudzha in the Second Balkan War established Romania as the dominant power in the Balkans, and enabled Bucharest to concentrate on its three irredentist aspirations. To the west, the objective was Hungarian-controlled Transylvania, which had a large Romanian population made restive by strictures imposed by Budapest. To the north, the goal was Bukovina, where a large Romanian population languished under the benign neglect of Austrian rule. In the east, the object was Russian-held Bessarabia, where the Romanian population was much less developed economically and nationally. But no activist organizations comparable to the Macedonian and Serbian secret societies existed in any of these regions, or in Romania itself.

As in the other Balkan countries, the king's role was central in Romanian affairs. Between 1881 and 1914, every government supported by the king won at the polls. The Romanian Army was dedicated to nationalist goals but, unlike the Bulgarian and Serbian militaries, remained firmly under government control. The Hohenzollern King Carol had overseen the negotiations for Romania's treaty with Austria-Hungary in 1883, and this connection to the Triple Alliance (renewed in 1913) was the mainstay of Romanian foreign policy. In the aftermath of the Balkan Wars, the Russians briefly flirted with Romania. To this end, Tsar Nicholas II visited the Romanian Black Sea port of Constanţsa in the first week of June 1914, generating alarm among Austro-Hungarian leaders, but nothing major developed – except further alienation of the jealous Bulgarians.

Beyond court and army, the Romanian political system was dominated by a land-owning aristocracy that retained control of most properties; and by a small educated urban class that ran most banking and commercial establishments. In foreign policy, the Conservative Party leaned toward the Triple Alliance, while the Liberal Party favored the Triple Entente, although these inclinations were by no means absolute. The prospect of gains from the European conflict fragmented the Conservative Party, but left the Liberal Party largely intact. The peasant majority, mostly landless, had demonstrated its regard for its debased circumstances in a bloody revolt in 1907. This effort brought 11,000 dead, much destruction, but little change. Still, the Romanian peasants, who as in the other Balkan countries formed the vast majority of military conscripts, stolidly answered the calls to duty in 1913 and 1916.

The European crisis initiated by the murder of Archduke Franz Ferdinand at Sarajevo on 28 June 1914 found Romania wavering. While King Carol assured the Austro-Hungarians that in the event of a general war Romania would side with the Triple Alliance, Liberal Prime Minister Ion Brătianu asserted Romania's determination to preserve the Bucharest peace settlement. But the deteriorating situation in Europe forced the Romanian leaders to take action.

On 3 August 1914 a Crown Council met at the royal palace at Sinaia to consider Bucharest's options. Only a few muted voices from the Conservative Party, most notably that of Petru Carp, a landowner from Moldavia, joined King Carol to advocate loyalty to Austria-Hungary. The Conservatives favored the Triple Alliance because of its superior strength and because of fears of Russian Pan-Slavism. News of Italy's defection from the Triple Alliance destroyed what little credibility these arguments had. A German offer of Bessarabia in return for adherence to the Central Powers failed to entice the Romanian government. Finally, a moderate Conservative leader, Alexandru Marghiloman, persuaded the king that the conditions for action specified in the treaty did not exist. At the end of the council, the German-born king, already sick with the illness that would kill him, lamented, "Gentlemen, you cannot imagine how bitter it is to find oneself isolated in a country of which one is not a native." Underlying the Romanian declaration of neutrality was a pervasive spirit of realism, dictated by geography. Fealty to the Austro-Hungarian alliance would ensure the hostility of Russia on Romania's eastern frontier; a tilt towards the *entente* could incur the wrath of Austria-Hungary on its western borders. To minimize this cruel choice, Bucharest waited and tried to determine who would win.

The death of King Carol in October 1914 left foreign policy firmly in the hands of Brătianu. While ostensibly maintaining neutrality, Brătianu initiated negotiations with the *entente* to obtain guarantees of Habsburg territory. Russia quickly promised support for the annexation of those Habsburg territories with a majority of Romanian inhabitants in return for benevolent neutrality. When the Italians entered the war on the side of the *entente* in May 1915, they provided Bucharest with a precedent for switching loyalties. Bulgaria's intervention on the side of the Central Powers in October 1915 intensified the danger on Romania's southern frontier. The German-Austrian-Bulgarian defeat of Serbia later that autumn further imperiled Bucharest. As a result of these developments, military talks between Bucharest and London and Paris assumed a new urgency.

The opening of the German offensive at Verdun in February 1916 prompted France to turn to Romania as a possible counterweight in the east. The apparent success of the Brusilov offensive in June 1916 impressed the Bucharest government of the *entente*'s resiliency. While Russian troops were overrunning Austro-Hungarian positions in Galicia, British and French staff officers planned an offensive at Salonika. General Joseph Joffre, the commander-in-chief of the French Army, predicted the "neutralization of the Bulgarian Army will allow Romania to enter the fray and precipitate the resolution of the war." *Entente* pressure on Bucharest increased. At the end of June 1916 London and Paris warned Bucharest to join the war or risk losing the prospect of obtaining Transylvania and Bukovina. At the same time, nationalist societies clamored for intervention on the side of the Triple Entente.

With the Austro-Hungarian Army in retreat in the East, and the Bulgarian Army fully engaged around Salonika, the time appeared propitious for intervention. First, Brătianu attempted to lever material benefits from the *entente* for the underequipped Romanian Army, thereby delaying the formal military convention for over a month. He finally signed on with Britain and France on 17 August 1916. At a Crown Council ten days later, he explained the decision to enter the war to the new King Ferdinand and to leading politicians. Some Conservatives, notably Marghiloman, refrained from active opposition. Others, however, rejected Brătianu's reasoning. Petru Carp thundered, "I wish that you will be conquered because your victory will be the ruin of the country!" Nevertheless, with the support of the king, the Brătianu government declared war on Austria-Hungary.

King Ferdinand stated that although a member of the Hohenzollern family, "I am the King of Roumania first, and therefore I have to do what my subjects wish." He "perceived" that "the majority of the people" were asking that Romania enter the war on the side of the *entente*, "and I therefore state to you that I am prepared to comply with their wish." This statement was rather disingenuous, since "the people" had not demanded war. Rather, it was Liberal politicians, under considerable pressure from London and Paris, who had decided that the time was right to intervene.

Initially, the Romanian Army achieved some successes against weak Austro-Hungarian resistance in Transylvania. But the force of the Brusilov offensive was spent by the time Romania entered the war and, contrary to Joffre's expectations, the *entente* offensive north of Salonika was unable to prevent the Bulgarians from joining the Central Powers in a punishing action against Romania in September. In

December the Central Powers occupied Bucharest and the Black Sea port Constanţsa.

The remaining Romanian forces retreated to northern Moldavia, but the Russian revolutions of 1917 soon isolated them. Romania had to acknowledge defeat. A change of government brought the Conservative leader Marghiloman to power. He signed the Treaty of Bucharest with the Central Powers on 7 May 1918, which took Romania out of the war. On 10 November 1918, with the defeat of the Central Powers evident, Romania returned to the war and gained the benefits and rewards of the *entente* victory.

Greece

The Greek decision to enter the First World War was the most difficult and convoluted of any country in southeastern Europe. Strong domestic political elements both favored and opposed intervention. At the same time, the warring alliance systems exerted considerable influence within the country. The resulting pressures on the Greek political establishment delayed Greek entry into the war until 1917.

Greece had not enjoyed the patronage of a great power before the war. Still, Athens pursued a nationalist agenda to acquire areas where Greek populations resided under foreign control. Their unification with Greece constituted the *Megale idea*, the gathering of all Greeks in one state. To realize this "great idea," Greek foreign policy focused on the Ottoman Empire. Concerned by the possible consequences of reform under the Young Turk regime, the Greek government turned to Bulgaria. This eventually led to the inclusion of Greece in the Balkan League of 1912. The Greeks achieved considerable military success against the Ottomans in the First Balkan War, and then against their erstwhile Bulgarian allies in the Second Balkan War. Greek lands increased by 70 percent and the Greek population by two million. Still, Greek national aspirations were not exhausted. Besides Cyprus, then under British control, and the Dodecanese, under Italian control, the *Megale idea* included areas of Albania and Bulgaria, but mainly parts of the Ottoman Empire.

At the outbreak of the Great War, many Greeks, notably the Anglophile Prime Minister Eleutherios Venizelos, favored the *entente*.

Venizelos was the leader of the Liberal Party and the dominant Greek political personality at the beginning of the twentieth century. After guiding Greece to success in the Balkan Wars, Venizelos saw the outbreak of the European war as an opportunity to utilize the power of the *entente* to realize the *Megale idea*. As early as 2 August 1914 he made his sympathies clear: "If the European situation results in a general conflict, *whatever happens* Greece will not be found on the side *opposed* to the Entente." This prediction, however, would not be realized for almost three years.

At the same time, the prime minister indicated that Greece would not uphold the terms of the alliance with Serbia. He informed Belgrade: "The Royal [Greek] government considers that it fulfills all its responsibilities of friendship and alliance by its decision to maintain, in regard to Serbia, a very benevolent neutrality, and to be prepared to repel any aggression undertaken by Bulgaria against Serbia." Like the Romanians, the Greeks declined to uphold their alliance commitments, seeing little to gain from a war against Austria-Hungary.

Venizelos encountered serious obstacles on his pro-*entente* course. King Constantine as well as the German-educated chief of staff, General Ioannis Metaxas, sympathized with Kaiser Wilhelm II, whose personal intercession in 1913 had been instrumental in securing the Thracian port of Kavala for Greece. Constantine, the kaiser's brother-in-law, enjoyed some prestige because he had commanded the victorious Greek Army during the Balkan Wars while General Metaxas had overseen the staff work. But there was little inclination in Greece to pursue a pro-German course, given the Royal Navy's dominance of the eastern Mediterranean. Thus, Constantine and many general staff officers steered a neutral course.

The entry of the Ottoman Empire into the war on the side of the Central Powers in November 1914 both simplified and complicated the Greek position. On the one hand, joining the *entente* made nationalist goals within the Ottoman Empire seem attainable. On the other hand, such action risked attacks from Bulgaria, still neutral, and from the Ottomans themselves. Moreover, the British did not help their cause when, upon Ottoman entry into the war, they annexed Cyprus, part of the Greek irredenta.

The Anglo-French attack on the Dardanelles in February 1915 brought the fighting close to Greek territory and increased Athens' importance for the *entente*. In a note of 23 January 1915 British Foreign

Secretary Sir Edward Grey offered Venizelos lands in Asia Minor in return for Greek help for both Serbia and the Dardanelles campaign. King Constantine and the General Staff opposed sending a Greek army to Serbia; General Metaxas warned that any intervention in Asia Minor was beyond the resources of the Greek Army. Russian interest in annexing Constantinople further complicated the question of Athens' entry into the war. Foreign Minister Sazonov warned on 5 March 1915: "Because of political and religious reasons the possibility of the Greek flag at Constantinople produces in Russia a sharp impression of disquiet and irritation." Under these circumstances, the British offer was problematic. His plans blocked, Venizelos resigned one day later.

The appointment of a new government by the king brought a hardening of the division in Greek politics, the so-called National Schism (*Ethnikos Dikhasmos*). Greeks, led by Venizelos, who favored intervention in the war on the side of the *entente* bitterly opposed those, led by King Constantine, who advocated neutrality. Venizelos' victory in the parliamentary elections of June 1915 and his subsequent return to power as prime minister that August only intensified the division.

Italy's entry into the war on the side of the *entente* in May 1915 further complicated the issue of Greek intervention. The Italians sought some of the same territories in Asia Minor that Greeks considered part of their irredenta. Moreover, Greek claims to southern Albania conflicted with Italian designs to make all of Albania a protectorate. Hence, the Italians were not strong advocates of Greek intervention.

On 24 September 1915, soon after Venizelos resumed office, the Bulgarian Army mobilized against Serbia. In response, Venizelos agreed on 3 October to the landing of *entente* troops at Salonika (Thessaloníki), on condition that they not violate Greek sovereignty and not occupy Macedonia (only to turn it over to Bulgaria). British and French troops disembarked at Salonika on 5 October. That same day Venizelos again resigned – because King Constantine held him responsible for the *entente*'s occupation of northern Greece. Elections held that December, boycotted by Venizelos and his followers, returned a neutralist–royalist government to power. By this time, Serbia's defeat had brought Bulgarian and German troops to Greece's northern frontier.

The continuing *entente* presence at Salonika and its January 1916 occupation of Corfu to secure an evacuation base for the defeated Serbian

Army trekking across Albania aggravated relations with Greece. In turn, the Greek government antagonized London and Paris by refusing passage across its territory by Serbian troops retreating from the Central Powers' advance. Athens further irritated the Triple Entente when it ordered the garrison of the important border defenses at Fort Duppel north of Salonika to surrender to Bulgarian troops. Control of the fort opened up northern Greece to the Central Powers. That summer, the Bulgarians used this advantage to occupy southern and eastern Macedonia. The situation became extremely precarious as both warring alliances violated Greek neutrality.

Under these circumstances, the interventionist party decided to act. On 30 August 1916 a cabal of pro-*entente* Greek officers, with the knowledge and encouragement of Venizelos, launched a coup in Salonika. On 9 October Venizelos joined them in Salonika, where he established a separate Greek government and army. The National Schism had produced a legitimate Greek government in Athens under King Constantine, which favored a neutral course, and an alternative Greek government in Salonika led by Venizelos, which advocated joining the *entente*.

Confident of the Salonika regime's support, British and French troops landed in Athens in December 1916 to coerce the legitimist government into capitulation. These landings met strong opposition from loyal Greek army units as well as armed civilians. After taking heavy casualties, the *entente* troops had to withdraw. A French report conceded the strength of the legitimist resistance: "The balance sheet for the allies and especially for France is most humiliating."

Having failed at armed intervention, Britain and France imposed a naval blockade around legitimist Greece, which by this time consisted mainly of the Peloponnesus and southern Thessaly. At the same time, they slowly increased their occupation of Greece. With Russia slipping into civil and military disarray, the Balkan front in stalemate, and the Americans still months away from appearing in force, the *entente* was desperate to strengthen its position in southeastern Europe. On 10 June 1917 France demanded that King Constantine abdicate within twenty-four hours and prepared to occupy Athens. Confronted with overwhelming force, the king complied with the ultimatum. His second son Alexander succeeded him and immediately agreed to form a united government in Athens under Venizelos. Greece duly declared war on the Central Powers on 30 June 1917, the last European state to enter the First World War.

Conclusion

The decisions to intervene in the First World War in Bulgaria, Romania and Greece were based on the same considerations that had led these countries to participate in the Balkan Wars. All sought to realize national aspirations. The victories of the First Balkan War and the defeat of the Second Balkan War added urgency to Bulgaria's acquisition of Macedonia, but precluded an immediate entry into the war. In summer 1914 Belgrade held most of Macedonia, and Serbia was firmly ensconced on the side of the *entente*. This meant that Bulgaria, despite a tradition of Russophilia, was likely to join the Central Powers unless Britain, France, and Russia could pressure the Serbs to surrender Macedonia. The Central Powers could guarantee Bulgaria immediate possession of all of Macedonia; the *entente* could not. This brought Bulgaria into the war on the side of the Central Powers in October 1915.

For Romania, participation in the war was more problematic. Its national aspirations to Austro-Hungarian Bukovina and Transylvania as well as to Russian Bessarabia were divided between the warring powers. This permitted Bucharest a certain freedom of negotiation, but it also ensured the enmity of whichever side the Romanian government decided to act against. Acquisition of the large Romanian-populated areas of Austria-Hungary proved more attractive than the annexation of a backward corner of the Russian Empire. But by the time the Romanians finally acceded to *entente* pressures and promises, their opportunity for success had largely passed.

For Greece, the question was not which side to join, but whether to intervene on the side of the *entente*. Vulnerability to the Royal Navy precluded Greek participation on the side of the Central Powers. The issue of intervention produced a rift in Greek politics, which resulted in a division of the country into a pro-interventionist north governed from Salonika and a pro-neutral south centered on Athens. This allowed both warring alliances onto Greek soil. The political battlefield raged for almost a year, until the Anglo-French ultimatum forced King Constantine to leave the country. Under these circumstances, the Greeks were fortunate to avoid civil war.

The decisions to go to war in Bulgaria, Romania, and Greece were difficult and prolonged. Domestic differences over which side to join complicated the decisions in Bulgaria and Romania. Also, the governments in both of these countries wanted to determine the likely victor before committing themselves. In Greece the great powers, increasingly desperate to break the military stalemate, played an important role in forcing the decision to intervene. In no case, however, did the great powers force the leading politicians – Radoslavov, Brătianu, and Venizelos – to act against their inclinations. Great power pressure was significant only in determining the timing of the intervention.

CHAPTER 10

Italy

Richard Bosworth describes Italy in 1914 as "the Least of the Great Powers." Italy's allies, Austria-Hungary and Germany, paid it scant attention that July. They excluded Rome from policy discussions in the aftermath of the murder of Archduke Franz Ferdinand. Nor did they inform the Italians of the terms of the ultimatum Vienna handed Belgrade on 23 July. During the crisis, neither Austria-Hungary nor Germany treated Italy as a valued ally, and much less as a great power.

Italy's first response to the war was a declaration of neutrality on 3 August 1914. That decision was largely the work of Foreign Minister Antonio di San Giuliano. Italy at that point was the Continent's largest neutral nation. Both sides in the struggle, accordingly, competed for its support, encouraging either continued neutrality or active participation. Italy's leaders welcomed these offers and for some nine months prepared for combat and weighed the options. This period, called the *intervento*, ended with the second response, the decision to enter the war on the side of Britain and France in May 1915.

War Powers

Italy was governed according to the Sardinian constitution of 1848. Article 3 of that document declared that the legislative power was to be "exercised collectively by the King and the two Chambers, the Senate and the Chamber of Deputies." But other articles assured royal dominance. Article 5 spelled out the war powers: "The King alone has the executive power. He is the supreme head of the state, commands all the armed forces by sea and land, declares war, makes treaties of peace, of alliance." Article 7 decreed that only the monarch could "sanction and promulgate laws." And Article 65 stated tersely: "The King appoints and dismisses his Ministers." He was not obliged to follow the advice of his ministers, who were responsible to him and not to parliament.

In July 1914 the sweeping powers accorded the occupant of the Quirinale, the royal palace, rested with Vittorio Emanuele III. He was cynical and sarcastic toward his soldiers and diplomats and detested the Roman Church to the point that he ate meat on Fridays and rarely went to mass. Despite his sweeping constitutional powers, he took little part in the actual running of the government, in effect, delegating power to his ministers. In May 1915 the German ambassador asked the king directly about Italy's imminent decision. He replied: "Speak with my ministers, I am a parliamentary King like the King of England and not like the Emperor Wilhelm or the Emperor Franz Joseph. It's up to my ministers to make such decisions." Bosworth states that Vittorio Emanuele III confined his politics to "pedantry" and to "malice." A more serious problem was the king's mental state during the July crisis. Bosworth reports he "was close to a nervous breakdown with scandal-mongers ascribing his problems variously to the Queen's pregnancy, to 'neurasthenia', 'meningitis', or 'attacks of madness and similar things'."

The Decision-Makers

The king, as indicated above, for all practical purposes was "an absentee ruler" who delegated the war powers to others. "Signs of positive interventions by him into foreign affairs," Bosworth reports, "are rare." The most obvious "others" were the prime minister and the foreign minister. In March 1914 Prime Minister Giovanni Giolitti, facing serious difficulties largely over Italy's imperialist venture in Libya, gave up office for what his enemies termed a "calculated political vacation." He was replaced by Antonio Salandra, the son of a family of wealthy landowners from Troia in southern Italy. Educated as a lawyer, Salandra taught briefly at the University of Rome and in 1886 entered the Chamber of Deputies as a representative from Foggia. In 1906 and again in 1909 Salandra served as finance minister. When he became prime minister in March 1914, Salandra had limited experience in international affairs, and according to William Renzi "had demonstrated no particular talent for statecraft."

It is not surprising, therefore, that these matters fell largely to Foreign Minister San Giuliano. The scion of an old noble family from Catania in eastern Sicily, San Giuliano took a law degree and then entered the Chamber of Deputies, where he specialized in colonial and foreign affairs. After a brief career as a professional diplomat, he was called to Rome (for a second time) in 1910 to lead the Foreign Ministry. A cynical but cautious man, it would fall to him to steer Italy through the July Crisis 1914.

In addition to the king and his political advisors, there was the Italian chief of staff, General Alberto Pollio. Appointed to this office in 1908, Pollio had risen rapidly through the ranks and had tied his career closely to the General Staff. A man of impressive intellect and author of several books on military history, Pollio nevertheless was marginalized by the politicians before July 1914 simply because he was a professional soldier. He suffered a heart attack on the day Archduke Franz Ferdinand was assassinated. Misdiagnosed as a gastric ailment, Pollio was given a purgative. He died on 1 July. The selection of a successor proceeded slowly and erratically. Almost four weeks passed, this in the midst of the July Crisis, before General Luigi Cadorna was installed in his place on 27 July. The son of a prominent Piedmontese military family, Cadorna suffered from a major persecution complex, convinced that Freemasons and Jews had blocked his promotion in the past. Above all, he was enamored of his putative strategic brilliance. In 1915 he would lead Italy into war.

It should be noted that some geographic difficulties and "facts of life" added to the decision-making problems. The king avoided the political hustle of Rome and spent much of his time on his estates at Castelporziano or in Piedmont. San Giuliano spent much of his time at Fiuggi, a spa located a two-hour drive to the east of Rome. Although continuing his work, he was dying. "Sometimes," Denis Mack Smith reports, "the foreign minister complained of an inability to sleep or eat, and ambassadors found him 'too ill to work'. He had to be regularly sedated with narcotics that must have affected his judgment, and before coming into Rome for meetings with Salandra had to take counter-injections that made him highly excitable." The end came in mid-October 1914.

And what about nongovernmental groups? Business and financial leaders in July 1914 desired peace, wishing an end to the violence of "Red Week" and restoration of productivity. Giovanni Agnelli of Fiat had contracts with Britain, Russia, and Germany. Gino Olivetti of Confindustria saw war as "a monstrous phenomenon" which would lead only to the "brutal destruction of men and wealth." The captains of Italy's hydroelectric industry, heavily dependent on German and Swiss technology, and those of its southern shipping industry, which feared French economic rivalry, were not among the "hawks" in 1914.

As well, the decision-makers had little contact with any domestic groups outside of their own narrow circle. There were nationalistic pressure groups – the Italian Navy League, Dante Alighieri Society, the Geographical Society, and the Italian Colonial Institute – but they never developed into mass societies capable of shaping government policy. Some intellectuals, some middle-class professionals, bureaucrats, lawyers, and journalists favored intervention, but their efforts had no significant impact.

Antecedents

Most Italian politicians were aware of the country's status as "the Least of the Great Powers." To shore up its fragile status, Italy in May 1882 had joined Austria-Hungary and Germany to form the Triple Alliance. The alliance was defensive, designed to shield the signatories from attack by "two or more Great Powers." In February 1887 the treaty was renewed, with the important addition of a new article, which offered "reciprocal compensation for every advantage, territorial or other," that one power might garner "in the regions of the Balkans or of the Ottoman coasts and islands in the Adriatic and in the Aegean Sea." In the third treaty of the Triple Alliance of May 1891 that statement became enshrined as Article VII. It would be of great importance in July 1914. Additionally, in January 1888 the Italian and German army staffs signed a separate convention wherein Rome promised to send six army corps and three cavalry divisions to the Rhine in case of a joint war against France.

The Triple Alliance, in the words of one expert, "rested uneasily on matters stated and unstated, on myth and on reality." It settled none of the outstanding differences between Rome and Vienna – and especially not those involving the *terra irredenta*, Italy's "unredeemed lands" which were mostly in Austrian hands. First and foremost, the irredentists wished to gain Trentino-Alto Adige (the Alpine watershed northwest of Venice) and Trieste, a port city on the Adriatic.

In addition to lands in the Austro-Hungarian Empire, Italy's leaders and nationalist spokesmen showed interest in Corsica, Malta, Nice and Savoy, Montenegro, Albania, Asia Minor, and northern Africa. In the Mediterranean, Italian aspirations ran head-on into British and French interests. Rome remained suspicious of French designs in North Africa. But on 30 June 1902, two days after renewing the Triple Alliance, the Italian foreign minister, Giulio Prinetti, in a secret exchange of notes with the French ambassador to Rome, Camille Barrère, obtained agreement that Morocco would fall into the French, and Tripoli-Cyrenaica (northern Libya) into the Italian sphere of interest. Italy promised neutrality if France were attacked by one or two powers; France offered reciprocal neutrality in similar circumstances. The Prinetti-Barrère Agreement posed an obvious problem. Mack Smith refers to Italy's "simultaneous and hardly compatible relations with both of the main rival alliances in Europe." But because the agreement was secret and remained so for some years, the implications did not surface immediately.

In 1911 Italy celebrated the Cinquantennio, the fiftieth anniversary of the *risorgimento*, with a new imperialist venture. On 29 September it invaded the Ottoman provinces of Tripolitania and Cyrenaica with an expeditionary corps of 44,000 troops under General Carlo Caneva. On 9 November Prime Minister Giolitti announced the annexation of what later would be called Libya. The Chamber of Deputies gave its blessings to this action in February 1912.

But the campaign proved both lengthy and costly. The Turkish garrison withdrew inland, aided and abetted by Arab guerilla forces soon numbering 25,000 men. The Italian army, the *Regio Esercito*, still smarting from its defeat at the hands of the Ethiopian Emperor Menelik II at Adowa in March 1896, proceeded cautiously. Rome had to send out 100,000 soldiers to press its invasion. Costs swelled to double the original estimate, and by 1914 had reached about 1.7 billion lire.

In the course of this war, the Italian navy, the *Regia Marina*, seized thirteen islands of the Dodecanese, including Rhodes. This, in turn, brought a demand for compensation under Article VII of the Triple Alliance (1891) from the Austro-Hungarians – who blithely ignored the fact that they had offered Italy none after their annexation of

Bosnia-Herzegovina in 1908. Giolitti carried the day by insisting in-genuously that the islands of the eastern Aegean were Asiatic, and by assuring Kaiser Wilhelm II that the occupation was only temporary. Important for future events is that Giolitti and San Giuliano ran the war in Libya by way of direct orders to General Caneva, thus bypassing the chief of the General Staff, Pollio, as well as the king's chief aide, General Ugo Brusati.

Italy avoided censure by two of the major powers for its Libyan ven-ture by hurriedly renewing the Triple Alliance on 5 December 1912 – eighteen months ahead of schedule and for a period of fourteen years. German-Italian military discussions began that same month during which General Pollio promised Helmuth von Moltke, the chief of the German General Staff, that "as soon as the *casus foederis* was estab-lished, Italy would mobilize all her forces and would take the offensive in the French Alps without delay." He also offered that Italian troops would be landed in the south of France. In addition, the Italian Navy would engage in joint action to block any movement of French rein-forcements from North Africa.

In January 1913 the German quartermaster-general, Alfred von Waldersee, visited Rome and Vienna to discuss matters. Pollio re-viewed Italy's troop commitments: five corps for the Alps and another five for "a possible landing" in southern France. And he "promised to make a full army available for service on the Rhine, after he got the approval of the king and the political leaders."

A steady exchange of information and mutual visitations to firm up and detail their arrangements continued through to the sum-mer of 1914. Italy's military leaders reiterated their commitments for the Rhine, in March 1914 agreeing that the Third Army would be present and would serve under direct German command. In April Italian, German, and Austrian general staff railroad specialists met to plan the movement of three Italian army corps through Habsburg territory.

Italy's military leaders provided strong assurances of their good faith. In 1913 King Vittorio Emanuele III attended the Kiel Regatta, Germany's premiere sailing event. Pollio, Moltke, and Franz Conrad von Hötzendorf, the Habsburg chief of staff, attended the German maneuvers in Silesia and again reviewed their arrangements. The Germans' key concern was that Italy tie down French forces. An energetic engagement by the Italians, Moltke thought, would mean almost certain success for their operation.

Germany's leaders based their optimism in the first months of 1914 on these assurances and promises. But a serious problem appeared in this connection: Italy's governance was characterized by a very "dysfunctional" compartmentalization, by an unwillingness to share information or even to inquire about the plans and operations of related departments. Italy's Foreign Ministry, for example, did not inform the nation's generals and admirals of the terms of the Triple Alliance. John Gooch writes that following renewal of the Triple Alliance, Pollio, in "accordance with Italian practice . . . was kept entirely in the dark about it and had no idea whether it contained any undertaking to support Austria-Hungary." Thus, late in July 1914, while political leaders were planning neutrality, the chief of the General Staff worked to meet Italy's "obligations under the Triple Alliance," specifically, planning the attack on France. No politicians had "consulted him, and no one disabused him."

One reason for this extreme compartmentalization was that civilian leaders were "repeatedly and scathingly dismissive of the army." Giolitti declared, in May 1915, that "the generals are worth little; they came out of the ranks at a time when families sent their most stupid sons into the army because they did not know what to do with them." The nation's army and naval officers simply were not part of the inner power circle. Chief of the General Staff Pollio was forbidden to communicate directly with cabinet members – because he was a subordinate of the minister of war. Military leaders in Berlin and Vienna were not aware of that compartmentalization. They believed that, like them, their Italian counterparts played an integral role in their nation's policy-making.

In the final prewar flurry of agreements with Berlin and Vienna, both King Vittorio Emanuele III and General Pollio again and again promised to transport at least three army corps to the Rhine in case of war. Further, Pollio assured the Germans that his troops would deploy in Alsace within four weeks of mobilization – under German command. At Vienna, he secured agreement to send them to the Rhine by rail via Austria. He also discussed with Conrad von Hötzendorf the possible use of Italian troops against Russia and Serbia! That the Austro-Hungarian railway system could never have handled these extra burdens apparently escaped both Pollio and Hötzendorf.

Despite all the official declarations of Triple Alliance solidarity, the arrangement, as of 1914, was more an appearance than a binding reality. For most Italian irredentists, Austria-Hungary remained the archenemy. The previous war minister, Paolo Spingardi, could hardly be accused of hyperbole when in 1911 he depicted Italo-Austrian relations as "insecure" and as susceptible to "conflict" following a single "spark."

The July Crisis: The Neutrality Decision

The "one spark" that War Minister Spingardi had feared turned out to be the assassination of Franz Ferdinand, an Italophobe. It caught Italy in the throes of the "Red Week" of June 1914. Peasant *jacqueries* broke out in Emilia and the Romagna. Shops were looted, churches assaulted, villas sacked, railroad tracks dug up, telephone poles torn down. Barricades were raised at Rome and elsewhere. Numerous towns witnessed protests against military service; some proclaimed themselves independent communes. Red flags flew from a number of city halls. Benito Mussolini, editor of the Milan socialist newspaper *Avanti!*, reveled in the violence. Landowners responded by forming mobile squads of "volunteers" for the "defense of order." Eventually, the government called out ten thousand conscripts to restore order.

News of the Sarajevo murder reached Rome on the afternoon of 28 June. The nation's leaders expressed outrage and ordered appropriate memorial ceremonies. But otherwise, there was an unmistakable sense of relief: a dangerous leader had been removed. The Italian General Staff was immobilized by news of Pollio's heart attack. Parliament began its normal summer recess on 5 July and was not recalled until December.

Italy's notorious compartmentalization problem meant that the new chief of staff, General Cadorna, was uninformed about the "larger political issues" facing the nation. On the day of his installation, 27 July, he assured the German military attaché that he would carry out all of the staff arrangements made by Pollio. In fact, Cadorna offered more than words. He ordered the four army corps on the French border to recall their effectives, cancelled all leaves and furloughs, reprovisioned storehouses, dispatched fortress artillery to the Mediterranean Alps, and brought the three army corps destined for the Rhine up to full strength.

Lamentably, Cadorna knew little of the realities of the army's readiness for a major war. Of Italy's 345,000 soldiers, about 60,000 remained in Libya as did also tons of ammunition, clothing, foodstuffs, and modern artillery. In March 1914 Pollio had warned the government about a severe shortage of 27,000 officers and noncommissioned officers and 200,000 sets of uniforms. Ten of Italy's 36 regiments of field artillery existed on paper only. In June 1914 Prime Minister Salandra, no champion of the *Regio Esercito*, learned that full equipment was available for only 730,000 of the 1,260,000 men of the fully mobilized army. There was no possibility of an immediate involvement.

The Italian Navy viewed the July crisis even more pessimistically. On 1 August 1914 Vice Admiral Paolo Thaon di Revel, the naval chief of General Staff, warned the government that the British and French had a 14 percent advantage over the naval forces of the Triple Alliance, rising to 26 percent when two new French dreadnoughts entered service in the next few months. The Capo di Stato Maggiore feared that the *Regia Marina* could not protect either Italy's coastal cities or the country's rail lines that ran along the coastlines and were thus vulnerable to naval bombardment.

Italy also faced a virtually insurmountable economic problem. Britain in 1913 supplied 90 percent of Italy's annual imports of about 10.8 million tons of coal. Loss of that coal would paralyze Italian industry, because domestic mines (mainly on Elba) produced a mere 701,079 tons of mostly low-grade coal that same year. While Germany in 1913 mined 220 million tons of coal, most of that would be used at home or, in case of war, exported to Austria-Hungary. The German railway system, moreover, would be taxed fully during mobilization and the Alps would be a major impediment to large-scale transfers of coal to Italy. In short, there existed a deep chasm between Triple Alliance planning and Italian military and economic realities.

Italy's naval situation in the Mediterranean, however, was not entirely hopeless. In July 1914 it had available three modern dreadnoughts; another would be ready in April 1915 and two more in May 1915 and March 1916. Austria-Hungary had two new dreadnoughts in service, with a third recently commissioned and a fourth to be completed in November 1915. The German Mediterranean Squadron consisted of the new battle cruiser *Goeben* and the light cruiser *Breslau*. According to the naval convention of June 1913, in case of war this force of potentially five capital ships was to be placed under the command of the Austrian Admiral Anton Haus. Its primary mission would be to prevent French troops in North Africa from reaching metropolitan France. By contrast, the British had but three battle cruisers and the French a mere two dreadnoughts in the

Mediterranean. But that comparison of forces represents a "best case" scenario. "The realities of the Austro-Italian antagonism," Paul Halpern notes, "remained and both navies realized that they were just as likely to be at war with each other instead of allies and planned accordingly."

The immediate decision facing Italy's government, whether to join with the Alliance or to remain neutral, was made in part by Prime Minister Salandra and mainly by Foreign Minister San Giuliano. The latter argued that Italy should prepare militarily and await developments. In the meantime, his course was one of "courageous serenity." Already in failing health, San Giuliano retreated to Fiuggi to work out the details of Italy's response. There he shared the waters with the chatty German ambassador, Hans von Flotow. From the latter, San Giuliano learned by 16 July that Vienna was prepared to use force against Serbia; the next day that Austria-Hungary, supported by Germany, was preparing an ultimatum with conditions unacceptable to Serbia.

San Giuliano was moved by several considerations. He was well aware of Italy's military weakness and of the vulnerability of vital coal imports. He also knew that the harvest, expected to be 10 percent below average, was not yet complete. He feared that the riots of "Red Week" might well flare up again. As well, he had learned from Flotow's indiscretions and Italian intelligence that Germany intended fully to back whatever play its Viennese ally planned for the Serbs. For the moment, he chose to avoid direct contact with the Austro-Hungarians for fear of jeopardizing Italy's chance for compensation under Article VII of the Triple Alliance. The hope for territorial compensation dominated Salandra's thoughts. Thus, he appealed to Berlin to pressure Vienna to offer the Trentino, Valona, or southern Albania as "compensation."

Germany had no problems with offering Italy extensive concessions in the Austrian border regions. Between 15 and 30 July, various leaders in Berlin – Chancellor Theobald von Bethmann Hollweg, Foreign Secretary Gottlieb von Jagow, and Chief of the General Staff von Moltke – urged Vienna to secure Italian military support by way of compensations. But Vienna stood firm, refusing, in the words of Kaiser Franz Joseph, to allow itself to be "pulled to pieces like an artichoke."

Vienna delivered its ultimatum to Serbia at 6 p.m. on 23 July. Two hours earlier, the Austro-Hungarian chargé d'affaires in Rome drove to Fiuggi and presented "a communication" to San Giuliano. It told of the ultimatum, of "a certain number of requests," and the 48-hour time limit but gave no details about the contents. Shortly before noon the next day, the chargé presented the specific demands to the Foreign Ministry in Rome – even though he knew San Giuliano was in Fiuggi where Salandra had joined him. The information was immediately telephoned to them but by then the Stefani News Agency had published the document!

The two men discussed matters for several hours. San Giuliano judged Vienna's actions to be aggressive. Rome had not been consulted beforehand as stipulated in the Triple Alliance treaty and therefore the *casus foederis* did not exist. But the two agreed that if Vienna provided "suitable compensation," Italy might still join its allies. Telegrams reporting their position went to Italy's ambassadors in Berlin and Vienna allowing them to open discussions.

Three days later, on 26 July, San Giuliano laid out his policy to Prime Minister Salandra: "No immediate decisions are required, indeed they would be extremely dangerous. We must for the moment leave everyone, at home and abroad, in doubt as to our attitude and our decisions, and in this way try to obtain some positive advantage." The foreign minister advised the government to work in silence, to be deliberate, and to remain away from Rome as much as possible.

Austria-Hungary declared war on Serbia on 28 July 1914. Vittorio Emanuele III returned to Rome that day, but left again the next morning as if to signal that nothing of importance was about to transpire. On 29 July General Cadorna, kept in the dark by San Giuliano concerning the state of diplomatic affairs, requested permission from the king to dispatch the Third Army to the Rhine. The Italian Navy, meanwhile, made plans to rendezvous with Austro-Hungarian and German naval units off Medina, Sicily.

At this point, Salandra and San Giuliano instituted a new governing arrangement, one that might be described as cabinet government. Despite the evident crisis, compartmentalization still prevailed, which meant "no serious discussion of foreign affairs." The Cabinet met again, at 10 a.m. on 31 July, to consider the pressing question.

San Giuliano reviewed the situation. He "stressed that Italian public opinion opposed war, and that in no event could Italy participate in a conflict against Britain." He concluded: "Fortunately, the casus foederis of the alliance does not exist. Neither the letter nor the spirit of the Triple Alliance obliges us in this instance to aid Germany and Austria." William Renzi's laconic summary is that the Cabinet "in effect agreed that neutrality was the only possible policy." That decision was tentative, he adds, because the king, still away from Rome, had yet to approve it.

A flurry of communication followed – by Italy's leaders, by the Alliance powers, and by some *entente* leaders seeking a clear and prompt declaration. The Cabinet met again the next morning, 1 August. A majority favored an immediate declaration but one member successfully argued for postponement. The ministers approved some military preparations – so that the "declaration of neutrality does not appear to be the result of weakness." On Sunday, 2 August, the king returned to Rome and "immediately approved" a declaration of neutrality. The Cabinet ratified the declaration, thus making Italy, for the moment, a neutral nation. The text was made public the next day.

Leaders in Berlin and Vienna were outraged. Kaiser Wilhelm II fumed that the Reich's allies were falling away "like rotten apples" even before the war had begun. General von Moltke spoke of revenge for "Italy's felony." "May God now grant us victory," he wrote his counterpart in Vienna, "so that later you can settle accounts with these scoundrels." Conrad von Hötzendorf blamed the situation on his Foreign Ministry's failure in the past to deal with the "snake" Italy. "Our future lies in the Balkans; our barrier is Italy; we must finally settle accounts with Italy."

Italy's decision for neutrality appears to have been popular with the nation's citizens. "There can be no doubt," Renzi writes, "that the great majority favored a pacific policy." Italy's peasants and farm laborers, who constituted the vast bulk of the army and who would suffer most casualties, were reported strongly opposed to fighting. The Revolutionary Socialists issued strong antiwar pronouncements. The secretary of the American embassy wrote that "the entire press of Italy" desired only continued peace.

Several days after the decision for neutrality, San Giuliano mused over his options. In an ideal world, Austria-Hungary would be beaten in the Adriatic and surrender Trieste; France would be beaten on land and surrender Savoy or Nice or Corsica or Tunis to Italy. San Giuliano died of severe gout in Rome on 16 October 1914.

The *Intervento*

San Giuliano had charted a "policy of temporization," a "wait-and-see" policy. Unlike the five major powers, where the decisions for war were taken in at best several weeks or at worst in a few days, Italy's leaders had much time for thought, negotiation, and their "considered judgment." Known as the *intervento*, this period is filled with activity, basically to encourage a decision either for continued neutrality or for participation on one side or the other.

For the first seven or eight months of the war, Italy set out to upgrade the military, to plan an intervention, and to solicit and negotiate terms from both contenders. Intervention, of course, was not the only option to be considered. Continued neutrality was also a negotiable offering, one that would be virtually costless. But the rewards for intervention would be considerably greater.

The negotiation of terms required a sense that Italy represented a plausible threat, that it could make a difference in the military outcome. But faced with continuing difficulties in Libya, Italy's "weight" was not clear and obvious. A persistent problem was that the leaders of the major powers did not view Italy as a significant force. The recent domestic disturbances also entered into the considerations of those potential allies. General mobilization could bring renewed insurgency requiring use of troops in Italian cities.

On the death of San Giuliano, Salandra temporarily took over the direction of Italy's foreign affairs. He quickly made a serious error, using an unfortunate expression to justify his policies – *sacro egoismo*. It would be used against Italy for some time thereafter. Overwhelmed by the tasks, Salandra chose Sidney Sonnino as his new foreign minister. Sonnino was from a wealthy Tuscan family, born in Pisa of a "Jewish–Italian" father and Scottish mother, both of whom were Protestants. He was "handicapped by inflexibility and intellectual intolerance," a serious failing when combined with limited experience in foreign affairs. Recognizing that Italy could make no move before the spring, Sonnino, within days of taking office, pursued negotiations with London, Berlin, and Vienna, which would last for the next six months.

The negotiations had a peculiar asymmetrical character. High on the agenda of wished-for territories were the Trentino and Trieste. But the Dual Monarchy went to war to stem the losses experienced over previous decades and thus was reluctant to give more. Germany urged concessions, seeing them as a small price to avoid Italian hostility and the opening of another front. A linked consideration was the possible involvement of Romania, seeking to gain its *irredenta*, lands that were also in Austro-Hungarian hands.

Germany's chancellor, Bethmann Hollweg, from the beginning resented the "pride, stubbornness, and stupidity, as if sent by the gods" with which Vienna refused "the necessary territorial concessions" to Rome and Bucharest. He failed to see that Italian ambitions went far beyond those modest properties to include the Alto Adige (German-speaking Süd-Tirol), the Isonzo frontier, Istria, the Dalmatian coast, Albania, the Dodecanese, and a share of the Turkish Empire.

On 11 December 1914 Count Leopold Berchtold, the Austrian foreign minister, told Giuseppe d'Avarna, the Italian ambassador, that Vienna was "entirely unwilling" to discuss any compensation under Article VII. In mid-December Prince Bernhard von Bülow, the former German chancellor, arrived in Rome as ambassador. He spoke fluent Italian and had an Italian wife, the stepdaughter of a former premier. He put forth suggestions that Austria might yield the Trentino in exchange for Italy's neutrality. But there could be no yielding on Trieste; the Dual Monarchy's only major port was its indispensable "lung."

Bülow provided lavish entertainment in his private residence, the Villa Malta, to win over Rome's "social aristocracy." Through intermediaries, he was in "fairly regular" communication with Giolitti. The German government awarded contracts to firms that favored neutrality, such as the influential Banca Commerciale. The services of Matthias Erzberger, a prominent Catholic politician and head of the Center Party, were enlisted. He was sent five million lire that were used to bribe deputies and some neutralists within the Cabinet. Some of that money came into the Vatican. A Bavarian priest, Rudolf Gerlach, serving as the pope's private secretary, was a very active "agent in German pay." All of these efforts, however, were to no avail.

The *entente* effort was even more extensive. The prominent socialist Mussolini, editor of *Avanti!*, abandoned party, newspaper, and neutralism, and in mid-November brought out a new publication, *Il Popolo d'Italia*. This appears to have been financed in part by two Italian industrial groups, Fiat and Ansaldo, and by French government and private sources. In February 1916 the director of the French Bureau de la Presse in Rome, a propaganda agency that sought to influence Italian publications, reported that Mussolini was "completely in our hands" and that he had "rendered us great service in the spring of 1915."

Behind the public light, on 21 December Cadorna completed his plan for an attack on Austria-Hungary. It would, on paper at least, bring Italian troops into the heart of Slovenia within 45 days, this in preparation for a drive on Vienna. But at a Cabinet meeting in late January 1915, the War Ministry declared that the army could not move before mid-April.

The pace of the war forced Italy's hand. Toward the end of February, Sonnino learned of the likely Allied move on the Dardanelles. Italy's negotiating position would be considerably enhanced by an early declaration; joining after the anticipated easy victory over the Ottomans would be of negligible value. On 4 March Guglielmo Imperiali, the Italian ambassador to Britain, opened discussions with Sir Edward Grey, presenting his country's territorial demands. Grey thought that Italy's entry "probably would, in a comparatively short time, effect the collapse of German and Austro-Hungarian resistance." It would be, he said, "the turning-point of the war."

Recognizing the changed situation, Austria now shifted position and offered to concede the entire Trentino. It was too little, too late. On 26 April representatives of Britain, Italy, Russia, and France signed the Pact of London. The terms were simple: Italy would enter the war on the *entente* side by 26 May in exchange for a generous promise of territories plus a loan of £50 million. The Austrians asked for further negotiations. But by then, Sonnino felt he could not again shift course.

By signing the London Pact, Italy's leaders were, in effect, giving a promissory note. Fulfilling that promise brought a major political crisis. The Triple Alliance had to be renounced, and the commitment for Italy's entry into the war had to be made public and justified. This posed an obvious problem since most Italians still approved the current policy of neutrality.

In mid-April Salandra decided to sound out "the state of public opinion" in the event of Italy's intervention. The vast majority of prefect reports indicated strong neutralist sentiment. One historian concludes that when the king, Salandra, and Sonnino authorized the signature of the Pact of London, there could have been no doubt in their minds that the overwhelming majority of Italians "would have stayed Imperiali's hand [the actual signer] had a plebiscite been held on the issue of war or peace." Another adds an important further observation: The prefect reports "give a general impression of a country with little desire to go to war but unlikely to offer active opposition."

Pro-war sentiment now became more overt. Mass meetings, demonstrations, and riots occurred at several universities. In Florence, Bologna, Genoa, and other cities, brawls between rival factions brought bloodshed and thousands of arrests. Leading neutralists were threatened. Austrian consulates were attacked. Mussolini urged people to occupy the streets and remain there to impose their will on the monarchy. His slogans: "War or revolution" and "War on the frontier or war at home."

Gabriele D'Annunzio, poet and demagogue, returned from his "exile" in France on 12 May to be welcomed by a massive crowd of nearly 100,000 in Rome. "For three days a stink of treason has been suffocating us," he shouted at the crowd, "Romans, sweep away all the filth, chuck all the garbage back into the sewer." The next day he declared: "If it is a crime to incite citizens to violence, I shall boast of this crime.... Form platoons, form citizens' patrols." A thousand students, led by professors, tried to storm the parliament building and then searched the streets "for friends of Giolitti to assault." Troops were called out to protect persons and property. The demagogues quickly termed these *le radiose giornate* – "the Radiant Days" – pointing to these events as evidence of "massive" support for intervention.

The Cabinet met again on 17 and 18 May and approved a measure for submission to the Parliament that would vest "full financial powers in the government in the event of war." On 20 May in two secret ballots Parliament backed the government, giving it overwhelming majorities. In the second, the decisive ballot, the vote was 407 to 74, most of the latter from Revolutionary Socialists. The body was recessed *sine die* "amidst the singing of the Garibaldi Hymn and a final outburst of enthusiasm for war." The next day the Senate gave the measure unanimous approval. Salandra and Sonnino were given ovations.

Mack Smith suggests that intimidation was one factor accounting for the conversion. Some deputies and senators, he feels, "were simply afraid of being attacked by the mob." Some were moved by concern for government patronage. Some were worried about the monarchy, a negative vote being seen as a challenge to the king. Perhaps for this reason, Giolitti instructed his followers to "save the honour of the country by putting up no opposition" to the intervention.

Mobilization was ordered on 22 May. Austria-Hungary was sent an ultimatum the next day. And on 24 May Italy was at war. With time, much more than Cadorna had anticipated, Italy assembled 35 divisions, some 400,000 men, along the Austrian border, the most difficult front in Europe. By the end of the year, four Italian offensives had been blunted.

Article 2 of the London Pact required Italy's "pursuit of the war jointly with France, Great Britain, and Russia against all of their enemies." But in May 1915 Italy declared war against and fought only Austria-Hungary. Italy declared war on the Ottomans in August and on Bulgaria in October. The Allies insistently reminded Italy's leaders of a further obligation but, despite much urging, Rome did not declare war against Germany until 28 August 1916, fifteen months later.

Conclusion

The Italian "case" differs from the experience of the five major European powers in that the process of decision was spread over nine months. And in sharp contrast to the experience of those five, where time did not allow it, in Italy much attention was given to discovering the attitudes of "the public" and developing some kind of response. The purpose of that effort, however, was not to respond to popular sentiment but rather to thwart the will of "the masses." As Renzi puts it, a "small minority of essentially conservative leaders had superimposed their will over that of the nation as a whole."

The process has implications for several of the theories reviewed in Chapter 1, specifically for those assuming some kind of "bottom up" influence. It simply did not work that way. The two key proponents, the men who more than any others brought Italy to war, were Salandra and Sonnino. Their efforts did require the consent of Vittorio Emanuele III, clearly a willing collaborator. The instigators of the "Radiant Days," the nationalist demagogues, played an important role as did also the press. "Without the newspapers," Salandra wrote later, "Italy's intervention would perhaps have been impossible." Especially important was *Corriere della Sera*, Italy's most influential newspaper, and its editor, Luigi Albertini. The support for intervention generated by this newspaper would be exerted by upper- and upper-middle class readers, certainly not by "the masses."

One might assume that a determined coterie would plan and coordinate policies with great care, and that some evident rationality would govern or guide their judgments. But both assumptions are unwarranted read-ins, that is, insistent, unfounded inferences. In fact, the king's "withdrawal" from politics put the "war powers" into the hands of the two key civilian ministers who then made the basic decision. One would assume that those ministers would work closely with the two key military leaders, carefully coordinating policies and timing. But that too was not the case.

Gooch reports that "Cadorna did not explain his strategic presuppositions to the politicians and they never bothered to explore them." He provides some clues to account for the decision-making pathologies:

> Cadorna's amazing strategic vision of a march on Vienna, and his complete disregard of the realities of trench warfare, were the product of a unique personality in a position of unquestioned and unquestionable authority.... The Italian general staff, unlike its German counterpart, was a small bureaucratic secretariat whose skills and training were narrowly functional....

Ahead lay numerous further futile engagements in the "howling wilderness" of stone that was the Isonzo River valley. And that was followed by Caporetto.

CHAPTER 11

The United States

In April 1917 the United States entered World War I on the side of the Allies. The decision-making process and the grounds for entry were very different from those reviewed in previous chapters. There has been, understandably, much contention about the causes and significance of this action. Most contenders have been Americans – historians, journalists, popular writers, and, occasionally, politicians. The contention was most intense, curiously, in the 1930s, as Americans again saw the breakdown of international order and the approach of another major war. Since that time, the argument has largely subsided and has usually involved only a few historians.

Evaluation has been one central concern in these discussions – whether intervention was a good or a bad thing? Did it bode well or ill for the future of the United States and the world? Many of these accounts made worthwhile contributions to our knowledge of the event, although many were highly colored with emotion and value judgments. A frequent element in those discussions was denigration of the role of individual actors. Partisans on both sides of the debate over the wisdom and morality of intervention have argued instead that some "great forces" of history – geopolitics, economics, and/or culture – largely determined what happened. With rare exceptions, these interpreters viewed individual decision-makers as witting or unwitting, honest or devious agents of great forces.

In the 1930s, when "revisionists" deplored intervention as wrong, President Woodrow Wilson was portrayed as either deluded or dishonest in his two-and-a-half-year effort to maintain neutrality and in his

subsequent justification of intervention. In their view, this son of an
English-born mother, admittedly a cultural Anglophile and an admirer
of British parliamentarism, could never have been anything but pro-
Allied at heart. As the historical detectives of that decade delighted
in discovering, his closest advisors, Colonel Edward M. House and
Secretary of State Robert Lansing, were covertly pro-Allied, while his
ambassador in London, Walter Hines Page, wrote weekly screeds ad-
monishing the president to side with Britain and the Allies. To these
interpreters, the pursuit of neutrality between 1914 and 1917 was either a charade to hoodwink an anxious public or a holding action until
the Allies' impending financial collapse required dropping the mask of
nonbelligerence.

If Wilson looked like a knave to the "revisionists," he looked like a
fool to their "realist" successors. To such critics as Walter Lippmann
and George F. Kennan, the fault in American policy lay in not joining
the Allied side sooner. To them, Wilson's belligerent critics, led by
Theodore Roosevelt and Henry Cabot Lodge, correctly recognized
America's strategic interest in an Allied victory and wanted to do
whatever they could to assure that outcome to the war. Even when the
president did the right thing by their lights, they saw him as acting per-
ilously late, when the Allies were teetering on the brink of disaster, and
having the wrong justifications. Rather than acknowledge the nation's
vital interest in an Allied victory and form a strategic alliance, Wilson
foolishly beclouded the issue with idealistic rhetoric about democracy, a nonpunitive peace, and international reforms to prevent future
wars.

Whatever the merits of either case, it is clear that the American system of government gave primary, at times exclusive, responsibility for
the response to the European war to a single person, President Wilson.
In 1923 Winston Churchill gave high praise for Wilson's unique contribution in directing "the fate of nations." A half century later, Lord
Devlin, Churchill's countryman, published a massive book examining
and supporting that judgment. In the meantime, in the United States
Wilson's greatest biographer and editor of the monumental edition of
his papers, Arthur S. Link, had been advancing similar arguments.

Still, the question remains: how could something so momentous for
the United States and the world depend on the thoughts and actions
of a single individual? Plainly, great influences had to have some impact, particularly in framing the choices before decision-makers. And
other people, obviously, had to be involved – some as advisors and

critics, multitudes of others as voters who put leaders in office and as followers who supported or opposed the decisions that were made. Indeed, under the American Constitution only Congress can declare war, which meant that several hundred elected officials had to approve the president's decision. Yet, when all such allowances are taken into account and all such background influences are noted, Wilson remains at the center, directing the nation's response.

Like nearly every American president of that era and later, Wilson was a foreign policy neophyte. Just after his election in 1912 he had remarked to a friend, "It would be an irony of fate if my administration had to deal with foreign problems, for all my preparation has been in domestic matters." But that statement, a comment on the nature of the recent campaign, is misleading. Wilson biographer Thomas J. Knock indicates that Wilson had been "a commentator on foreign policy since the 1890s... [and that] From the intellectual standpoint, the body of Wilson's written work in the fields of comparative government, contemporary history, and international law constituted a preparation unrivaled by any incoming president since John Quincy Adams."

That "irony of fate" came early in Wilson's presidency in the protracted and painful dealings with the revolution in Mexico. By and large, however, he had been able to concentrate on domestic affairs in his first year and a half in office during which he produced an impressive record of legislative accomplishment. A mundane reason accounted for Wilson's dominant role during the first year and a quarter of the war. Congress was out of session for all but three months between August 1914 and the end of 1915. The war broke out just as a marathon session devoted to domestic reform was adjourning before the off-year elections in November 1914. The three-month "lame duck" session between December 1914 and March 1915 predictably did little. While Wilson unsuccessfully tried to buy interned German ships, German-Americans attempted to embargo arms and munitions sales to the Allies. Thereafter, until the next Congress, elected in 1914, convened in December 1915, Wilson acted largely on his own.

Wilson sought advice from his principal advisors and delegated a great deal of authority. He did consult, with his Cabinet and others, but he decided. Biographer Knock describes his "method" as follows:

> He approached the administration of foreign affairs, like most other things, with unshakable certitude.... Wilson the diplomatist made all final decisions himself, routinely composed important diplomatic notes

on his own typewriter, and, in many instances, conducted diplomacy without informing the State Department of his actions. With the possible exception of Franklin D. Roosevelt, no other president in American history exerted more personal control over foreign policy.

The other person most directly involved in shaping American foreign policy was the secretary of state. Three-time Democratic presidential nominee William Jennings Bryan possessed an independent power base and felt free to weigh in with advice and take initiatives of his own. Some commentators have depicted Bryan as an inexperienced, inept, and woolly-headed diplomatist. But John M. Cooper reports that Wilson "formed a harmonious, productive relationship" with Bryan, one based on "almost daily meetings and consultation and mutual respect." They developed a division of labor with Bryan managing "most Latin American matters, except Mexico." He also "promoted schemes for peace and arbitration." Knock, somewhat less positive, reports that Wilson "regarded the Nebraskan's fundamentalism as naïve and his thought process as unsophisticated; he doubted Bryan's skill as a diplomatist. . . . " But, despite those reservations, until he resigned in June 1915, "no one exerted a stronger influence on Wilson's foreign policy."

Despite differences in temperament and background, Arthur Link writes that Wilson and Bryan shared

> certain assumptions and ideals. . . . They were both dedicated to the democratic ideal, at least theoretically, and obsessed with the concept of America's mission in the world. . . . They were both fundamentally missionaries, evangelists, confident that they comprehended the peace and well-being of other countries better than the leaders of those countries themselves.

Bryan "served as the major link between the administration and the American peace movement, then in the prime of its life." He also "championed arbitration and conciliation with particular effectiveness and therein," Knock points out, he "contributed one of the main components of Wilson's program."

The president had two other advisors in foreign affairs. One was Lansing, an experienced international lawyer then serving as the second-ranking officer in the State Department with the title of "counselor." The other was Colonel House, a wealthy Texan who held no office but enjoyed a close personal friendship with Wilson. Cooper sees both men as, to the say the least, problematic. He describes

Lansing as "the worst appointment Wilson ever made" and House as showing a "characteristic deviousness." Both from time to time proceeded independently of Wilson, both on occasion undermined his policies. Neither Secretary of War Lindley M. Garrison (and later Newton D. Baker) nor Secretary of the Navy Josephus Daniels played a major role in the decision for or against intervention in the war. They, unlike their European dynastic counterparts, were civilians with little or no military experience. Nor did Wilson consult the two service chiefs – Admiral William S. Benson and General Hugh L. Scott.

The American ambassadors in the major belligerent capitals were a mixed lot. The envoys in Paris and Berlin, William C. Sharp and James W. Gerard, were financial contributors to the Democratic Party who were not expected to do much more than convey messages back and forth. The envoy in London, Walter Hines Page, was a former magazine editor and an old friend and political backer of Wilson's, but he had become an ardent admirer of the British before the war and soon became a shrill, uncritical partisan of the Allies.

In many ways, the United States was unique among the great powers of 1914. It was, and always had been, a republic. It was the world's oldest continuous democracy. Its lawmakers had a powerful fear of monarchs and distrust of military leaders. It was a "melting pot" that had absorbed many of the Old World's disgruntled minorities. It had waged a bloody Civil War to preserve the Union. It had fought only two wars with major foreign powers – Britain in 1812 and Spain in 1898. Indeed, the parallel to 1812 was constantly on the president's mind. In the fall of 1914 Wilson, who was an historian, told his confidant, Colonel House, "Madison [James Madison, president during the War of 1812] and I are the only two Princeton men that have become President. The circumstances of the war 1812 and now run parallel. I sincerely hope they will not go further."

Of the great powers that eventually joined in World War I, the United States was the only one with a written constitution that assigned the "war powers" to an elected legislature. Article I, Section 8 of the Constitution stated: "The Congress shall have Power . . . To declare War, grant letters of Marque and Reprisal, and make Rules concerning Captures on Land and Water." Any declaration of war therefore required majority assent of both the House of Representatives and the Senate. Acting in accordance with that provision of the Constitution, on 2 April 1917 Wilson asked Congress for a formal

declaration of war against Germany. Four days later the House and
Senate granted that request.

The "Great Forces"

One obstacle to American involvement in World War I was the tradition
of noninvolvement in power politics outside the Western Hemisphere,
a policy first formulated in George Washington's warning to "steer
clear of permanent alliances" and then in Thomas Jefferson's call to
avoid "entangling alliances." Even Roosevelt and Lodge, who wanted
to abandon isolation and plunge the United States into the great power
game, did not directly challenge this tradition. An apparent exception,
the recent Spanish-American War, was seen as consonant with this
tradition; that conflict removed another of the troublesome European
powers from the hemisphere. Threats of involvement in the current
struggle, it was thought, would revive and strengthen those isolationist
sentiments.

   Among the "great forces" that presumably favored American entry
into World War I was the Anglo-Saxon common "culture." Traditional
Anglophobia had gradually eroded since its last major flare-up during
the Civil War and in its place a sentimental Anglophilia developed,
this based on a common language and shared literary heritage. The
attitude was prevalent among social and cultural elites, most of whom
traced their ancestry back to England, Scotland, and Wales. Later, the
children of wealthy American families occasionally intermarried with
the British aristocracy. Churchill, first lord of the Admiralty in 1914,
had an American mother, while his cousin, the Duke of Marlborough,
had married the heiress Consuelo Vanderbilt. On an immediate and
popular level, the German "rape of Belgium" in 1914, exaggerated
by clever British propaganda, made the Allies and especially Britain
stand in American eyes as defenders of freedom and civilization against
autocracy and barbarism.

   But the diffuse Anglophilia among elites gave rise to scant interventionist sentiment. As well as public opinion can be gauged, popular
anti-German sentiment over Belgium was neither so widespread nor
so strongly felt as later interpreters imagined. According to a nation-
wide poll of newspaper editors conducted in the fall of 1914 by the
magazine *Literary Digest*, about half declared themselves impartial between the belligerent camps; the proportion rose to three-quarters in

the Midwest and West. Nor should pro-Allied attitudes be confused with interventionist sentiment. In April 1915 the British ambassador in Washington reported, "It is, I think, useless and misleading to depend on these people for help or practical sympathy. . . ." Later, in 1916, even detached pro-Allied attitudes waned in reaction to such high-handed British practices as stopping and opening the mails and blacklisting American businesses and, even more, out of revulsion toward British brutality in Ireland. For the British and, by extension, the Allies, Ireland besmirched their moral standing in American eyes the way Belgium had done earlier for the Germans. When the United States finally did enter the war in 1917, the newspapers' "plague-o'-both-your-houses" dismissals of the belligerents were more frequent than at any time since the outbreak of the war.

Two sizable ethnic groups were opposed to intervention, especially to a move in support of the Allies. The largest, wealthiest, and best organized of these had family and cultural ties to Germany. Hardworking, disciplined, often highly educated, the 8 million German-Americans attracted both admiration and envy as what a later generation would call a "model minority." Many members of another potent, though not so well organized ethnic group, some 4 million Irish-Americans, held an ancient grudge against Britain, an attitude that received powerful reinforcement with the suppression of the Easter Rising in 1916.

Thanks to British control of the seas, American contacts and relations with the belligerents during the first six months of the war were largely with the Allies, mostly with Britain. The Allied blockade of Germany and Austria-Hungary and neighboring neutral nations wrought hardship in sensitive export sectors of the American economy, particularly cotton. Inasmuch as Wilson's was a Democratic administration whose strongest political base lay in the South, anti-British political pressures there could be particularly potent.

Pressure groups were formed, some favoring "preparedness," some favoring "peace." For the former, the basic question was the condition, or readiness, of the army and navy. Both sides had the support of dozens of eminent persons. In December 1915 a group favoring intervention was formed but, until March 1917, Link reports, they "remained only a fractional minority . . . devoid of influence on the masses of people." The readiness question was particularly difficult for Wilson since many members of his party, notably the Bryan faction, were "progressives" who opposed any efforts of "preparation."

There was also a strategic concern: the century of peace between America and Britain after the War of 1812 had seen a diplomatic rapprochement based on British appeasement of American advances in the Western Hemisphere and acceptance of rising American naval power and expansion in Asia. Correspondingly, since the 1890s a tiny band of geopolitically savvy Americans, including Roosevelt, Lodge, and Alfred Thayer Mahan, had recognized that the two countries held a common interest in maintaining the international balance of power and that the United States benefited from British naval supremacy, especially in the Atlantic. For such strategic-minded Americans, therefore, an Allied defeat and a weakening of British sea power would constitute a security threat to the United States.

But Wilson and his Cabinet gave little attention to strategic arguments, those involving a balance of power. Few people outside Roosevelt's immediate circle of friends and associates subscribed to such strategic views, and even Wilson's pro-Allied advisors appear to have given little weight to such concerns. Even Roosevelt based his passionate partisanship of the Allies on moral rather than strategic grounds. He subscribed to a more sophisticated version of the popular revulsion over Belgium, and he based his fervent interventionism, which he never advocated in public, on a wish that his countrymen share in what he saw as the uplifting, ennobling experience of the war. And for the strategic argument for siding with Britain and France to have an impact, people had to believe that the Allies might lose. Thanks to British secrecy and optimistic propaganda, few Americans at the beginning of 1917 knew of the Allies' dire circumstances. Roosevelt and his friends did not know, and neither did Lippmann, who later made so much of this argument.

Intervention, some have argued, was due to "the economic factor." Both Britain's control of the seas and its dependence on overseas trade quickly made the United States, with the largest industrial and agricultural economy in the world, the Allies' supply house, especially for munitions and foodstuffs. The vast, urgent demand for American products necessitated borrowing on a huge scale by the British on behalf of themselves and the Allies, mainly through J. P. Morgan and Company. That borrowing soon turned the United States into the Allies' banker. By 1917, Britain had exhausted its sources of collateral and faced a credit crisis that could have crimped or possibly even cut its overseas lifeline of supplies. Such fears, some have argued, prompted the United States to intervene in 1917. The decision was made to save the Allies from financial collapse, or, as some left critics claimed, "to save the Morgan loan."

Of all the great forces, "economics" would seem to have the clearest connection with intervention, but this also evaporates under scrutiny. British secrecy effectively masked knowledge of their financial plight, not only in the United States but also among their adversaries. After the war, the Treasury's brilliant young expert on war finance, John Maynard Keynes, was amazed to discover that his German opposite numbers had no inkling of how bad off the British had been. The only influential person who seems to have grasped the Allies' precarious financial situation was President Wilson, and he used that knowledge, not to aid them, but to threaten them as part of his peace offensive at the end of 1916. Moreover, even if the Allies' desperate condition had been widely known, their Wall Street supporters had limited influence with Wilson and the Democratic Party, whom they had opposed in the 1916 election. Nor would an Allied financial collapse have necessarily done much economic damage to the United States since all of the loans before 1917 were secured.

On examination, each of the "great forces" appears to have problematical links with the intervention. The historical-precedent argument proves to be the weakest of all. Besides apparently favoring an American stance against rather than alongside the Allies, those precedents were dated and tenuous. Much had happened, on both sides of the Atlantic, in the century since the Napoleonic wars. The development of military technology had revolutionized warfare, as the slaughter on the Western Front quickly showed. The United States had been transformed from a small, struggling, newly independent federation of states into a large, populous centralized nation and an economic giant. Foreign trade, important though it was in certain places, counted for comparatively little in the new twentieth-century economy. Maritime shipping had withered into a minor industry. Blockades and economic warfare by European powers thus touched a smaller minority of Americans in their livelihoods and pocketbooks than was the case a century earlier.

The effects of those great forces could better explain why the United States almost did *not* enter the war on the side of the Allies. Here was a big, geographically removed nation with a largely self-sufficient economy and a polyglot population, many of whose most recently arrived members had ties and feelings on opposing sides in the war. A tradition of diplomatic isolation and a century of nearly unbroken

noninvolvement in overseas affairs had made foreign policy only a minor and intermittent concern in the nation's politics. As nearly every
observer at the time and every scholar since has noted, the great majority of the population showed no appetite for intervention right down
to April 1917, while a large minority opposed intervention under any
circumstances. The lesson, in short, is that the "great forces" do not
provide an adequate explanation.

What explains American intervention is an element that has lain
outside the conceptual framework of most interpretations – individual
actors and their decisions. One choice came easily to both Wilson and
Bryan: they declared neutrality on 4 August 1914. A second choice,
the struggle over preparedness, also termed "armed neutrality," was
very contentious, lasting throughout 1915 and most of 1916. To understand this struggle, some understanding of the progressive tradition
shared by Wilson and Bryan is needed. Arthur Link has provided a
useful portrait of the "progressive-pacifistic movement" at that time:

> [P]rogressivism concentrated largely on economic and social justice at
> home. . . . To the large majority of progressives, particularly in the South
> and Middle West, America's unique mission was to purify and offer
> herself to decadent Europe, an example of democracy triumphant over
> social and economic injustice. This self-purification involved also an end
> to America's experiment in imperialism and a weakening of American
> naval power. . . . Wars were mainly economic in causation and necessarily
> evil because bankers with money to lend, munitions-makers with sordid
> profits to earn, and industrialists with markets to win were the chief
> promoters and beneficiaries of war.

It followed from these two assumptions that the path of progressive righteousness led straight to disarmament, an international system
based upon compulsory arbitration, and an unequivocal repudiation
of war. To progressives, therefore, the call of duty was unmistakably
clear in the summer and fall of 1915. The forces against which they
had been battling at home since 1898 – big-navy imperialists, armor-
plate monopoly, industrialists, and bankers – were arrayed solidly in
support of a great military effort. That fact alone would have sufficed
to arouse their hostility; much more important was their repudiation of
the principle of using power as an instrument of diplomacy. To them,
preparedness signified turning America into an armed camp, the glorification of force, and, worst of all, an end to the reform movement
at home.

Wilson's foreign policy was based on these progressive assumptions. He called for self-determination (democracy) for all and for an international "concert" to arbitrate future conflicts (subsequently termed the League of Nations). At a later point, he asked the belligerents to accept "peace without victory." Those guiding principles, it should be noted, were strikingly at variance with the agendas of the five major European powers and the other contending nations reviewed in previous chapters. For some participants, he was asking for a regime change. For all involved, the "without victory" demand would seem virtually impossible, especially for states that appeared to be winning.

Without abandoning those progressive principles, Wilson did "deviate" in two important matters – in the decision for preparedness and later with the choice of intervention. The preparedness struggle was long and difficult. The complexities can be only briefly sketched. In October 1914 Wilson had deprecated the preparedness talk, calling it a "good mental exercise." In his Annual Message in December he declared "We shall not alter our attitude. . . . " In January 1915 he consulted with Democratic leaders and reviewed the question of army and navy appropriations. The unanimous opinion was that "in view of the decrease in federal revenues, the military budgets would have to be cut. . . . "

Wilson reversed his position following the sinking of the *Lusitania* on 7 May 1915. His response, a series of tough demands, brought the resignation of Bryan early in June. From that point, Wilson single-handedly directed the nation's foreign affairs. In July he asked Secretaries Garrison and Daniels to prepare programs to strengthen the army and navy. These were made public on 4 November. Wilson's shift from "pure" to "armed" neutrality was strongly opposed by the progressives in his own party. With the Bryan forces in control of key positions in the Congress, he found support for this policy now largely from Republicans and "the great financial and industrial interests."

Garrison's plan to enlarge the regular army was stalemated in the House of Representatives. To generate support, Wilson went on a speaking tour through the Midwest, but this was largely without effect. He gave up the plan and, on 10 February 1916, Garrison resigned. After some negotiation, a modified plan to double the regular army to 175,000 was approved by the House, overwhelmingly, on 23 March. An important factor here was a change in the tax law – a progressive measure increased taxes on higher incomes. The author of the measure declared, "the forces of big business should put up the money."

The second "violation" of progressive principles came with the decision to intervene, with America's declaration of war. The old saw – "It takes two to make a fight" – applies here. The two decision-making coteries stood on opposite sides of the Atlantic, in Germany and in the United States. The German group created a situation to which American leaders had to respond. Intervention on the side of the Allies would not have happened had the German leaders not resumed submarine warfare.

Germany's leaders made two pivotal decisions. The first, at the beginning of 1915, was to commence submarine warfare against Allied and neutral shipping and to sink those ships without warning. After strong protests, this effort was stopped. But then, in January 1917, the second decision was taken – to resume and expand submarine warfare, now with no restrictions. In both cases, the major factors were not great historical forces or influences, but rather human credulity, poor judgment, and wishful thinking. The first decision stemmed almost entirely from such failings, with little to be said in its favor. In early 1915 Germany had a total of 29 small U-boats, mostly antiquated craft powered by paraffin-oil engines, of which no more than a third could be deployed on the vast expanses of the Atlantic at one time. Obviously, such a force was ill prepared to inflict serious damage on Britain's maritime supply lines. The German threat to sink all shipping headed for Allied ports was not grounded in reality, and the imperial government appears to have decided for this action through a desire to test a new military technology.

At the beginning of 1915, given British dominance on the seas, Germany and the United States had few contacts other than through diplomacy. In the first weeks of the war the British had cut Germany's undersea cables, thereby hampering contacts with the United States. Direct trade between the two had halted and Britain's blockade also stopped shipping through ports in neutral countries neighboring Germany. With this choice, German leaders did the one thing that might bring the largest neutral and richest nation in the world into the war against them.

The second submarine decision was both better and worse than the first. It was better in the sense that it appeared to embrace sound military calculations. German shipyards had been working overtime, and submarine advocates could now argue that there were enough U-boats (105) to accomplish the goal of severing Allied supply lines. But those advocates falsified their data, greatly exaggerating both the numbers and firepower that were deployable. In January 1916 the Admiralty Staff had declared that 350 U-boats would be required for the Atlantic; in January 1917 there were 92 boats on hand. Nearly a dozen U-boats were in secondary theaters, such as the Baltic, Black, and Mediterranean seas. Even so, the unlimited submarine campaign of 1917 did sink significant tonnage. Most authorities credit the fortuitous Allied adoption of the convoy system, which provided some defense against the submarine, with foiling the Germans' plans. A more vigorous prosecution of industrial and agricultural policies by David Lloyd George's new coalition government after December 1916, together with more massive and efficiently delivered supplies from the United States, also offset the impacts of the submarine campaign.

This decision by Germany's leaders was worse than the first because there was nothing lighthearted about it. On 9 January 1917 an Imperial Council of War met at Pless to consider a renewed submarine campaign. Kaiser Wilhelm II had already sided with the advocates, and after impatiently listening to opposing arguments, ordered unrestricted submarine warfare to commence on 1 February. The German decision-makers now were under no illusions – the move would almost certainly bring the Americans into the war against them. They were confident that they could win the war before the militarily unprepared Americans could make any difference.

This decision, this "calculated risk," ignored both diplomatic hints that a renewed and expanded submarine campaign might provoke American intervention and also the evidence of Britain's financial difficulties. While some policy-makers in Berlin knew of those difficulties, enough to justify reconsideration, the government discounted that concern, apparently moved by the exciting prospect of a sweeping military victory. Through a combination of ignorance and willfulness, German decision-makers did the one thing that could have saved the Allies from financial collapse and a supply disaster.

Nothing was foreordained about that response – not at the beginning of 1915, nor in the months that followed, not even in 1917. Submarine warfare offered odd and unsatisfying reasons for plunging America into the conflagration. The nation's merchant marine had shrunk to a minuscule size; few ships involved in the combat flew the stars and stripes. Only in February and March 1915, at the outset of submarine warfare, and again in 1917, with the unrestricted campaign, were any American ships attacked or sunk. In between, strict orders from the German naval command forbade assaults on American vessels, and, despite grumbling about the difficulty of identifying ships at sea, U-boat commanders largely followed those orders.

The main matter of contention was the safety of American citizens on board Allied ships, mainly British, as passengers and crew. There were not many people involved. Few Americans worked as merchant officers and seamen under any flag. The outbreak of the war had curtailed transatlantic travel, and many of those who persisted in crossing the ocean were wealthy, privileged folk. Broader issues of freedom of navigation in wartime and regard for civilian safety entered into the diplomatic disputes, as did questions of the nation's prestige. But there was a huge disparity between cause and effect, between the small number of Americans whom submarine warfare actually touched and the enormous costs of involvement in the war.

President Wilson's basic approach to the submarine issue, to the war, and to foreign policy in general, fell into two radically different phases. The dividing point came in May 1915 with the sinking of the *Lusitania*. During the first nine months of the war, Wilson's affirmation of neutrality was unquestioned, virtually an automatic response. In one famous formulation, he urged Americans to be "neutral in fact as well as in name, . . . impartial in thought as well as in action." Initially, he allowed Bryan to forbid loans to belligerents, but when it became clear that this ban would hamper foreign trade, Wilson, with Bryan's consent, quietly reversed the decision.

The first major issue for the United States arising from the war involved whether to challenge the Allies' expanded blockade practices in the fall of 1914. With the agreement of all his advisors, Wilson declined to mount a full-fledged diplomatic challenge and adopted a wait-and-see attitude. Not even Germany's opening of submarine warfare in February 1915 changed his approach. His initial response – to hold the Germans to "strict accountability" for losses of life and property – adopted Lansing's harsh-sounding phrase, this after consultation and approval by Bryan. But "strict accountability" had little impact since no sanctions were threatened for failure to comply.

Two poles of thought about the problem formed within the administration. Lansing took a hard line against acquiescence with any kind of attacks by submarines, while Bryan sought a face-saving way to avoid trouble, forbidding or warning Americans against travel on belligerent vessels. Wilson did not identify himself with either approach but instead shifted the focus. In April he stated publicly, "our whole duty, for the present, at any rate, is summed up in this motto: 'America first'. Let us think of America before we think of Europe, in order that America may be fit to be Europe's friend when the day of tested friendship comes." A neutral United States, in his view, would be available to arbitrate the conflict.

Wilson's approach to foreign policy changed with the sinking of the *Lusitania*, the great British liner. In the course of a few hours on the afternoon of 7 May 1915 the country's relation to the war was changed. Wilson's first response was again to counsel calm. In a public statement he declared: "There is such a thing as a man being too proud to fight. There is such a thing as a nation being so right that it does not need to convince others by force that it is right." He almost instantly retracted that statement, not because Roosevelt and other pro-Allied stalwarts lambasted it as cowardly, but because he recognized that the sinking of the *Lusitania*, which killed 128 Americans, had completely altered the context of foreign policy.

The press response was not belligerent. Out of 1,000 newspaper editors who responded to a telegraphic poll, only six called for war. But with submarine warfare now clearly a major concern, the question facing Wilson was how to respond. His immediate aims, he told Bryan, were twofold: "I wish with all my heart that I saw a way to carry out the double wish of our people, to maintain a firm front in respect of what we demand of Germany and yet do nothing that might by any possibility involve us in the war."

Wilson now took virtually complete charge of foreign policy. This move was aided by Bryan's decision on 9 June 1915 to resign as secretary of state rather than incur what he regarded as wrongful risks of war posed by Wilson's demands on Germany. Accepting Bryan's resignation posed some difficulty for Wilson since the secretary still stood high in the Democratic Party. Its congressional leaders had recently informed him that they would not support any belligerent response to the sinking of the *Lusitania*. That knowledge meant that Wilson could not take the country to war at that time. The prerequisite to any such declaration was conversion of the Congressional Democrats.

At first, Wilson wanted to find someone of comparable stature to replace Bryan. William Gibbs McAdoo, secretary of the Treasury and Wilson's son-in-law, told Colonel House that Wilson balked at appointing Lansing because "he did not think he was big enough." House agreed but made a virtue of that inadequacy. Lansing, he told Wilson, "could be used to better advantage than a stronger man. . . . I think the most important thing is to get a man with not too many ideas of his own and one that will be guided by you without unnecessary argument." Whether because of this advice, Wilson named Lansing as Bryan's successor.

But for Wilson, House's usefulness was now seriously diminished. Someone else had replaced him as the president's closest advisor: this was Edith Bolling Galt, whom Wilson had begun courting in spring 1915 and whom he married in December. Galt had taken an instant dislike to the Texas colonel and early on began to undermine his influence. Wilson continued to use House as a negotiator, and he allowed him to pursue his scheme to mediate the war that culminated in the House-Grey Memorandum of February 1916. Yet, as earlier, Wilson seems to have indulged House more than he relied upon him. One example: at the place in the House-Grey Memorandum, which stated that if a joint effort at mediation by the United States and Britain failed, the president inserted the fateful word "probably" in the statement that America would then enter the war on the Allied side.

For almost a year following the sinking of the *Lusitania*, Wilson engaged in a protracted, frustrating diplomatic sparring match with the Germans over submarine warfare. In August 1915, after an attack on another passenger liner, he informally threatened to break diplomatic relations – a likely prelude to war – unless attacks without warning stopped. The Germans agreed to cease attacks on passenger ships, but they resisted demands to apologize and give compensation for the sinking of the *Lusitania* and not to attack freighters.

Meanwhile, Wilson, reversing Democratic policy, now advocated the previously discussed buildup in the army and navy, thus undercutting the efforts of bellicose critics like Roosevelt. Matters came to a head in March 1916 when a U-boat attacked a French Channel steamer, the *Sussex*, wounding several Americans. Wilson responded now with a formal threat to sever relations. This prompted the Germans to restrict submarine warfare, pledging not to attack merchant vessels without warning. The concession was a diplomatic triumph for Wilson.

The dramatic events of the Great War must be seen in conjunction with the realities of American domestic politics. "Local issues" remained on party agendas and 1916 was an election year. Wilson and his party continued their fight for progressive legislation and several important measures were passed in the first months of 1916. Foreign affairs issues, understandably, continued to be major concerns and both parties indicated their commitment to peace. Wilson's achievements in both areas brought his uncontested renomination at the Democratic convention in mid-June. To win the election, he had to make substantial gains over his 41.8 percent vote share in 1912 against divided Republicans. He did make substantial gains, taking 49.2 percent of the total (against Republican Charles Evans Hughes' 46.1 percent), much of that increase coming from the 1912 Progressives and from Socialists. Wilson was the first Democrat since Andrew Jackson to win a second consecutive term.

A key slogan used in support of Wilson's effort was "He Kept Us Out of War." That phrase was not his choice and Wilson was uneasy about its significance and use. Link thought Wilson never used it. Although clearly a salient issue, some commentators had judged the peace issue as less important in the outcome than domestic reform concerns and the troubles of the Republican opposition, Hughes having run a poor campaign.

Wilson was occupied with the campaign during much of 1916, a task that allowed little room for foreign policy initiatives. Given uncertainty over the outcome, or more precisely, a general sense that he would lose the election, no credible initiative was possible. By the time of the election, Wilson received warnings that the German restraint in submarine warfare might soon be ended. He took the danger so seriously that, in the event of his defeat, he secretly outlined steps to have his opponent, Hughes, succeed him at once, thus avoiding the four-month interregnum until the next inauguration on 4 March 1917. Under the law of succession then in force, the secretary of state stood second in line after the vice president. Wilson planned to appoint Hughes to that position following which he would secure the resignation of the vice president. Wilson would then resign, thereby making Hughes president immediately.

Instead, once his own victory was assured, Wilson moved boldly to moot any renewed submarine threat by bringing the war to an end. In December 1916 and January 1917 he mounted peace offensives on multiple fronts. First, he tried to soften up the British by threatening to curtail financial support. Next, he dispatched a public diplomatic note to all the belligerents asking them to state their peace terms, offering mediation, and promising American membership in a postwar league of nations empowered to maintain peace. Third, boldly disregarding both hostile and lukewarm responses from Europe and a plot by Lansing to derail the effort, Wilson unveiled his grand design for world peace on 22 January 1917 by calling for a nonpunitive settlement to the war – "a peace without victory." He also specified such terms as restoration of Alsace and Lorraine to France, an independent Poland, a restored and indemnified Belgium, and freedom of the seas – all to be incorporated later in his Fourteen Points – and he again pledged American membership in a league of nations.

The Intervention

But Germany's leaders had already decided to resume and expand submarine warfare, the move that precipitated the final crisis and brought American intervention. Still, even now that was not the only possible outcome, at least not as long as the decision lay in Wilson's hands. For some other leaders, the German move would have instantly brought the United States into the war. Roosevelt and Lodge, whom Wilson's call for "peace without victory" had enraged, declared their unambiguous support for intervention. Lansing and, more cautiously, House likewise urged war on the president, as did several cabinet members. Ambassador Page from London weekly urged war. He personally felt that Wilson was "constitutionally unable" to go to war. "He has no quality of *real* leadership." Page demanded that the U.S. Navy "immediately" send to British waters "every destroyer and other craft that can be of anti-submarine use." In fact, Page's blatant Anglophilia so annoyed Wilson that he informed a cabinet member, "Page meddles in things outside his domain. I do not mind if he gave us his own opinions but he is giving... English opinions."

Wilson refused to accept arguments for war. He broke relations with Germany at the beginning of February, but in a speech to Congress explaining the action held out an olive branch. "We do not desire any hostile conflict. . . . We shall not believe that they [the Germans] are hostile to us unless and until we are obliged to believe it." As a defensive measure, he proposed legislation to arm American ships, which was overwhelmingly passed in the House. But a Senate filibuster led by the anti-interventionists Robert M. La Follette of Wisconsin and George W. Norris of Nebraska prevented its passage. Wilson denounced these opponents as a "little group of willful men, representing no opinion but their own," and, backed by a legal opinion from the attorney general, issued an executive order to arm the ships. The votes in the House indicated a major shift on the part of the Democratic majority.

The strong words and deeds did not mean, however, that Wilson was ready to go to war. But now a quick succession of events made that decision more urgent. The publication of the Zimmermann Telegram on 1 March, which British intelligence operatives had intercepted on 19 January and artfully disclosed to Wilson on 24 February after covering their tracks, caused a sensation. Therein, the German foreign secretary offered Mexico not only "generous financial support," but also an alliance – and recovery of "former lost territory, Texas, New Mexico, and Arizona" in the likely event of war with the United States. More, he suggested that Mexico and Germany "together make war" against the United States, thereby tying down American forces along the Rio Grande and simultaneously curtailing arms shipments to the Allies. Next, the U-boats sank five American ships. Then two American women passengers died when a U-boat sank a British liner, their deaths prompting expressions of editorial outrage. The overthrow of the tsarist regime in Russia in March 1917 removed a big contradiction to Allied claims to be fighting for democracy. Interventionist sentiment was growing in America, although still not an "irrepressible" force. The best available evidence showed substantial opposition to war; an outraged public was not forcing a reluctant Wilson into war.

Reluctant he was. As late as the third week in March, just before he called Congress into special session, the president showed unmistakably how unwarlike he felt. On 19 March he had a long talk with Frank Cobb, a leading Democratic newspaper editor, in which he declared that war:

> would mean that we should lose our heads along with the rest and stop weighing right and wrong. It would mean that a majority of people in this hemisphere would go war mad.... A declaration of war would mean that Germany would be beaten and so badly beaten that there would be a dictated peace, a victorious peace.... Once lead this people into war, and they'll forget there ever was such a thing as tolerance. To fight you must be brutal and ruthless, and the spirit of ruthless brutality will enter into the very fiber of our national life.... If there is any alternative, for God's sake let's take it!

At a cabinet meeting the next day, 20 March, Wilson answered one member's assertion that Congress and the public demanded war: "I do not care for popular demand. I want to do right, whether popular or not." At that meeting, all the members recommended war, some enthusiastically, such as Lansing and McAdoo, and others reluctantly, most notably Secretary of the Navy Daniels, an old friend and former political associate of Bryan's. Daniels' reluctance did not spring from any advice from his senior service commanders, nor did the detached attitude of Secretary of War Baker. At the end of this cabinet meeting, Wilson greeted the secretaries' pleas for war with the noncommittal remark: "Well, gentlemen, I think that there is no doubt as to what your advice is. I thank you." When Lansing pressed him to call Congress into session to be ready to declare war, he replied, "Oh, I think I will sleep on it." The next day he did issue the call for Congress to meet on 2 April 1917, but gave no indication about what actions he might recommend. More than two months had passed since Germany's announcement of unrestricted submarine warfare.

Given Wilson's clearly expressed aversion, why did he now call for intervention? This apparent contradiction created an aura of mystery about Wilson's decision that has never disappeared. Conclusions about his motives must be largely inferential since, as Knock states, "There is no direct evidence that reveals why Wilson decided to lead the country into war." When the president went to Capitol Hill to address a joint session of Congress on the night of 2 April, no one except he and his wife knew what he was going to say. Here is Link's inference:

It is this writer's opinion that the most important reason for Wilson's decision was his conviction that American belligerency now offered the surest hope for early peace and the reconstruction of the international community. Wilson, we may be reasonably confident, believed that the European conflict was in its final stages.... He certainly believed that American participation, as decisive as possible, would hasten the end of the ghastly carnage, if not end it quickly. American entry would spell Germany's inevitable defeat, or at least frustration of German plans. The German people, or their leaders in the Reichstag, might take control as liberals had done in Russia and refuse to fight for imperialistic ends.

Link then added "a final tempting thought," one for which we have a fragment of documentary support. It was that "American belligerency would enhance his ability to force an early settlement... [and that] he would have a seat at the peace table...." Jane Addams and other members of the Emergency Peace Federation had visited the president at the White House on 28 February. She later remembered Wilson saying that "as head of a nation participating in the war, the President of the United States would have a seat at the Peace Table, but that if he remained the representative of a neutral country he could at best only 'call through a crack in the door'." In a later work, Link cites this statement and declares the seat at the table to have been "the compelling reason for Wilson's decision to accept belligerency...."

Woodrow Wilson's war address ranks among the three or four greatest presidential speeches in American history. He began with a factual recitation of what had happened since the resumption of submarine warfare, calling the German actions "a warfare against mankind...a war against all nations." He had tried armed neutrality, but the Germans' response had made that policy "worse than ineffectual," drawing the nation "into the war without either the rights or the effectiveness of belligerents." He asked Congress to declare that a state of war existed between the United States and Germany.

Wilson stated he was still seeking "a peace without victory." The further aim "is to vindicate the principles of peace and justice in the life of the world as against selfish and autocratic power and to set up amongst the really free peoples of the world such a concert of purpose and of action as will henceforth ensure the observance of those principles." Here he added the most famous (and often misquoted) sentence of the speech: "The world must be made safe for democracy." Wilson asserted that "the right is more precious than peace" and that Americans would be fighting "for democracy,...for a universal dominion of right by such a concert of free peoples as shall bring peace and safety to all nations and make the world at last free. To such a task we can dedicate our lives and our fortunes...."

Wilson carried substantial majorities in both houses of Congress with him. The war resolution passed the Senate by a vote of 82 to 6 on 4 April, and the House by a vote of 373 to 50 on 6 April, Good Friday. No other American war in the twentieth century would have so many dissenting voices raised in Congress at the outset. For comparable opposition, it is necessary to look back at such earlier conflicts as the War of 1812 and the Mexican-American War. The small band of opposing senators included such principled critics as La Follette and Norris. In the House the Democratic majority leader, Claude Kitchin of North Carolina, broke with his party to oppose the war, as did the first woman elected to Congress, Republican Jeannette Rankin of Montana. A substantial number of the dissenting votes in both houses came from the Midwest. There was some correlation with concentrations of German-Americans, but the strongest correlation was with left-leaning politics, particularly anti–big business "progressive" insurgency of the kind championed by La Follette and Norris. The lone Socialist in Congress, Representative Meyer London of New York, also voted against the war resolution.

Many of the congressmen and senators who spoke in favor of the war resolution expressed reluctance and believed little more than money, ships, and supplies would have to come from the United States. Aside from Roosevelt and other "hawks," few wanted to see a large-scale commitment of ground forces on the Western Front or imagined that such operations would be necessary. Significantly, no one expressed any sense that American intervention would make a critical difference in the outcome of the war. Nobody recognized that this move was likely to save the Allies from defeat.

Conclusion

The American decision for war, as indicated, differs from all of those reviewed previously. The decision-making coterie was smaller than most and the role of the chief executive more pronounced. Wilson consulted with his Cabinet and with several others, but their collective judgment, as seen, was not the compelling factor. Churchill judged the importance of Wilson's thoughts and actions as follows:

> [I]t seems no exaggeration to pronounce that the action of the United States with its repercussions on the history of the world depended, during the awful period of Armageddon, upon the workings of this man's mind and spirit to the exclusion of almost every other factor . . . he played a part in the fate of nations incomparably more direct and personal than any other man.

The American decision for war differed from all of the others in that approval by the Congress was a requirement that could not, as in the French case, be circumvented by a simple declaration by the Cabinet that the nation already was at war! A substantial shift in congressional attitudes occurred between the end of 1916 and April 1917. Most of those changes, probably, came within the Democratic ranks, most of them among the progressives. We have no detailed study of their attitudes, of the sources of the changes, but two factors, unrestricted submarine warfare and the Zimmermann telegram, were probably decisive. Put differently, the provocative actions of Germany's leaders brought the conversion.

Another important difference should be noted: while Congress authorized intervention, the nature of that intervention was left to President Wilson as commander-in-chief of U.S. armed forces. Thus it was Wilson, a civilian, who made the basic military strategic decision to dispatch an American Expeditionary Force to France in order to concentrate land power on the Western Front and to defeat the German Army. His only caveat was that the United States would mobilize an independent army under its own flag in its own sector of the front and with its own commanders, staff, and supply. In short, there was to be no "amalgamation" with the British and French armies.

Finally, a third difference should be noted: Wilson's program and actions had a major impact on the conclusion of the conflict. Most previous wars ended with the defeated regimes still in power. But in this instance, the end phase was accompanied by regime change in Austria-Hungary and in Germany. Knowing the hopelessness of the military situation, facing revolution at home, and well aware of the Allies' expectations, Germany's military leaders pressed the kaiser to abdicate and to leave the country. A new regime, the Weimar republic, would follow. To guarantee the peace, a new "concert," the League of Nations, was established.

CHAPTER 12

On the Origins of the Catastrophe

World War I, the Great War, began with the decisions taken by the leaders of five major European powers: Austria-Hungary, Germany, Russia, France, and Great Britain. The decision-making coteries saw "their" nation either as in decline or as seriously threatened. To halt the decline or to block the threat, the decision-makers felt that the choice of war was necessary. Our view, in short, is that those "strategic" considerations were the paramount concerns in July and August 1914.

The Major Powers

Austria, once the commanding central European presence, the state that had defeated and pushed back the Ottomans, was now tagged as the second "sick man of Europe." An important Balkan satellite, Serbia, had been lost in 1903 as a result of a coup d'état. It appeared as if "the Serbs" were going to repeat the Italian *risorgimento*. A "Greater Serbia" would provide an example for others, for Croats, Romanians, Poles, and Czechs. Two Balkan wars in 1912 and 1913 led senior leaders in Vienna to a now-or-never conclusion. The Dual Monarchy had to end the Serbian threat, or else, like the Ottomans, it would proceed to an ultimate decline. Thus, their decision, the first act of war, was to move their armies south, to defeat and eliminate "upstart" Serbia.

Germany's leaders also felt that their empire was threatened. Their image was one of "encirclement," the prime concern being the Franco-Russian *entente* but with Britain always in mind. Austria-Hungary, their loyal ally, was a weak and declining power; Italy, their other ally, was perceived as both weak and unreliable. Watching Russia's economic and military recovery after the Russo-Japanese War of 1904–05, Germany's leaders sensed that they faced a decline in power relative to Russia and France. For the decision-makers, especially those of the military, the solution was a preemptive war. And for them, timing was essential: it was "now or never."

Germany's leaders pursued two separate and distinct agendas. Their prime concern was defensive, to shore up the gains of 1871 – to preserve, and if possible to enhance, their position within Europe against the French and Russian "threat." The other agenda, *Weltpolitik* – power in Africa and Asia – was offensive, requiring a reach beyond the European metropole. Both agendas appeared in official discussions, before and after August 1914. In the July Crisis, Germany's leaders were moved by the defensive concern.

Germany followed its long-standing operations plan, pushing its armies into France. Following that short campaign, it was expected, these troops would be shifted to the Russian front. Although discussions of the Great War regularly use the singular, it is important to note that by early August two wars were "in process," the Austro-Serbian war in the Balkans and the German war in Belgium and France. In a matter of days, however, Austrian-Hungarian forces would be called out of Serbia and sent off to a third war, against the Russians on the Galician front.

Russia's leaders also saw their state as seriously threatened. As of 1914, it had experienced six decades of defeat from the Crimean War (1853–56) to the Russo-Japanese War (1904–05). It had been humiliated in 1908 by the Austro-Hungarian power play in Bosnia-Herzegovina, one backed by Berlin. In the next six years, Russia's leaders struggled to rearm, to reorganize their land and sea forces, and to industrialize the empire without surrendering power to the various groups demanding political and social reform. In the July Crisis, Russia's leaders concluded that a demonstration of the nation's strength or capacity was necessary; they had to come to the aid of "the Serbs." The alternative, backing down, would mean still another humiliation, ending Russia's standing as a great power.

France, like Austria, had also been a major European power. Four world wars had been fought, in Europe and overseas, to contain its expansion. France had been thoroughly defeated in the last of those struggles, the Napoleonic wars (1803–15). Six decades later, it suffered another humiliating defeat, this one by Prussia and the other German states, in the Franco-Prussian War (1870–71). This war brought the establishment of a much larger, unified, and stronger Germany. For France it meant the loss of much of Alsace-Lorraine. But over time, Frenchmen forgot the "gap in the Vosges" and cries of "revenge" for 1871 abated.

German Chancellor Otto von Bismarck sought to keep France isolated and encouraged colonial distractions. For several decades, France did "stand alone." But after Bismarck's dismissal in 1890, Kaiser Wilhelm II dropped the Russian connection (the Reinsurance Treaty of 1887), allowing the Russo-French links of 1892 and 1894. France now had a strong ally on Germany's eastern flank. Its key aim was to "fasten the bonds" and to encourage Russian military plans that would serve France's needs. That meant speeding Russia's mobilization, allowing it, in case of war, to concentrate forces quickly for an attack on Germany.

Thus, the various foreign policy decisions made by the four continental powers in 1914 were based on what might be termed defensive considerations. The concern, as the diverse leadership groups saw it, was to protect or to prop up a weakened or threatened state. The driving concern was to remove imminent threats to the state's power and prestige.

Put differently, the decisions for war in July 1914 were not based on offensive considerations. Territorial expansion was not the immediate consideration. Austria-Hungary explicitly disclaimed any interest in annexing Serbia. Russia had no immediate territorial aims. Coming to the defense of Serbia would perhaps garner Slavic allies for Russia in the years to come, but new possessions were not a factor. The Dardanelles was always a general European security concern and in July 1914 preventing German dominance there was a pressing issue, especially for St. Petersburg and London. As for the *Weltmacht* thesis, Germany stood to lose all of its overseas possessions as a result of a general European war. That was an easy prediction, the probability of loss escalating dramatically with Britain's involvement. For France, one can always point to Alsace and Lorraine as ultimate aspirations. But in July 1914, the prime concern was defense against a likely German attack, French leaders knowing the broad outlines of the Schlieffen plan.

Great Britain, the fifth European power, was not directly threatened. Historically, Britain stood secure behind the "moat" of the
English Channel, protected by the guns of the Royal Navy. There was
no interest in acquiring European territory. But ever since the wars
of Louis XIV and Napoleon I, British policy had been to maintain a
"balance of power" in Europe. London had shown time and again that
it would tolerate no hegemon on the Continent; hence the concern to
come to the aid of France.

The Lesser Powers

Six later entrants – Japan, the Ottoman Empire, Bulgaria, Romania,
Greece, and Italy – are best described as negotiators, as dealers. They
solicited terms, judged the likely winners, and, based on those calculations, joined the fray. The contrasting goals of the major powers and
the late entrants are striking. The former, as indicated, were largely
defensive, basically protecting a threatened enterprise. The latter were
expansionists, offering intervention in exchange for territorial gains
(and possibly some prestige, some recognition).

Surprisingly, the first of the "lesser powers" to enter the war was
Japan. Allied with Great Britain since 1902, Japan had no vital interests
at stake in the European power struggle. But those European powers
had claimed large pieces of real estate in the Far East, either as outright
colonies or as so-called leaseholds. Japan's leaders saw in the war an
opportunity to affirm their "rights" and influence in Asia, primarily in
China. Japan's decision for war on 8 August 1914 was largely the work
of one man, Foreign Minister Katō Takaaki.

The Ottoman Empire, the second lesser power to enter the war,
had been in manifest decline. Tagged as the "sick man of Europe,"
other nations believed they could, more or less at will, pick up some of
the "pieces." France took Tunisia, Italy took Libya, and in 1913 the
states of the Balkan League defeated the Empire and removed more
of the pieces. In August 1914, as Europe became engaged in general
war, there was little the exhausted Ottomans could do militarily, hence
their initial incentive was to avoid involvement. But then, with the
German offer, first of a treaty of alliance and then of two warships,
the Young Turks who had seized power in 1905 decided for war on the
side of Germany and Austria-Hungary, thus extending the Great War
into the Middle East. Two very different participants, David Lloyd

George and Erich Ludendorff, concluded that this move, by diverting British Empire troops from the Western Front, lengthened the war by two years.

National aspirations and territorial aggrandizement were central agenda items for the four other "lesser powers" reviewed here. In August 1914 Italy's government concluded it was not obligated by the terms of the Triple Alliance and declared neutrality. Over the next months, leaders in Rome debated entry into the war, assessing the terms received from both sides. In this period – the so-called *intervento* – they sought to discern the outcome of the conflict and negotiated with both warring coalitions what Italy might receive for its intervention. In April 1915 they obtained highly favorable terms of alliance with London and Paris. Although facing open opposition from many organized groups and passive hostility from among the peasantry, on 25 May 1915 King Vittorio Emanuele III declared war against Austria-Hungary alone. Italy's leaders had weighed their options and chosen war on the side of the *entente* as being in their best interest.

The Italian decision to enter the war moved Bulgaria's leaders. Tsar Ferdinand, the scion of the German house of Coburg, and his prime minister, Vasil Radoslavov, aspired to a "Greater Bulgaria" which translated into claims to Macedonia against Greece and Serbia. For the first few months of the war, Ferdinand and Radoslavov wavered, eagerly following the battlefield fortunes of both sides. But when, in the spring of 1915, Berlin and Vienna promised Sofia the immediate occupation of all Macedonia, Radoslavov accepted the offer as his chance to claim Bulgaria's "historical and ethnographic rights" to the region. On 14–15 October 1915 Tsar Ferdinand announced Sofia's entry into the war.

Romania, allied to Austria-Hungary and Germany since 1883 and to Italy since 1888, also undertook tortuous negotiations before finally entering the war. Its national aspirations in Bukovina and Transylvania on the one hand, and Bessarabia, on the other, were divided between the warring powers. But the ascent of the Liberal Party in the summer of 1914 and the death of the German-born King Carol in October 1914 shifted the balance away from Berlin and Vienna. Italy's entry into the war on the side of the *entente* in May 1915 and the success of the Russian Brusilov offensive in June 1916 proved decisive. Already in the summer of 1915, Romania had secured Russia's assent to the annexation of large parts of Hungary and Bukovina. And when the *entente*, a year later, confronted Romania with the choice of either joining the war or risk losing those prospects of territorial expansion, Prime Minister Ion Brătianu on 27 August 1916 committed the nation to war.

The political establishment of Greece was badly divided from the first days of the war. While the Liberal and Anglophile Prime Minister Eleutherios Venizelos favored the *entente*, King Constantine sympathized with his brother-in-law, Kaiser Wilhelm II. Greek nationalist aspirations focused on territories in the Ottoman Empire, but the British annexation of Cyprus, part of the Greek irredenta, was also a concern. The allied attack on the Dardanelles in February 1915 brought the war closer to home, and further divided the Athens leadership. While Venizelos was receptive to British offers of an alliance and extensive territories in Asia Minor, Greek army leaders argued that any intervention was beyond its resources. In October 1915 Venizelos agreed to the landing of *entente* troops at Salonika and in January 1916 to their occupation of Corfu. In December 1916 British and French troops landed at Athens, only to be confronted by Greek forces and eventually forced to withdraw. An allied naval blockade of Greece and a French ultimatum to King Constantine to abdicate finally proved decisive: on 30 June 1917 Greece became the last European state to enter the war. It had taken this step through a combination of nationalist enthusiasm and direct *entente* intervention and blackmail.

The sixth major power, the United States, was not a threatened or declining power, nor was it moved by a wish for new territory. When war came in 1914, the United States found itself caught in the classic dilemma of neutral nations during a large-scale war. For three years, President Woodrow Wilson kept the nation out of the conflict. His policy of intervention came about reluctantly and largely because of an incredible German miscalculation, unrestricted submarine warfare against allied as well as neutral shipping.

On the Causes

We offer three principal conclusions. First, World War I resulted from decisions taken by the leaders of the five major European nations. Second, in each of those nations the decision for war was taken by a coterie, by a group of no more than eight or ten individuals. And third, an adequate explanation for the war's origins must center on the considerations that moved those groups of decision-makers.

Decision-making by individuals, by a small coterie, makes contingency highly likely. Misinformation, misjudgment of intentions and consequences, time pressures, ego-strength, and weak nerves all were evident in the discussions leading to those final decisions. One implication is that in all settings many choices were possible. The other implication is that the received explanations, reviewed in Chapter 1, are inadequate.

The first of those explanations holds that the alliance system "caused" the war. But as seen, the alliances were first and foremost defensive. None called for any of the contracting powers to behave as they did in July 1914. None triggered the *casus foederis*. Not a single major leader, to the best of our knowledge, argued the recourse to war primarily on the basis of alliance obligations. All the treaties of the Triple Alliance became active only if one of the contracting powers was forced to resort to war "without direct provocation on their part." The decisions to resort to war, beginning with Vienna, were made entirely independent of treaty stipulations. In all cases, the "strategic" argument – the need to halt a perceived decline or to block a serious threat – proved decisive. The leadership groups made their choices for war according to their readings of national interests and needs, not according to formal contractual obligations.

Treaties are words on paper that by themselves have little or no determinative impact. Not cast in stone for eternity, their import is bound by time and circumstance. Their terms will ordinarily be upheld only insofar as they serve "the national interest." The age-old argument of alliance determinism assumes an effective international rule of law and honorable alliance partners. But most experts in international affairs would count those as among the most naïve hypotheses imaginable.

The focus on coterie decision-making is simultaneously an argument against four of those "big causes" – nationalism, militarism, imperialism, and social Darwinism. All four are essentially cultural arguments, the claim being that those attitudes were present in the general population, all of them presumably constituting demands compelling responses from the nation's leaders. All four are best described as incomplete and unverified arguments.

Nationalist sentiments were "out there," present to some degree in all of those nations. But the key considerations in July and August 1914 were the outlooks or mindsets (*mentalités*) present among the decision-making coteries in each of the five nations, not the diffuse (and largely unknown or unmeasured) sentiments of some millions of citizens. The decisions to go to war, as seen, were extemporizations, choices based on assessments of recent events, on perceptions of threats to the nation, and the alliance needs posed by the immediate events.

Cultural arguments, as seen, typically fail to specify the causal connections. An initial and fundamental problem is the failure to determine the frequencies: how many citizens, for example, shared those nationalist sentiments? And how many would give priority to those aims, choosing war over all other considerations? Second, most accounts, as seen earlier, are selective, focusing for example on nationalist demands but neglecting the countering or "growing" internationalist sentiments. Third, what were the channels of influence? How did the diffuse sentiments of some millions of citizens impact on the decision-makers? And fourth, there is the related question of timing: why did those mass attitudes impact at this specific point in time, "forcing" those leaders to choose war? One might note also a difficulty in the logic: while the monarchs in three of those European regimes are routinely portrayed as committed authoritarians, in July 1914 they are being depicted as "pawns," as men forced to respond to popular sentiments.

The factors reviewed to this point are routinely said to have had "powerful" impacts on the decisions taken. The next argument, the "slide-into-war" thesis, has a strikingly opposite character, one that might be classified as an indeterminacy hypothesis. This easy analogy was first enunciated by David Lloyd George with his declaration that Europe's leaders had "slithered" over the brink into the "cauldron of war." The evidence reviewed in the previous chapters provides no support for this claim. In each of the countries studied, the decision-making coterie weighed its options, calculated its chances, and decided for war. Each of the chapters reports intention as opposed to inadvertence.

A variant argument, one going beyond the easy analogy, is that of the "calculated risk." The decision-makers planned a limited war, one in which astute deterrence policies would discourage wider involvement. But then, it is claimed, the prudent calculations somehow, inadvertently, proved mistaken and a general war resulted. But, as seen in previous chapters, many key decision-makers knew the risk, knew that wider involvement was probable, yet proceeded to take the next steps. Put differently, fully aware of the likely consequences, they initiated policies they knew were likely to lead to war. The statements of many participants attest to that conclusion.

The European crisis began in Vienna where Foreign Minister Count Leopold Berchtold counseled an aggressive policy "even though our operations against Serbia should bring about the great war." Count Alexander Hoyos, the man entrusted with securing Germany's "blank check" to support their effort, put it perhaps most bluntly: "It is immaterial to us whether the world war comes out of this." General Franz Baron Conrad von Hötzendorf confided his innermost thoughts on the coming European struggle to his mistress: "It will be a hopeless struggle, but nevertheless it must be because such an ancient monarchy and such an ancient army cannot perish ingloriously." When the likelihood of a Russian intervention was raised at the Foreign Ministry, Section Chief János Forgách laconically commented: "Well then, it [the European war] will just have to come." And even the aged Kaiser Franz Joseph, with whom the "war powers" ultimately rested, accepted the risk of a general European war. "If we must go under," he confided to Conrad von Hötzendorf, "we better go under decently."

Addressing the likely Russian intervention, Wilhelm II told Austro-Hungarian representatives that they could count on "Germany's full support," even if "serious European complications" – a diplomatic euphemism for war – resulted. He further counseled Vienna not to "delay the action" against Serbia, and he informed Hoyos that Germany fully expected war with Russia and for years had made all preparations with this in mind. Chancellor Theobald von Bethmann Hollweg also pressed Vienna to move aggressively against Belgrade, describing this as the "best and most radical solution" to the empire's Balkan troubles. Helmuth von Moltke, the chief of the German General Staff, had stated as early as 1911 that he believed a general European war to be inevitable, a statement that he repeated at the so-called war council of 8 December 1912. During the July Crisis, and especially during the critical days of 28 to 30 July, the general, with but one brief relapse on the night of the 29th, pressed the case for war.

If Russia's leaders had refused involvement, what remained would have been the Austro-Serbian venture, effectively a third Balkan war. But early on, Foreign Minister Sergei Sazonov demanded that Russia "fulfill her historic mission" – to defend Serbia, a threatened "Slavonic nation." To do otherwise, he argued, would transform Russia into a "decadent State" and a "second-place" power. Agriculture Minister A. V. Krivoshein, effectively the leader of the Cabinet, claimed that "opinion," both public and parliamentary, demanded war. War Minister V. A. Sukhomlinov and Chief of the General Staff

N. N. Ianushkevich likewise insisted on the "bold" policy. Russian leaders knew that their decision to block Austria-Hungary in its Serbian venture was likely to bring German intervention and hence force St. Petersburg to a simultaneous move against Berlin. And that move, they knew, would bring the German action against France. Just as Russia could not leave Serbia at the mercy of Austria-Hungary, so Germany could not leave Austria-Hungary at the mercy of Russia.

There is even less evidence of a "slide" in the French case. President Raymond Poincaré exercised an influence over French foreign policy that far exceeded his constitutional authority. For him, and French leaders generally, the imperative in 1914 was simple and clear: to preserve the tie to Petersburg at all cost. France could not afford to "decide" whether to stand by Russia. Premier René Viviani declared publicly his concern to "resolve the conflict...in the interest of the general peace." But simultaneously, he stated that France was "entirely ready to support the action of the [Russian] imperial government." France's ambassador to St. Petersburg, Maurice Paléologue, throughout the July Crisis counseled an aggressive stance on the part of France and Russia, including if need be recourse to war. On 25 July and again on 28 July Paléologue assured Sazonov of "unequivocal French support."

The decision for war by the British Cabinet came after the other four powers had made their decisions, ones that had already assured a sizable conflict. At the outset, most cabinet members were opposed to intervention, but Foreign Secretary Sir Edward Grey and First Lord of the Admiralty Winston S. Churchill eventually generated a majority, arguing Britain's interest in maintaining the balance of power on the Continent. The calculation in this case was to assure that no European power was able to sever or seriously to constrain its seaborne commerce or to pose a legitimate threat to the home islands or to the Empire. The decision, largely the work of Grey, was for a commitment to the defense of Belgium and France. The discussion focused on France, but Germany's violation of Belgian neutrality and Bethmann Hollweg's ill-chosen words about the 1839 Articles constituting but "a scrap of paper" did much to persuade reluctant members of the Cabinet.

Germany's submarine offensive brought about America's eventual response. The sinking of the British liner *Lusitania* on 7 May 1915, with the loss of 128 Americans, changed the nation's relation to the war. William Jennings Bryan's decision to resign as secretary of state on 9 June allowed President Wilson to take charge of foreign policy. Following Berlin's decision in January 1917 to resume unrestricted submarine warfare, Wilson abandoned his "double wish" policy and called on Congress for the declaration of war, steps that could hardly be described as a "slide" into war.

For decades, the leaders of the major European powers had "gamed" the likely war scenarios and had recognized the danger of diplomatic escalation leading to a wider conflict. They accepted those risks in July and August when deciding for war. There was, in fact, a surprising single-mindedness of purpose in their decision-making. They recognized almost to a man the strategic argument, that perceived decline or the threat thereof required a resort to arms. In short order, the murder of Archduke Franz Ferdinand receded from the forefront of their considerations. Instead, the leaders in Vienna and Berlin, Petersburg and Paris, persisted in their view that war alone could alter their perceived precarious positions. Strikingly, when at the last moment two monarchs, Wilhelm II and Nicholas II, tried to reverse the direction, their coteries forced them back on course.

The "slide" thesis is rendered untenable also by the actions undertaken by decision-makers in three capitals – Vienna, Berlin, and St. Petersburg – to block possible mediation of the crisis. Vienna refused a state funeral for Archduke Franz Ferdinand in part because a gathering of the crowned heads of Europe might have provided an opportunity to discuss and perhaps to coordinate peaceful responses to the assassination. Foreign Minister Berchtold as early as 3 July boldly informed the German ambassador, Heinrich von Tschirschky, of his government's need for a *"final and fundamental reckoning"* with Serbia. Wilhelm II at Berlin endorsed that initiative with the terse marginal note, "now or never." Once Russia had decided to block the proposed Habsburg "punitive expedition" against Serbia by mobilizing, Foreign Minister Sazonov, to forestall further discussion and possible resolution of the crisis, instructed Chief of Staff General Ianushkevich to smash his telephone!

Perhaps the last words on the "slide" thesis should go to one of the key players, the chief of the German General Staff. Already in March 1913 General von Moltke confided to the Italian military attaché Germany's intention to violate Belgian neutrality in case of war. The next war, Moltke stated, would be between France and Germany. In brutal terms, he declared that this war would be "a question of life or death for us. We shall stop at nothing to gain our end. In the struggle for existence, one does not bother about the means one employs." And in retirement in June 1915, Moltke in a private letter to Field Marshal Colmar von der Goltz spoke openly of "this war which I prepared and initiated."

All of the explanations reviewed here – the alliance system argument, the four "cultural" claims, and the slide theory – present a further difficulty, that of relativizing. The focus on those "big" causes suggests no difference in the decision-making of the leaders in Vienna, Berlin, Petersburg, Paris, and London. But as seen in the most easily measured of those factors, military expenditures, the patterns were markedly different. The relativizing arguments, with their assumption of shared responsibility, raise two basic questions, those of accuracy and of fairness.

Until at least 1919, the dominant explanations for the coming of the war were arguments of intention, of premeditation, basically of aggressive purpose. A year or so after the end of the war, a "sea change" occurred and arguments of inadvertence – no one wanted war – gained wide approval. Both positions were basically political in character, serving first as an aid in the conduct of the war, then in the conduct of the peace. Since little serious documentation was available at either time, the actual bases of the decision-making were essentially unknown.

The most striking instance of the shift in usages appears in the case of David Lloyd George who, in less than a year, changed from a committed intentionalist to become the principal author of the nonjudgmental slide thesis. In January 1920 he demanded that Kaiser Wilhelm II be formally tried as a war criminal. Then, in December of that year, he made a famous speech in which he argued that the nations had "glided, or rather staggered and stumbled" into war. As late as 1936 Lloyd George still maintained, "No sovereign or leading statesman in any of the belligerent countries sought or desired war – certainly not a European war." The "slide" thesis renders careful reexamination of the July Crisis unnecessary: no motive, no intention, no responsibility. We argue instead a consistent pattern, multiple instances of moves for engagement, all of these to effect some "larger" strategic purpose.

Theoretical Implications

In this section we wish to provide the rudiments of a theory, something intermediate between the Big Causes and Ultimate Particularism. All five major powers in 1914 were constitutional regimes, meaning that the four monarchs and the one president were subject to some legal, or in the case of Britain some agreed-upon, limits to their power. But that categorical formulation, as indicated, hides significant differences. Austria-Hungary, Russia, and Germany had written constitutions but all three left important powers in the hands of the monarch – most importantly, the power to declare war. Those three, moreover, were not parliamentary regimes since the monarch chose the ministers. The latter were responsible to the monarch, and, when no longer in favor, could be dismissed by him. The elected legislative bodies provided the principal check on the monarch's power by wielding the power of the purse. While an important achievement, that formal power on some occasions was not easily exercised. If the empire faced a hostile or threatening power, a vote against a military budget would be a very problematic move.

Many of the authoritarian leaders believed that "time was running out." Britain's Hanoverian kings, recognizing the "tide of events," had compromised and accepted new developments. But the authoritarian rulers on the Continent continued the fight. Wilhelm II's first speech after his accession in 1888 was a message addressed to the Prussian Army. He spoke of the death of his grandfather and father, emphasizing their ties and those of many other Hohenzollern ancestors with the army and its glorious heritage. His conclusion: "Thus we belong together – I and the army – were born for one another, and thus we will remain together forever, whether, through God's will, in peace or war." Not too surprisingly, he and some of his ministers considered the use of the military, of a *coup d'état*, to stop or reverse the pervasive tendencies.

France, the most progressive of the major powers, had a republican regime, the third in its history after several tries at other arrangements. The president named a premier who chose cabinet members from among the parties represented in the legislature. The premier and his government were responsible to, and could be removed by, a vote of that legislature. The government could also be voted out in a subsequent election. Formal constitutional arrangements are one thing; actual practice could be quite another. Formally, the premier headed the government. But in midyear 1914, as seen, President Poincaré was clearly the *de facto* head of the government. In August he finessed the required parliamentary vote for war by simply announcing that France already was at war with Germany!

Great Britain was nominally a constitutional monarchy, but the king was a figurehead with very limited powers. Generally, the monarch called on the leader of the largest party in Parliament to form a government. That leader, the prime minister, then chose the other cabinet members from among the elected members of his party. That government was responsible to Parliament, not the king. It could be removed by a no-confidence vote in Parliament or, of course, it could be voted out in the next general election. The Cabinet, as seen, was empowered to take the nation into war.

Dynastic Elites

In Austria-Hungary, Germany, and Russia, the decision-making coterie consisted of the monarch and his chosen ministers. Among the latter one would find a prime minister, a minister of foreign affairs, a finance minister, a minister of the interior (police), and so on. Those ministers were usually civilians. In addition, one would find the war minister, possibly the head of the General Staff, and the minister of the navy. Even for these people, the chosen ones, no hard-and-fast rules determined participation. Much depended on the ego strength (and whim) of the ruler who could make *ad hoc* decisions about inclusion. Influence could also be exerted in the opposite direction. A capable (or tactically adept) subordinate could ingratiate himself and might, possibly, change the monarch's mind. But it was a chancy business, given the monarch's "last word" and the deference expected of subordinates.

Something needs to be said about the "formative experiences" of these decision-makers. Most were drawn from the aristocracy. While that statement is accurate, if not qualified it is also misleading. Most aristocrats were landowners, persons involved in agriculture and estate management. The civilian ministers left the estates at an early age and, typically, would have studied law. They then would have undergone a long apprenticeship moving up the ranks within the government. Military ministers joined the forces at an early age and normally would spend their entire lives there. The estate-owning aristocrat, the inheritor, was the *de facto* ruler within his domains. The aristocrats in government, in contrast, were subordinates during their entire professional careers. Many were tough-minded and arrogant, but all, to some degree, had to "play the courtier." This was especially the case at the topmost level, for those directly responsible to the monarch.

The training of monarchs, what might be called the social psychology of monarchy, has been generally neglected by the social sciences. Heirs apparent were subjected to a most unusual child-rearing program. Given the careers for which they were destined, they were typically subjected to very demanding and insistent routines, initially in the palace nursery under the direction of carefully chosen tutors. Later, in their early teens, the male inheritors were given a military rank and assigned to a unit under the supervision of a trusted officer. Here the young man would find some easy-going companions who, not surprisingly, were deferential, supportive, and very helpful in attending to his needs and wishes.

Coming of age within the latter highly permissive environment gave rise to two problematic character traits. Few of those companions would challenge the prospective monarch, neither contradicting nor correcting him. Accordingly, for him there would be no serious "reality testing." One result would be an unusual assurance about the validity of his judgments. With no "controlling" logic to govern his thinking, another result was irresolution, vacillation, continuous and unpredictable changes of positions. Both pathologies were found, in especially egregious form, in the mental processes of Kaiser Wilhelm II.

Finally, something needs to be said about the outlooks, or *mentalités* of the monarchs. Given their training, given the focus on "the state," it should come as no surprise that "the national interest" figured prominently in their thoughts. The power, prestige, or influence of the nation, on the Continent and in the world, had a central place in their thinking – as may be seen in the justifications they offered during the 1914 crisis. That expression, "national interest," is misleading in its suggestion of realism, as if one were dealing with an objective reality (such as troop strength, industrial capacity, or food supplies). In fact, those interests are definitions, declarations of perceived needs and of appropriate actions, plus some ordering of priorities. A striking feature of the coteries of the three threatened monarchical powers is the high degree of consensus evidenced with respect to "the imperatives" presented by the July Crisis. All three coteries "recognized" that a demonstration of their nation's power was necessary. And all three signaled they were willing to take enormous chances, or more precisely, willing to pay enormous costs for the sake of that aim.

Party Elites

The decision-making coteries in Britain and France had a very different composition. The members, basically, were party leaders, men heading the dominant party or party coalitions plus some others who had shown some degree of competence, enough to be entrusted with cabinet positions. In Britain civilians usually headed the war and naval ministries. In France members of the military usually held those offices but they had little say in governance. The chiefs of staff were not ordinarily members of the governing coterie. France, of course, had no monarch. The British monarch was, essentially, "off stage."

The British and French decision-makers came to their positions through routes that differed significantly from the paths of the three dynastic coteries. All of them were elected officials, members of Parliament or of the National Assembly. An individual's presence among the decision-makers depended on three processes: first that his party won favor with the voters, second that it was chosen to form the government, and third that the party leader (or leaders) then chose that individual for a cabinet position. Ordinarily, the successful official would have held several cabinet positions, being promoted to more demanding posts as he accumulated experience.

For the British and French ruling coteries, party and party advantage were high-priority continuing concerns. They too, like the dynastic coteries, would be concerned with "the national interest." But their definitions of that interest differed substantially from the obsessive concerns of the dynastic regimes. One difference deserves special emphasis: in Britain and France military elites were not ordinarily part of the ruling coterie. No prestige-obsessed monarch was present in their decision-making circle and there was no chief of staff insistently pressing military needs. In contrast to the concern with power, prestige, and military affairs in the monarchic regimes, one biographer reports that Prime Minister Herbert H. Asquith, at least in the early years of his government, "was generally lax about defence issues." He regarded the Committee of Imperial Defence, established in 1903, "with indifference and only on occasion set it to work on central issues." Lloyd George after the war recalled, "During the eight years that preceded the war, the Cabinet devoted a ridiculously small percentage of its time to a consideration of foreign affairs." Some ministers, those who attended the Committee of Imperial Defence, were familiar with "certain aspects of foreign policy," but "the Cabinet as a whole were never called into genuine consultation upon the fundamental aspects of the foreign situation."

French and British strategic concerns were markedly different from those of the "threatened" powers. Dynastic elites initiated events; party elites reacted to them. French leaders knew long before the fact of the German plan to attack, leaving them a basic choice, to resist or to concede. Since the latter was never a serious option, the key choices involved "presentation." The principal task was to influence events so as to yield the most positive reading, for French citizens and for audiences elsewhere; basically, to show France as the victim of unprovoked aggression. The German threat provided the agenda and set the basic directions for the Cabinet. Under Poincaré's direction, a consensus was achieved on the major policies with much greater ease than in the case of Britain.

Unlike France, Britain was not directly threatened by that "distant" struggle. Germany's leaders, in fact, were desperately providing assurances, doing all they could to discourage British intervention. Moreover, many Liberals saw war as an alien, inappropriate procedure, one that had no proper place in the modern age. That view, shared by a majority of the Cabinet in 1914, was an integral part of the liberal worldview, a heritage going back at least as far as Adam Smith. Party leaders who argued for intervention were constrained both by constitutional and party considerations. They could not initiate anything without substantial cabinet support. And that support was not available until Germany moved into Belgium and France. Here too, as in France, there was an important "style" element. For public consumption, most especially in the case of Lloyd George, emphasis was placed on the violation of Belgian neutrality. Cabinet discussions, however, centered on France. Britain could not let France fall; it could not allow German dominance on the Continent. That was the view advanced by Asquith, Grey, Churchill, and later by Lloyd George. The German advance across the Meuse, belatedly, brought a majority of the Cabinet to accept the view that intervention was necessary. Their rationale was to maintain the continental balance of power.

Absent Elites: The Bourgeoisie

An agreement that a given coterie will rule means that others will be excluded. Concretely, that means the choice of a monarchical or party coterie excludes industrial and financial leaders, press lords, religious and labor leaders, heads of advocacy groups, intellectuals, and so on. That conclusion, a truism, is substantiated in the previous chapters where, with rare exception, those other groups simply do not appear.

The exclusion of other elites does not necessarily mean opposition or even indifference. Collusion is an easy and often-alleged possibility. Those "in power," for example, are sometimes said to be acting "in the interest of" other groups. Or, in another familiar image, those others, working "behind the scenes," are said to be "pulling the strings." That "fact," the assumed convergence of interests, was taken as the explanation for the bourgeoisie's continued acceptance of "old regime" rule. In its most familiar formulation, those "in power" were acting on behalf of industrialists, bankers, or, more generally, of the bourgeoisie.

The argument, as applied to World War I, would go as follows: industrialists were seeking raw materials and new markets; bankers were looking overseas for new investment opportunities. When blocked in those endeavors by the other powers, war was the "obvious" or "necessary" solution. In this reading, the choice of *Weltpolitik*, and specifically the choice of war by Wilhelm II, Chancellor von Bethmann Hollweg, Chief of Staff von Moltke, and a few others, served the needs of Germany's business interests.

The key questions here: do we have documentary evidence showing that business groups shared and supported the views of the decision-making coteries? Do we have evidence demonstrating their influence with the governing coteries? If not, then obviously we should look for such evidence and, at the same time, consider other hypotheses, other "plausible logics." One immediate possibility would be that "business" generally did not want war. Put simply: war would be bad for business. A case in point: in September 1914 Jack Morgan, head of the famous banking house, saw the war bringing "the most appalling destruction of values in securities which has ever been seen in this country."

One distinctive characteristic of the accounts provided in the previous chapters is the absence of "the bourgeoisie." There were no bankers or financiers, no industrial magnates, no representatives of commercial interests, no press lords, and no arms manufacturers among the decision-makers. If they were "operating behind the scenes," if they were "pulling the strings," that should be evident somewhere in the extensive documentary record. Big business representatives do figure prominently beginning with the first weeks of the war.

They oversaw the sudden demands for weapons, munitions, vehicles, uniforms, and so forth. But those activities occurred after the fact; in the initial decision for war, their "voices" were absent. The bankers and industrialists of all participating nations did of course have opinions and in one way or another communicated their views. But here one discovers lessons for which most school-trained intellectuals are not prepared.

In Austria-Hungary, in the days immediately following the assassination, Jonathan French Scott reports that the Vienna Bourse "viewed the situation with some uneasiness...but without intense alarm." Traders assumed "the need for peace in the Monarchy had increased." Stock prices "dropped but little." But then, the calling of a meeting of the Council of Ministers on 7 July "had a depressing effect on the market." Although the substance of those discussions was not known, the meeting itself resulted in a "sharp fall in values," these reaching levels lower than they had been since the outbreak of the First Balkan War. The subsequent publication of the note to Serbia "wrought havoc on the Bourse." Investors, clearly, did not see war as "serving their interests."

Bernard Michel provides a detailed picture of the relationship between "the banks" and "the government" in Austria-Hungary. The Dual Monarchy, he points out, avoided "the wave of militarism" that broke over Germany, opposition to that course being found, more than anywhere else, from the major banks. In the eyes of the financial bourgeoisie, "the army constituted a reserved domain of the aristocracy, a world totally foreign to the banking universe." Banks had ties with arms manufacturers such as Škoda and Vitkovice, but it was those firms that maintained the relationships with the military, not the banks. The bankers, Michel reports, were "profoundly pacifist," not hiding "their hostility to every warlike enterprise." And as for their governmental contacts, "the bankers exercise no real influence on the aristocratic Ministry of Foreign Affairs. The diplomats live in a totally different universe from theirs, one in which [the bankers] are rarely admitted."

Eduard März confirms those judgments and adds other supporting evidence. "The financial world's most prominent representatives were as good as debarred from influence on the nation's foreign affairs," he states. "These remained the province of the dynasty and a small exclusive group of the higher nobility." Rudolf Sieghart held an important position in the Office of the Council of Ministers prior to his appointment as governor of the Creditanstalt. But those connections yielded little information and less influence. His view was that "hostilities could, indeed must, be avoided." This account provides a striking contrast between this banker's "mindset" and that of the "small exclusive group" setting policy.

> To the last moment I did not believe that war would happen. I could not imagine that Austria-Hungary, of all the Great Powers that with the weakest periphery, with an exposed situation on several fronts, and with the magnetic attraction exercised by numerous nations beyond its borders on their co-nationals inside them, would plunge into so risky an adventure. I still do not understand the folly of the erstwhile rulers, and least of all their childish faith that Austria-Hungary would be dealing solely with Serbia.

Michel concludes that none of the bankers were consulted, "and no name of a banker, no mention of influence by the press, or that of the bourse appears in the official documents." His summary conclusion: "It was the Austria of the diplomats and the generals, not the Austria of the bankers, who, at the end of July 1914, pulled central Europe into the war."

German business leaders, too, were strongly opposed to the war but, clearly, had no effective political influence. Hugo Stinnes, one of Germany's leading industrialists and one with extensive international holdings, was an advocate of peaceful development. An associate summarized Stinnes' prewar views as follows: "Let things develop quietly for three or four years and Germany will be the uncontested economic ruler of Europe. . . . Only three or four years of peace, and I can assure you the silent attainment of German predominance in Europe."

Stinnes was very poorly informed about political developments during the July Crisis. On 22 July his son reported from London, "the relationship between Germany and England gets better from day to day." On the 28th, the day the Dual Monarchy mobilized, Stinnes and his colleagues were still "hopeful that the war between Austria-Hungary and Serbia would be localized."

Carl Duisberg, the great chemical industrialist,

> hoped for peace to the last minute and believed that the war would set back German economic development for a decade. . . . Germany's extraordinary economic growth in the prewar period depended on increasing international trade and interdependence and on international stability. . . . In the end, politics ruined economics.

In Great Britain, Lloyd George was Chancellor of the Exchequer in July 1914 and, from that position, was in touch with many leading businessmen. He reported that on Saturday, 1 August, "the Governor of the Bank of England called on me ... to inform me on behalf of the City that the financial and trading interests in the City of London were totally opposed to our intervening in the War." Lloyd George addressed the claim that the war had been "intrigued and organised and dictated by financiers for their own purpose." His comment: "I was Chancellor of the Exchequer and, as such, I saw Money before the war; I saw it immediately after the outbreak of war ... and I say that Money was a frightened and trembling thing: Money shivered at the prospect. It is a foolish and ignorant libel to call this a financiers' war." That reading is seconded by Prime Minister Asquith, who on 30 July wrote that London's financial community was "in a terrible state of depression and paralysis" and "for the time being all against English intervention." The next day he wrote, "the general opinion at present – particularly strong in the City – is to keep out at almost all costs."

Britain's bankers anticipated serious losses as a result of the war and that, in fact, was their experience. The Rothschild firm "lost close to £1.5 million in 1914 – an immense sum equivalent to 23 per cent of its capital." London had been the central lender in previous wars. During the Great War, that centrality shifted to New York. Niall Ferguson summarizes, "what united the Rothschilds after 1914 was decline – and it was a decline that was to continue for at least half a century."

No discussion of the Great War would be complete without some discussion of the arms merchants, of the Merchants of Death. An arms manufacturer such as the House of Krupp might make a lot of money, that seeming an obvious conclusion. But other options are always possible. A firm might sell more armaments at home but lose most or all of its foreign market, leaving a negative balance. The Krupp firm, William Manchester reports, was one of the losers: "At the outbreak of the war Krupp had been 130 million marks in the black; the day the chimneys stopped he was 148 million in the red, and the first year of peace was no help – at the end of 1919 the firm had lost another 36 million."

The dominant rationale of the business elites differs considerably from those of the dynasts or the party leaders. Putting profits ahead of national power, prestige, and party advantage, they sought steady economic growth, extending their activities wherever it appeared advantageous. That meant they could manufacture, trade, or invest across borders. Other things being equal, for them questions of power and prestige would be matters of indifference. Those "other things," however, are never equal and where those "larger" national issues come "into play," businessmen, most of them, would be concerned. Both war and the rumors thereof would threaten their foreign activities, reducing profits or, in the extreme case, bringing confiscation of holdings. Increased arms expenditures in peacetime, moreover, would pose some threat to profits in that someone had to pay the costs. Tax increases are usually a source of domestic unrest. They might be charged to the businessmen themselves. If charged to others, to the middle classes, workers, and/or farmers, this would mean a reduction of aggregate purchasing power that in turn, for most businesses, would mean reduced profits.

The three coteries discussed to this point (dynasts, party leaders, and business leaders) operated with markedly different assumptions, with different mindsets, or *Weltanschauungen*. The dynastic coterie, the monarch, ministers, and military, gave precedence to a distinctive conception of the national interest. Their concern was with the nation's historic territory, with its defense and, perhaps, its extension. Their policies sought, in one way or another, to demonstrate that nation's prestige and power. In their view, a threatening or competing "upstart" must be "put down." Austria-Hungary's leaders in July 1914 provided the key example, it being obvious to them that Serbia had to be "taught a lesson." Similar orientations were seen in the efforts of German and Russian decision-making coteries; they too recognizing the urgent "need" for defense of the threatened empire.

There are some obvious correlates of this mindset. The dynasts gave strong emphasis to autarchy; a proper defense of "the territory" required self-sufficiency. Theirs, accordingly, was essentially a fortress mentality, one that laid considerable emphasis on the military, given their view of war (or the threat thereof) as a proper and legitimate means for achieving their goals. Dynastic decision-makers, civilian and military, saw the nation's economy as serving the requirements of those higher goals, power and prestige. Their preferred "design" for the economy emphasized autarchy as opposed to free trade and interdependence; the economy should provide ample and secure funding for the needs of "the fortress." They would, at best, advocate a "national liberalism," as with Friedrich List, rather than the free trade and world markets commended by Adam Smith.

The party leaders, the decision-makers in France and Britain, were also autonomous, proceeding independently of big business. But they operated on different principles, following a different rationale or logic. They combined concerns for "the national interest" with the requirements of party (or coalition) support. A significant difference appears in this connection: where the dynasts initiated events, party leaders reacted to others' initiatives. French leaders were responding to a known threat, that posed by the Schlieffen plan, a threat followed by an actual attack. British leaders also responded, not to direct threat, but to the more extended implications of the July events, to that of a powerful continental hegemon. The British case involved the entire Cabinet, which contained several important factions – pacifist, neutralist, and interventionist. In contrast to the high cohesiveness of the dynastic coteries that made quick decisions possible, the British decision to intervene took several weeks.

The third elite delineated here, economic leaders, as seen, were not present in decision-making circles in July 1914. And, just as important, their urgent demands to avoid war were given no serious attention. It is an unexpected lesson because many intellectuals give much emphasis to the power of big business. The logic is easy: industrialists and bankers have immense resources; anxious and deferential politicians, supposedly, must respond to their demands. But the realities were quite different. At one point a German banker, Arthur von Gwinner, "had the audacity to point out Germany's dire financial straits" to Wilhelm II. The monarch's reply: "That makes no difference to me." From one perspective, the limited power of "big business" is easily explained. Unlike tsar and kaiser, "the bourgeoisie" would, at any time, have only modest police forces and no army at its disposal. Paraphrasing a famous question, one may ask: how many troops did big business have?

The decisions made by the dynasts and party leaders in July 1914 brought disaster for many businesses, a disaster that was easily foreseen, the implications clearly indicated in previous crises. Mobilization removed a large part of the labor force in the firms of all warring nations. Family incomes were suddenly diminished. And, at the same time, product shortages brought instant inflation, led by food prices. For the firms, the transition from peacetime to wartime production was both cumbersome and costly. There would be costs also at the war's end with the shift back to a peacetime economy. The limited review of evidence presented in this chapter suggests an important counter-factual conclusion: if big business had been "in power" in 1914, it is likely that their preferences would have prevailed and that the Great War would not have happened.

Other Elites

What were the outlooks and behavior of other elites, of other potentially influential groups in July 1914? What impact, if any, did they have? One might give consideration to the press lords. One of them, Lord Northcliffe, advocated British intervention and proceeded on the course despite strong "business" opposition. Other British newspapers, however, argued for noninvolvement. Some newspapers in Serbia were generous in their provision of provocative content. And those comments were picked up and used for opposite purposes by many newspapers in Austria-Hungary. But elsewhere, on the whole, there does not appear to have been any strong or consistent press influence. Few commentators have assigned an important role to the press in shaping key decisions. After the fact, however, with rare exception, the press provided subsequent legitimation, giving enthusiastic support for the nation's patriotic efforts.

Religious elites had long since disappeared as decision-makers in the nations discussed here. Little attention has been paid to the efforts of the clergy, whether Roman Catholic, Orthodox, Protestant, or Jewish. Their contributions also appear to have been dependent, coming after the fact, after the political leaders had set the nation's course. And their role too, as far as we can tell, was supportive, arguing the justice of the nation's cause.

Still another elite deserves attention, another group whose activities in July 1914 have been generally neglected, namely, the intellectuals. Like "the bourgeoisie," this group too had been gaining in numbers and influence over the course of the previous century. Given intellectuals' self-depictions, their contributions in July 1914 are rather surprising. In the self-portraits, they insistently announce their "critical" mission. Intellectuals comment, analyze, criticize, and reject handed-down beliefs, most especially those put forth by "established" authorities.

In a comprehensive review of intellectuals' productions in July 1914, Roland N. Stromberg documents a curious phenomenon – "the almost manic bellicosity of the European intellectuals, writers, artists, scientists, at the crucial beginning of the terrible war." Two striking findings are: a near-instant acceptance and defense of their nation's position, and exuberant declarations of support such as are not to be found in any other context. Intellectuals were not decision-makers, to be sure, but they helped to legitimate the effort, generating greater support for the decisions taken than would have been the case otherwise.

Since so unexpected, a handful of quotations may prove useful. Rudolf Eucken, the creator of a then-fashionable Life Philosophy, hailed the war as "a mighty spiritual movement." Max Scheler published a book in 1915, *Der Genius des Krieges und der Deutsche Krieg*. Stromberg describes it as "sheer bellimania," one that "hailed the war chiefly for renewing human contacts, breaking down the isolation of individuals from their fellows, and inducing a renaissance of belief." Three composers – Alexander Scriabin, Alban Berg, and Igor Stravinsky – welcomed the war as "necessary for human progress." The sociologist Max Weber wrote, "No matter what the outcome will be, this war is great and wonderful." Emile Durkheim thought the war would contribute to "reviving the sense of community."

Stromberg offers a third striking finding, an unusual frequency distribution – these intellectuals giving near-unanimous support for their country's position. Although unaware of the previous decision-making, in other words, ignorant of "the facts," they nevertheless proved fervent advocates of the national cause, showing more zeal even than the dynasts. Intellectuals were ecstatic, transported by mystical visions of redemption and community, and glorifying the imminent catastrophe. In those same countries, "the masses," the people who would pay the costs, reacted with fear, anguish, and concern. As opposed to the otherworldly orientations of those advanced intellectuals, they recognized the imminent realities of pain, suffering, misery, and death.

On the Later Experience

In 1917–18 three major powers, Austria-Hungary, Germany, and Russia, saw the end of dynastic rule. For the three royal houses – Romanov, Hohenzollern, and Habsburg – the Great War proved to be "the final conflict." The tsarist regime was replaced by a new-style authoritarian regime, this led by a coterie purporting to represent the interests of workers and peasants. Kaiser Wilhelm II fled to the Netherlands following revolution and defeat and Germany, for fourteen years, became a democracy. The Habsburgs were expelled from Austria-Hungary and those lands were divided among various successor states.

Following some unanticipated "dynamics," new authoritarian regimes made their appearance. In 1922 Italy's constitutional monarchy was set aside and the government was taken over by Benito Mussolini and his Fascists. Eleven years later, Germany's Weimar Republic was replaced; the new regime, like Italy's, was also headed by nationalist authoritarians. The key agencies in both regimes were paramilitary organizations, war-trained veterans, the Fasci di Combattimento and the Storm Troops, each arguing an unjust settlement in the previous conflict. The Italians, it was said, had been denied the promised fruits of victory. And the Germans, "undefeated in the field," were victims of a "stab in the back." Adolf Hitler and his party, the National Socialists, were often said to be "agents" of big business, but that claim has been shown to be erroneous.

The operating rationales of these two regimes were similar to those of the dynastic regimes. They too favored autarchy; they too were much concerned with the nation's power and prestige; they gave much emphasis to the military; and they advocated national "expansion." On the other side of the world, Japan continued with its authoritarian regime, basically a monarchy dominated by a powerful military elite, one also rejecting basic liberal initiatives. Japan's constitution and military institutions were based on prewar German originals and this gave military elites a substantial voice in policy-making.

World War II was initiated by this trio of neo-authoritarian regimes in Berlin, Rome, and Tokyo called the Axis powers, each reaching out, with varying degrees of initial success, to capture a new empire. With some important modifications to be sure, this war also had its origins with the initiatives of nonliberal coteries. The democracies, those headed by party elites, were again slow and hesitant in their responses; again they were reacting rather than initiating. The democracies were slow to react to Japan's efforts in China, to Italy in Ethiopia, and to the fascist Putsch in Spain.

The most notorious policy of Europe's democracies was the appeasement of Hitler's Germany, the first event in that history being the acceptance of the dictator's occupation of the Rhineland. A prompt French response might have changed the course of history because France had decisive military superiority. But both the French and British governments failed to react and Hitler achieved a complete victory.

The outcome of World War II differed significantly from its predecessor. The "total" victories of 1945 meant that no group within the perpetrating countries could question the result, or, put differently, could construct an unjust-settlement myth. There was no possibility for a *revengiste* movement. After brief periods of occupation, the victorious allies instituted democratic regimes managed by political party elites. The imposed settlements, moreover, removed the military elites and dismantled their institutions. One important consequence: the new arrangements gave business elites a stronger voice than ever before. In Europe the new arrangement allowed the development of the Common Market, originally with six members, then, with later additions, of the European Union that in 2004 has twenty-five member nations. The plan involved, effectively, a substantial extension of the liberal economic program.

Two principal correlates should also be noted, namely, a substantial increase in the wealth of the participating nations and an extended period of peace. As of 2004, central and western Europe had experienced 59 years of peace. For Japan the new liberal arrangements also brought both wealth and peace.

Recommended Reading

Books dealing with the origins of World War I are legion. They range from general anthologies to sophisticated national studies. Many are reprinted, with or without updates, on a regular basis. Among the most recent general anthologies in English by scholars active in the field are:

Herwig, Holger H., ed. *The Outbreak of World War I: Causes and Responsibilities.* Boston: Houghton-Mifflin, 1997.
Joll, James, ed. *The Origins of the First World War.* London: Longman, 1999.
Langdon, John W., ed. *July 1914: The Long Debate, 1918–1990.* New York: Berg, 1991.
Martel, Gordon, ed. *The Origins of the First World War.* London: Longman, 1996.
Mombauer, Annika, ed. *The Origins of the First World War: Controversies and Consensus.* London: Longman, 2002.
Remak, Joachim, ed. *The Origins for World War I, 1870–1914.* Fort Worth: Harcourt Brace College Publishers, 1995.

To this list of recent paperbacks should be added one thorough hardback classic:

Albertini, Luigi. *The Origins of the War 1914.* 3 vols. London and New York: Oxford University Press, 1952–57.

Some twenty years ago, St. Martin's Press in New York commissioned a series of regional studies on the origins of the war. Some have remained on their list, unrevised, while others have been taken over by new publishers. They include:

Berghahn, Volker R. *Germany and the Approach of War in 1914.* Basingstoke and London: Macmillan, 1993.

Bosworth, R. J. B. *Italy and the Approach of the First World War*. New York: Palgrave Macmillan, 1983.

Keiger, John V. *France and the Origins of the First World War*. New York: St. Martin's Press, 1984.

Lieven, D. C. B. *Russia and the Origins of the First World War*. New York: St. Martin's Press, 1983.

Steiner, Zara S. *Britain and the Origins of the First World War*. London: Palgrave Macmillan 2003.

Williamson, Samuel R., Jr. *Austria-Hungary and the Origins of the First World War*. New York: St. Martin's Press, 1991.

Readers wishing to delve further into Austria-Hungary's decision for war in July 1914 should look at:

Fellner, Fritz. "Austria-Hungary." In Keith Wilson, ed., *Decisions for War 1914*. New York: St. Martin's Press, 1995. Pp. 9–25.

Leslie, John. "The Antecedents of Austria-Hungary's War Aims, Policies and Policymakers in Vienna and Budapest before and during 1914." *Wiener Beiträge zur Geschichte der Neuzeit* Bd. 20. Vienna: Verlag für Geschichte und Politik, 1993. Pp. 307–94.

Tunstall, Graydon A., Jr. *Planning for War Against Russia and Serbia: Austro-Hungarian and German Military Strategies, 1871–1914*. New York: Columbia University Press, 1993.

Williamson, Samuel R., Jr. "Vienna and July 1914: The Origins of the Great War Once More." In S. R. Williamson and P. Pastor, eds., *Essays on World War I: Origins and Prisoners of War*. New York: Columbia University Press, 1983. Pp. 9–36.

Events in the Balkans leading up to the Great War have been covered in a myriad of books – at least 3,000 on the murder at Sarajevo alone – and hence only a few pertinent works can be cited here:

Cornwall, Mark. "Serbia." In Keith Wilson, ed., *Decisions for War 1914*. New York: St. Martin's Press, 1995. Pp. 55–96.

Dedijer, Vladimir. *The Road to Sarajevo*. New York: Simon and Schuster, 1966.

Dragnich, Alex N. *Serbia, Nikola Pašić, and Yugoslavia*. New Brunswick: Rutgers University Press, 1974.

Hall, Richard C. *Bulgaria's Road to the First World War*. New York: Columbia University Press, 1996.

Leontaritis, George B. *Greece and the First World War: From Neutrality to Intervention, 1917–1918*. New York: Columbia University Press, 1990.

Petrovich, Michael Boro. *A History of Modern Serbia, 1804–1918*. 2 vols. New York: Harcourt Brace Jovanovich, 1976.

Torrey, Glenn E. *Romania and World War I.* Portland: Center for Romanian Studies, 1998.

France's largely reactive posture during the July Crisis has received a fair share of attention:

Becker, Jean-Jacques. *The Great War and the French People.* Leamington Spa: Berg, 1993.

Hayne, M. B. *The French Foreign Office and the Origins of the First World War, 1898–1914.* Oxford: Clarendon Press, 1993.

Porch, Douglas. *The March to the Marne: The French Army 1871–1914.* Cambridge: Cambridge University Press, 1981.

Schuman, Frederick L. *War and Diplomacy in the French Republic.* New York: Whittlesey House, 1969.

Wright, Gordon. *Raymond Poincaré and the French Presidency.* Stanford: Stanford University Press, 1942.

Not surprisingly, the literature dealing with Germany's role in the outbreak of the First World War is immense – especially in the wake of Fritz Fischer's spectacular charges of a predetermined pro-war policy in Berlin. A sampling of the most recent and most relevant works includes:

Cecil, Lamar. *William II,* vol. 2: *Emperor and Exile, 1900–1941.* Chapel Hill: University of North Carolina Press, 1996.

Fischer, Fritz. *Germany's Aims in the First World War.* New York: Norton, 1976.

———. *War of Illusions: German Policies from 1911 to 1914.* New York: Norton, 1975.

Geiss, Imanuel, ed. *July 1914: The Outbreak of the First World War. Selected Documents.* New York: Norton, 1968.

Herwig, Holger H. *The First World War: Germany and Austria-Hungary 1914–1918.* London: Arnold, 1997.

Mombauer, Annika. *Helmuth von Moltke and the Origins of the First World War.* New York: Cambridge University Press, 2001.

Röhl, John. *1914: Delusion or Design? The Testimony of Two German Diplomats.* London: Paul Elek, 1973.

Verhey, Jeffrey. *The Spirit of 1914: Militarism, Myth and Mobilization in Germany.* New York: Cambridge University Press, 2000.

The origins of the war have not been heatedly debated in Britain, given that the government of Prime Minister H. H. Asquith and Foreign Secretary Sir Edward Grey believed (or hoped) that the war could somehow be avoided. Recent treatments include:

Gooch, John. *The Plans of War: The General Staff and British Military Strategy c. 1900–1916.* London: Routledge and Kegan Paul, 1974.

Hinsley, F. H., ed., *British Foreign Policy under Sir Edward Grey*. Cambridge: Cambridge University Press, 1977.

Robbins, Keith. *Sir Edward Grey: A Biography of Lord Grey of Falladon*. London: Cassell, 1971.

Williamson, Samuel R., Jr. *The Politics of Grand Strategy: Britain and France Prepare for War, 1904–1914*. Cambridge, MA.: Harvard University Press, 1969.

Wilson, Keith. "Britain." In Keith Wilson, ed., *Decisions for War 1914*. New York: St. Martin's Press, 1995. Pp. 175–208.

Italy's decision not to stand with her allies Germany and Austria-Hungary in 1914 and instead to join the *entente* in 1915 surprisingly has produced few analyses in English. Those few include:

Bosworth, R. J. B. *Italy, the Least of the Great Powers: Italian Foreign Policy before the First World War*. London: Cambridge University Press, 1979.

Clough, Shephard B., and Salvatore Saladino, eds. *A History of Modern Italy: Documents, Readings and Commentary*. New York and London: Columbia University Press, 1968.

Gooch, John. *Army, State and Society in Italy, 1870–1915*. New York: St. Martin's Press, 1989.

Renzi, William A. *In the Shadow of the Sword: Italy's Neutrality and Entrance into the Great War, 1914–1915*. New York: P. Lang, 1987.

Sullivan, Brian R. "The Strategy of the Decisive Weight: Italy, 1882–1922." In Williamson Murray, MacGregor Knox, and Alvin Bernstein, eds., *The Making of Strategy: Rulers, States, and War*. Cambridge: Cambridge University Press, 1994. Pp. 307–51.

The difficulty of the Japanese language and the lack of English-language translations of Japanese historical works for long have denied readers useful accounts of Japan's decision to enter the war on the side of the *entente*. The situation is now only slowly beginning to be remedied:

Dickinson, Frederick R. *War and National Reinvention: Japan in the Great War, 1914–1919*. Cambridge, MA.: Harvard University Press, 1999.

Harries, Meiron, and Susie Harris. *Soldiers of the Sun: The Rise and Fall of the Imperial Japanese Army*. New York: Random House, 1991.

Nish, Ian. *Alliance in Decline: A Study in Anglo-Japanese Relations, 1908–23*. London: Athlone Press, 1972.

———. "Japan." In Keith Wilson, ed., *Decisions for War 1914*. New York: St. Martin's Press, 1995. Pp. 209–28.

The same problems of mastery of a difficult language and of lack of translations also plague the case study of the Ottoman Empire and the Great War. By and large, students remain dependant on general surveys or on specific analyses of the Porte's relations with outsiders:

Shaw, Stanford, and Ezel Kural Shaw. *History of the Ottoman Empire and Modern Turkey.* 2 vols. Cambridge: Cambridge University Press, 1976–77.

Trumpener, Ulrich. *Germany and the Ottoman Empire, 1914–1918.* Princeton: Princeton University Press, 1968.

Turfan, M. Naim. *Rise of the Young Turks: Politics, the Military, and Ottoman Collapse.* London: I. B. Tauris, 2000.

Yasamee, F. A. K. "Ottoman Empire." In Keith Wilson, ed., *Decisions for War 1914.* New York: St. Martin's Press, 1995. Pp. 229–68.

Historical interpretations of Russia's role in the outbreak of the Great War received a great impetus from the (however brief) opening of former Soviet archives in the 1980s and 1990s. Among the more recent interpretations of the official actions taken in St. Petersburg during the July Crisis are:

Fuller, William C. *Civil-Military Conflict in Imperial Russia 1881–1914.* Princeton: Princeton University Press, 1985.

Gatrell, Peter. *Government, Industry, and Rearmament in Russia, 1900–1914.* Cambridge: Cambridge University Press, 1994.

Kennan, George F. *The Fateful Alliance: France, Russia, and the Coming of the First World War.* New York: Pantheon, 1984.

Lieven, D. C. B. *Nicholas II: Emperor of all the Russias.* London: John Murray, 1993.

Menning, Bruce W. *Bayonets before Bullets: The Imperial Russian Army, 1861–1914.* Bloomington: Indiana University Press, 1992.

Last but not least, the American entry into the First World War has largely revolved around the actions of one man: President Woodrow Wilson. Only a small sampling of the vast literature on Wilson and his statecraft can be given:

Ambrosius, Lloyd R. *Wilsonian Statecraft: Theory and Practice of Liberal Internationalism during World War I.* Wilmington: SR Books, 1991.

Cooper, John Milton. *The Vanity of Power: American Isolationism and the First World War, 1914–1917.* Westport, Conn.: Greenwood, 1969.

Gregory, Ross. *The Origins of American Intervention in the First World War.* New York: Norton, 1971.

Knock, Thomas J. *To End All Wars: Woodrow Wilson and the Quest for World Order.* New York: Oxford University Press, 1992.

Link, Arthur S. *The Higher Realism of Woodrow Wilson and Other Essays.* Nashville: Vanderbilt University Press, 1971.

———. *Wilson: Confusions and Crises, 1915–1916.* Princeton: Princeton University Press, 1964.

———. *Wilson: The Struggle for Neutrality, 1914–1915.* Princeton: Princeton University Press, 1960.

May, Ernest R. *The World War and American Isolation.* Cambridge: Harvard University Press, 1959.

Readers should also consult the "Suggested Readings" in the larger book from which these selections were culled:

Hamilton, Richard F., and Holger H. Herwig, eds. *The Origins of World War I.* Cambridge: Cambridge University Press, 2003. Pp. 525–31.

Index